The Postw

*Militaries, Masculinities and _____ ~eacekeeping
Bosnia and the ~~~erlands*

Lawrence and Wishart Limited
99a Wallis Road
London
E9 5LN

First published 2002

British Library Cataloguing in Publication Data.
A catalogue record for this book is available from the British
Library

ISBN 0 85315 946 7

Text setting E-Type, Liverpool
Printed and bound by Redwood Books, Trowbridge.

The Postwar Moment

*Militaries, Masculinities and
International Peacekeeping
Bosnia and the Netherlands*

Edited by
Cynthia Cockburn and Dubravka Zarkov

Lawrence & Wishart
LONDON 2002

Contents

Acknowledgements

We are seriously in debt to many people in connection with this book, and are very happy that we have a chance here to say thank you. A great deal has flowed from an initiative by the University for Humanist Studies (UvH) in Utrecht, Netherlands. They awarded Cynthia Cockburn the Chair of Feminism, Humanism and Emancipation for the year 2000, providing her with a stimulating academic environment in which to complete her work with Medica Women's Association on women's organizations in postwar Bosnia-Herzegovina. Cynthia Cockburn would like to express appreciation not only to the University for Humanist Studies for this academic hospitality, but also to the late Mrs Ribbius Peletier for the endowment of the Chair, and the Peletier Board for her appointment and for funding the related seminar on *Gender Relations After War* in October 2000, which generated several chapters for this book.

Dubravka Zarkov also wishes to express appreciation to UvH for the opportunity of a one year lectureship in the year 2000 and to thank the students who attended her course on gender and war for sharing their thoughtfulness with her. Thanks, too, to the colleagues of the Department of Spiritual Care of the Netherlands Ministry of Defence who lead her through the intricacies and paradoxes of the Dutch Military. Additional thanks to the Department for funding and logistical support for yet another seminar, in December 2000, on *Power and Powerlessness in Bosnia: Gender Aspects of Peacekeeping*, that generated further chapters for the book.

We both of us feel special gratitude for the way these initiatives brought us into contact and gave us a chance to work together. It led to an unanticipated friendship, a lot of fun and a project more far-reaching and mind-bending than either of us had dreamed of when we embarked on the first year of the millennium.

In addition, Cynthia Cockburn wishes to thank, very warmly, the funders who made her initial work in Bosnia a possibility. They are: The Ajahma Charitable Trust, the Network for Social Change, the

Lipman-Miliband Trust and the Open Society Fund of the Soros Foundation. Dear funders, thank you for your faith in the project we called *To Live Together Or To Live Apart*. I hope you will receive this book as the second instalment of my end-of-project report.

Most penitently, we thank the authors of the chapters gathered here. Several of them out of sheer kindness travelled to the Netherlands to give a talk at a seminar and found themselves swept into a book-writing project for which we had ill prepared them, and which we know cost them time and energy they could scarcely afford. We were in blessed ignorance, at the outset, of how perilous the process of editing a book can be, wantonly threatening to relations with colleagues and friends. All the contributors responded with extraordinary patience and creativeness to the outrageous demands we made on them as editors. We very much hope they like the book that is the result of their labours and their wisdom.

Finally, we would like to thank Sally Davison at Lawrence and Wishart for her enthusiasm for *The Postwar Moment*. That she gave us a contract for the book on the basis of an idea, without prior sight of the material, was a gesture of faith that kept us all going. Thanks to you all at L&W, too, for skilfully guiding the book through to publication.

Cynthia Cockburn and Dubravka Zarkov, editors.

Introduction

DUBRAVKA ZARKOV AND
CYNTHIA COCKBURN

In this book we explore the impact of peacekeeping and postwar reconstruction on Bosnia-Herzegovina and the Netherlands, two countries
involved in one war in very different ways. A concern with the experience
of Bosnia-Herzegovina itself, as a society affected by war, needs no
explaining. We shall see this devastated region stumbling out of a blood-
bath into an insecure and unsatisfactory constitutionalism and statehood.

But when people speak of 'a society affected by war' we should not
hear this as referring only to a country that has participated in the
fighting, or on whose territory the war was fought. A country sending
peacekeepers to a conflict zone may also be touched and changed by its
experience. And in this book we link the experience of Bosnia and the
Bosnians with the experience of the Netherlands and the Dutch, who
played a significant role in the international peacekeeping operation
during the war and after it. Countries that contribute soldiers to international peacekeeping missions have been largely neglected in war
studies. The war in which the Dutch military were involved in Bosnia
was not considered 'their war'. Yet their engagement in it has, as we
shall see, shaken Dutch society, causing some soul-searching and a
rethinking of Dutch national identity.

What is also particular about the articles collected in this book is
that they consistently deploy gender concepts in analyzing these
matters of war and peacekeeping, militarism and nationalism. The
experience of war fighting and peacekeeping – being expected to die,
and even to kill, whether for your own 'nation' or for a just cause in
'someone else's war' – can be seen, if we have the eyes for it, to affect
the nature of the relationship between the nation, its military and the

men and women that constitute them. It also affects relations between men and women themselves, and between masculinity and femininity.

The 'postwar moment'

Does it make sense to speak of a 'postwar moment'? Observed with a detached historical eye, war can surely never be said to start and end at a clearly defined moment. Rather, it seems part of a continuum of conflict, expressed now in armed force, now in economic sanctions or political pressure. A time of supposed peace may later come to be called 'the pre-war period'. During the fighting of a war, unseen by the foot soldiers under fire, peace processes are often already at work. A time of postwar reconstruction, later, may be re-designated as an *inter bellum* – a mere pause between wars.

There are several good reasons for not breaking up cycles of war and peace into discrete labelled chunks. A continuum of violence runs through the social sphere, and the economic and political spheres. To focus on outbreaks of armed conflict could thus have the effect of diminishing the significance of structural violence, long-term oppression and impoverishment. When our analysis is gendered, the prevalence of male sexualized violence against women and children, in both war and peace, calls this continuum strongly to mind. So too does a focus on cultures – since a culture of militarism may dominate a country in the name of 'pacification'.

Nonetheless, from the point of view of the individual caught up in armed conflict, at whichever end of the barrel of the gun, the moment that gun is silenced has something to be said for it. Arms may be cached for another day and the landmines may remain in place for a generation, but a cease-fire, especially if a peace agreement follows, brings an opportunity worth examining in its specificity.

During open warfare, military strategy has consumed politicians and military commanders alike. Postwar comes as a moment when policy can diversify. There will be policy moves on several fronts simultaneously: demobilization, the reconstruction of the economy, the shift from emergency services to social rehabilitation, the reconception of state, political structures and law in a new constitution. For democrats and socialists the moment is one where much may be lost and much gained. Will economic class relations be rebuilt on the exploitative model of those that structured pre-war society? Will all groups within society gain a share in political power?

To those of us who have a concern with gender power relations it also seems a crucial moment, when social upheaval might open a door to the changes we hope for. In the rebuilding of social structures, the renewal of democracy and the reworking of cultures, will the familiar old exclusions and oppressions be reproduced? Or will policy-makers be alert to the possibilities of reshaping the relationship between women and men, the feminine and the masculine? Will they understand, with hindsight, a certain causal implication of gender relations and gendered cultures in the mobilization of national sentiment and the recruitment of armies? Is it thinkable that the postwar moment be used as an opportunity to turn a society towards gender equality, the diminution of 'difference' and the valorization of women and the feminine? Could policy-makers recognize such a transformation of the gender order as a necessary component of any lasting peace process, as itself an underpinning of peace?

An influential force in some postwar moments may be an international peacekeeping operation, fielded by the United Nations or some other international institution. But a failure to understand the politics of masculinity and femininity in causing and sustaining violence, and in working to redress violence, has till now rendered such operations less effective than they might have been. At worst, by playing in to the existing gender order, some have reinforced aggressive and predatory forces, and entrenched violent and unstable environments. In one of three opening chapters of this book – each of which offers a conceptual framework for the remainder of the contributions – Dyan Mazurana discusses the significance of recent moves towards gender awareness in United Nations peacekeeping operations.

Nations, militaries and militarism

The answer to the question of what kind of peace will follow the cessation of hostilities is of course linked to another: how fast and how purposeful will be the process of de-militarization of society? In looking at this we need to examine the interaction of nationalism, militarism and patriarchy,[1] which have historically been brother ideologies, mutually supportive. This does not mean, of course, that each of the three comes in a singular model, or that the articulation between them does not vary over time and place. Nationalism has its modes and its periods. National feeling can be mobilized for liberation, and in such movements it may be relatively open, promising the establishment of democracy. It may be self-aggrandizing, imperialist and deeply racist. It may be mean-minded, defensive and reactive, re-telling some essentialist fiction of common origins. But because all nationalisms appeal to the individual to identify with a 'people', they are inevitably more or less concerned to foster internal cohesion and control, and to maintain external boundaries, naming and excluding the non-belongers, the not-us. They therefore have tendencies, now modulated, now manifest in extremist form, on the one hand to patriarchalism (structuring gender relations hierarchically and emphasizing gender difference), on the other to ethnic and cultural differentiation and a reification of race.

The majority of nations are born in or through warfare. Militarism is the culture, and national militaries supply the force, that usually sustains the national movement and achieves its goals. Historically, the societies of the European nations that were formed in the nineteenth century have been deeply shaped by linked structures and ideologies of nationalism, militarism and patriarchy. But even militarism is, as Cynthia Enloe (2000) reminds us, the outcome of a process – *militarization*. And as such it has many phases and manifestations. The raising of armies is one of them, and it has normally been associated with nationalisms and wars. But, once the guns are silenced, we would be naïve to assume that militarization will disappear on its own. In Chapter 1 Enloe shows us that there is a persistent tension between processes of demilitarization, transformation of militarized masculinities and the democratization of gender relations. In a postwar society such as Bosnia-Herzegovina, militarization is deep and widespread, and the criteria Enloe offers for assessing demilitarization are essential tools for feminist anti-militarist politics and theorizing.

A significant shift in militarism in the twentieth century has been its association with international and multinational peacekeeping. These variations of expression of the relationship between nationalism and militarism open also onto the possibility of variations in the traditional link between these two and patriarchy. As Enloe asked in a previous book, is the manliness of the international 'blue beret' the same as that of the national squaddie? And if international peacekeeping is a different kind of military culture, what are the implications of the new forms for relations between men and between men and women (Enloe 1993)?

In this book we shall see in Bosnia-Herzegovina a society in which it is difficult not to be aware of just how deeply it is militarized, and the adverse bearing this has on everyday life. In the Netherlands we shall see, on the contrary, a society that represents and imagines itself as barely militarized at all, and only then in blue-beret style, for peaceful purposes. But we shall see too just how, for all that, the military is a live issue for Dutch people.

Masculinities and gender regimes

Which brings us to the third term in this title: masculinities. Two features characterize our approach to masculinities in this book. The first is signalled by our use of the plural form of the noun. We presume that masculinity is not a singular phenomenon but has variant forms. The second is that, unlike many 'masculinity studies', we do not isolate masculinity from the other half of the gender dyad, femininity; men from their bearing on women; or gender specificities from gender power relations. In none of this, of course, are we breaking new ground, but benefit from recent work by other analysts of gender.

First – the plurality of masculinities. Since R.W. Connell's theorization of gender and power (Connell 1987), his terminology has become widely accepted. He uses 'gender order' to signify a particular structuring of gender relations on the large historical and spatial plan, while institutionally, gender relations manifest themselves in differing 'gender regimes'. Latterly Bob Connell has been arguing that we cannot speak simply of 'masculinity' – we have to differentiate hegemonic from marginalized masculinities, emphasized from resistant feminities (1995). In this volume (Chapter 2) he further emphasizes the plurality of masculinity, and offers some strategies for changing dominant forms of masculinity, embedded in violence, and developing more democratic alternatives.

Connell's and other analyses have furnished a terminology now widely deployed in problematizations of dominant forms of masculinity, in fields such as anthropology, cultural studies, media studies and (post-) colonial histories, along with a new awareness of alternative, subordinated and even subversive, masculinities.[2] Within gender studies, the traditional militarized gender regime is rightly identified as generating a form of masculinity, hegemonic in all too many societies, that is deeply oppressive of women and also of many men.[3] It is a regime that exaggerates gender difference and inequality, and dictates complementary worlds for men and women, during and after wars. In war, militarist discourses (like the nationalist discourses with which they often elide) elevate men to the world of arms and glory; women they relegate to the world of birthing and mourning. Different sacrifices are expected of men and women, different rewards are offered them. After war, the traditional militarized gender regime endows men with the power in politics and locates women's importance within the family. Of course the genders generated in this way, and their inter-relationships, are no more than injunctions and aspirations. They are never fully determinant of reality, and never altogether erase individual agency. Nonetheless they are influential on the individual and her or his experience.

In this book we seek to show modulations of military masculinity – on the one hand men that seek glory in battle, on the other men that seek glory precisely in averting battles. In studying Bosnia-Herzegovina, a society that has recently emerged from war, there is no avoiding a concern with traditional militarized masculinity. It is pervasive, a factor in everyday life that can hardly be ignored. In studying the Netherlands we have found ourselves looking at another, divergent, form of militarized masculinity – one that is less aggressive and less overtly nationalistic than traditional militarism. The Dutch military represents itself differently from the armies that fought the war in Bosnia, in softer guise, aspiring to constitute a different, gentler, kind of culture.

Such a comparatively gentle, soft-yet-armed, masculinity does not spring ready-made from a void. It has emerged in the Netherlands through a specific history of war, in a specific national and international context. Three contributors to the book try to unravel this knot of military, masculinity and Dutch national identities. Stefan Dudink's analysis (Chapter 9) of different masculinities in Dutch nationalism shows that an alternative masculinity, moderate and moral, may still serve the purpose of the military and the nation. Marc De Leeuw's investigation of an encounter between the Bosnian Serb General Mladic and Dutch Colonel Karremans attests that war has its perils for patriarchy, and that peace-making involves not only the persistence but the active restitution of patriarchal authority. Finally, in her analysis of the media representation of the fall of Srebrenica in the Dutch press, Dubravka Zarkov shows how crucial are peacekeeping missions for the formation of national self-image, even in a society that imagines itself as the least militarized of all.

If plurality is the first feature in our approach to masculinity in this book, the second is our sustained feminist concern with positioning masculinity *within gender relations*. To do so may seem obvious, but in studies of war and militarism it has not always been the case. Some studies of masculinity have tended to consider manhood as a phenomenon in and of itself, prioritizing relations between men. Gender power relations between men and women have sometimes slipped out of the picture. Feminist gender studies have sometimes had the contrary fault of focusing on women while abstracting from gender relations. But ideally feminist work, whether by women or men, has given us a body of knowledge concerning both men and women, in relation to each other, on masculinity and femininity within the gender relations that shape and are shaped by them.[4]

Studying different manifestations of militarized masculinity within a context of gender power relations can, we believe, bring new insights into old fields of study. Understandings of nationalism and, more specifically, the role of war and militarism in the formation of national identities, change with the perception that there is more than one way in which masculinity can be militarized, and more than one way that a military can shape its gender regime.

The peace agreement and peacekeeping in Bosnia-Herzegovina

Some background is called for here on the role of international peace-keepers in the Bosnian postwar moment. The United Nations positioned on Bosnian territory, even while the war was at its height, what was termed a United Nations Protection Force (UNPROFOR). Then in August 1995, 12 days of bombing by NATO, authorized by the United Nations, ended the Bosnian Serb forces' siege of Sarajevo and tipped the balance of the war.[5]

The peace agreement, titled *The General Framework Agreement for Peace in Bosnia and Herzegovina*, was drafted and initialled in negoti-ations at the Wright-Patterson Air Force Base in Dayton, Ohio, on 21 November 1995. Thus the Agreement also became known as the Dayton accords, or simply 'Dayton'. It was actually signed in Paris on 14 December 1995. Of particular importance, from our point of view, is Annex 1A of the Dayton accords, titled *Agreement on the Military Aspects of the Peace Settlement*.[6]

The authority structure of the international intervention was complex. The military Annex authorized an international Implementation Force (IFOR) to take over from UNPROFOR in B-H. The Peace Implementation Council (the body of nations responsible for the peace agreement) sought United Nations approval for delegating to NATO the military aspects of the implementation of Dayton, while NATO was authorized also to involve non-NATO countries in contributing troops. Thus IFOR came to furnish, at the start of its operations, 60,000 troops from a diverse array of countries and cultures.

IFOR were required to establish a buffer zone between the two entities (the Federation of Bosnia-Herzegovina and the Republika Srpska) created by Dayton, separate the warring parties' forces and sequester their heavy weaponry. They were also authorized to disband the irregular forces that had been such an important factor in the war.

In December 1996, when the mandate of IFOR expired, but tension was still running high, its function was renewed and extended in the form of a Stabilization Force (SFOR). Now the civilian aspect of NATO's role came to the fore. SFOR's attention was increasingly directed to supporting the socio-political concerns of the Peace Implementation Council, that is: 'deepening economic reform, accelerating refugee returns and fostering functional and democratically accountable common institutions'.

Two aspects of the Dayton peace accords and the subsequent international peacekeeping operation in Bosnia are of special interest in relation to this book. The first is their implication for militarism and demilitarization in Bosnia. There is a contradiction inherent in international armed peacekeeping. To 'maintain a security environment' in order to return quickly to 'normal conditions of life' after war (NATO's brief under Annex 1A of the Dayton accords) requires the potential for, and from time to time the actual use of, considerable armed force. Dayton has not decommissioned and abolished the military might of the warring forces in Bosnia, it has merely corralled them. And, ironically, its own 20,000 personnel and their bases, barracks and weaponry, add to the overall militarization of the country.

The second aspect of the peace arrangements calling for comment is their bearing on gender relations. Militarization of itself favours militarized forms of gender and gender relations. Militarized masculinities (whether the traditional verson, in the local forces, or the modified peacekeeping version, in SFOR) remain hegemonic. But additionally, it has been widely remarked that the peace agreement did not address the problems inherent in prewar and wartime gender relations and as a result did no favours to women or femininity in postwar Bosnia.

Overwhelmingly influential in the postwar development of Bosnian society, the international community has not applied any of the political strategies, theoretical insights or institutional provisions on gender equality that existed in the region prior to the war, or that have been developed in many of the countries contributing to peacekeeping as a consequence of three decades of feminist thinking and women's movements.

Two authors – Madeleine Rees and Suzanne Williams – analyze the dire consequences of this neglect of gender for war-ravaged societies such as Bosnia. Rees gives us an account of the opportunities that the supra-national organizations such as the United Nations, the Organization for Security and Co-operation in Europe and the European Union have missed in addressing gender issues, and the tough struggle women in these organizations have had even to begin to counteract this neglect. Williams shows us the efforts and the effects of introducing gender policies in Oxfam, one international humanitarian NGO that has been a significant actor in Bosnia. They amplify, with their concrete examples, Dyan Mazurana's concerns in Chapter 3.

Furthermore, while women's needs (or rather those of 'women and children') have been a subject of concern to international agencies involved in humanitarian missions, the international community has been slow to recognize women's strengths – and their potential value in the postwar moment. In Chapter 5 Cynthia Cockburn analyzes women's ethnically-integrative, local, non-governmental organizations in Bosnia, and suggests that women's empowerment and the transformation of gender culture can in themselves be work for peace and democracy. The continuous struggle for the recognition of women's work for peace is seen in Chapter 7, where Cynthia Cockburn and Meliha Hubic analyze the unsatisfactory relationship between the peacekeeping army and women's organizations in Bosnia.

International peacekeeping:
the involvement of the Netherlands
In recent years forces from the Netherlands have taken part in operations in Yugoslavia, Cambodia and Cyprus, and most recently in Ethiopia/Eritrea. In Bosnia, Dutch troops were part of UNPROFOR.

Due mostly to the Dutch military's policies on homosexuality, the Dutch are often seen as being the most liberal of all participating troops. Discrimination in the military is prohibited on various grounds, one of which is sexual orientation. The Dutch armed forces, in general, also include a respectable proportion of women and ethnic minority soldiers, and even have a relatively high percentage of ethnic minority officers (Richardson and Bosch 1999). Furthermore, the Dutch military is perceived, by the country's policy-makers, as one of the most significant players in Dutch international aspirations.[7]

Consequently, a lot of thought is given to the way the armed forces are run – and rewarded. But things are no longer going as smoothly as they once did. For some years now the Dutch military have been struggling to fill their ranks. Each year there are fewer young white men eager to join up. And they can no longer be forcibly drafted. In 1996 the Dutch military became a voluntary force, an army no longer of conscripts but of professionals.

This mix of high national aspirations and hard military realities has a significant bearing on the way Dutch soldiers and their commanders, once they become peacekeepers, perform their tasks and behave in the field or in the barracks. And, as several authors in this book show, their behaviour matters – not only for the country in which they keep the peace, but also back home. In Chapter 8 Jolanda Bosch and Desiree Verweij look at the disturbances that have ensued in the gender regimes and cultures of the Dutch military. They ask what kind of masculinities and femininities are nourished within its ranks, and what this means for the men, and the growing numbers of women, in the Dutch armed forces. The answers they offer are sobering evidence of the limits of democratization in institutions built upon militarized masculinities.

The origins of this book

Unlikely as it may seem, this volume, so critical of militarism and militarized masculinities, owes its existence largely to the military. It results from an unusual co-operation between a Dutch university (the University for Humanist Studies, or Universiteit voor Humanistiek) and the Dutch Ministry of Defence (its Department for Humanist Spiritual Care, or Dienst Humanistisch Geestelijke Verzorging). Both institutions are quintessentially Dutch, to the extent that it is difficult to imagine them existing anywhere other than in the Netherlands.

The University for Humanist Studies in Utrecht is a small but growing state-funded university, currently with around three hundred students. It is one among several Dutch institutions and associations founded on the principles and philosophy of humanism, dating back to Erasmus from Rotterdam (1466-1536). The University developed from a vocational college in which students acquired the skills necessary to become counsellors in prisons, hospices and the military. Today, while its students prepare for similar employment, the University also has a lively research programme. There is debate among staff and students about the interpretation of humanism, both with regard to atheism versus religious belief, and with regard to political society and action.

The Department of Humanist Spiritual Care also needs some explanation. The Dutch state has a tradition of being even-handed towards the principal religious groups in the Netherlands. This is applied to the corps of priests and pastors employed within the armed forces to carry out the role of pastoral care. In recent years this even-handedness has been extended to Humanism, and minority religious are also recognized. Thus the Dutch military currently has humanist, Catholic, Protestant, Jewish, Muslim and Hindu counsellors.

The University of Humanist Studies was endowed by the Ribbius Peletier Foundation with a temporary chair for a visiting professor in 'Feminism, Humanism and Emancipation Studies'. Each year a topic is chosen for the chair, and a Dutch or foreign feminist invited to associate her work with the University. In the year 2000 the topic for the year was 'Meanings of Gender and War Violence', and Cynthia Cockburn was invited to pursue her current research interest in gender, women's organization and democratization in postwar Bosnia-Herzegovina in association with the students and staff of the University for Humanist Studies.

At the same time, the Dutch Ministry of Defence was showing increased interest in gender issues. Women in the Dutch military had for some years been lobbying the Ministry for more attention to these issues, organizing networks, study days and conferences, with little response from the military authorities. Now, with the changes in the Dutch military noted above, attitudes shifted (Joachim & Zarkov, 2001). So an agreement was made in 2000 between the University of Humanist Studies and the Ministry of Defence. The Dutch army has about forty humanist counsellors, and it was the Department of Humanist Spiritual Care, particularly a few dedicated women and men in it, that were instrumental in this partnership with the University. They financed a Dutch counterpart to Cynthia Cockburn, who would, for a year, introduce the study of gender relations in war to the curriculum, and further explore their specific relevance for the Dutch Army. The position was offered to Dubravka Zarkov. Born in Yugoslavia, and naturalized in the Netherlands, her prior research on femininity and masculinity in the Yugoslav wars complemented Cynthia Cockburn's interest in women and gender in Bosnia-Herzegovina.

It was from these strange encounters of institutions and people that the productive series of activities emerged that eventually led to the creation of this book. The first was an expert seminar organized in October 2000 on 'Gender Relations After War: Peace-building, Peacekeeping and Social Transformation'. This focused on three inter-related domains in war-torn societies. First, the gender dimension of international peacekeeping and violence control as an issue within peacekeeping militaries and between militaries and local populations. Second, the gender dimension of the activity of international organizations responsible for humanitarian aid and development after war. And third, the gender dimension of the voluntary sector in the restoration of civil society postwar – in particular the role of local women's organizations.

The seminar's objectives were to present empirical facts and effects revealed in recent research and practice; to highlight gaps in knowledge and analysis and thus inspire new research and theoretical debates; and to create a space for exchange of experience between academics, activists and practitioners. To accomplish this rather ambitious agenda we involved speakers and participants with a great deal of experience of such postwar situations, well regarded for their contribution to academic and policy thinking on these issues. Among them were three of the contributors to this book: Cynthia Enloe, Madeleine Rees and Suzanne Williams (Chapters 1, 4 and 6). We ourselves also gave papers that appear here as Chapters 7 and 11.

A second activity from which we drew contributions for the book was a seminar on 'Power and Powerlessness in Bosnia: Gender Aspects of Peacekeeping', held in December 2000.[8] This was organized specifically for military personnel in the Dutch army: those going to or coming back from Bosnia, policy-makers in the ministries of defence and foreign affairs and the teaching staff of military academies. This seminar had a dual purpose. On the one hand it aimed to provide a space where the participants – and especially the military personnel – could reflect on their experiences of peacekeeping in Bosnia. Both their encounters with the local population and the internal dynamic of the army were in question. On the other hand, we wanted to offer Dutch military, policy-makers and lecturers an opportunity to hear, and speak with, outstanding experts who had direct experience in dealing with the gender aspects of complex realities in Bosnia, were familiar with the peacekeeping role of the military in conflict zones, and were knowledgeable about gender relations within the Dutch military. Among these experts were Jolanda Bosch, Meliha Hubic, Madeleine Rees, and Desiree Verweij, each of whom contributes to this volume. Regretfully, Nancy Paterson, a lawyer in the Prosecutor's Office of the International War Crimes Tribunal for Yugoslavia, who also participated in the seminar, was not able to develop her presentation into a chapter, due to the increased work-load in the Court. Besides the contributions to these two seminars, the book includes four more texts, those by Bob Connell, Dyan Mazurana, Stefan Dudink and Marc de Leeuw. We found their work and the perspectives they introduce highly relevant for the discussion to which we wish to contribute.

On the wider scene, the context for the book is an active and inspiring women's movement worldwide to which, as authors and editors, we acknowledge a great debt. Many countries have been swept by hurricanes of killing and destruction in the last decade. In all those war-ravaged places, women have not just suffered and survived the violence. Sometimes they have participated in it. Elsewhere they have actively resisted it. And in many cases they have intelligently analyzed it. Some of the most overwhelming displays of firepower, in Iraq for instance, and in Yugoslavia, have been enacted by powerful countries claiming to act for justice and human rights. Women in the countries from which the bombers fly (and the peacekeepers are despatched) are also part of the growing women's movement against militarism and war. Careful feminist analyses of the gendered processes of war and peace making, as well as feminist protests against masculine militarized violence, are at last awakening, slowly but surely, glimmers of gender awareness in the international institutions and national governments mounting peacekeeping operations. We hope that this book will contribute to the debate and, more important, inspire action.

Notes

1. While recognizing shortcomings in the term 'patriarchy', we use it here as a succinct term to signify a long-lived, but adaptive, sex-and-gender order characterized by a hierarchy among men, and of men over women, that structures and is structured by other hierarchical systems, notably those of class and ethnicity.

2. See especially Chapman and Rutherford 1988, Gilmore 1990, Craig 1992, Easthope 1992, Sinha 1995, de Almeida 1996 and Bowker 1998.

3. See especially classics such as Huston 1982, Enloe 1983, 1989, 1993, and Elshtain 1987; or Connell 1985 and Theweleit 1987.

4. See for example studies such as Cooper, Munich and Squier 1989, Farmanfarmaian 1992, Cooke and Woollacot 1993, Brouke 1996, Melman 1998, Cockburn 2001 and Zarkov 2001.

5. From NATO Fact Sheets, *Nato's Role in Bosnia and Herzegovina*. This and the information in subsequent paragraphs is drawn from the website <www.nato.int/docu/facts>.

6. The text of the General Framework Agreement can be consulted at <www.nato.int/ifor>.

7. Tweede Kamer (2000), *Defensie Nota*, vergaderjaar 1999-2000, 26 900, nrs.1-2.

8. The first seminar was sponsored by the Department of Humanist Spiritual Care, Ribbius Peletier Foundation and the University for Humanist Studies, the second by the Department of Humanist Spiritual Care of the Dutch Ministry of Defence.

PART 1:
DISMANTLING MILITARISM, DECOMMISSIONING MASCULINITIES

Demilitarization – or more of the same? Feminist questions to ask in the postwar moment

CYNTHIA ENLOE

To explain why, even after the guns have gone silent, militarization and the privileging of masculinity is each so common, we need to surrender the oft-cherished notion that when open warfare stops, militarization is reversed. One of the insights garnered by feminist analysts from the recent experiences of women and men in societies as different as Bosnia and Rwanda is that the processes of militarization can continue to roll along even after the formal cease fire agreement has been signed.

Persistent militarization in a postwar society serves to re-entrench the privileging of masculinity – in both private and public life. Thus, if we lack the tools to chart *postwar* militarization, we will almost certainly be ill-equipped to monitor the subtle ways in which – democratic rhetoric notwithstanding – masculinity continues to be the currency for domination and exclusion.

In a given social group at any particular time – for instance, the Netherlands in the mid-1600s, Yugoslavia in the late 1990s, Oxfam and the UN in the early 2000s – there are likely to be at work certain processes that bestow influence on those men who manage to meet the currently accepted (versus existing, but commonly disparaged) standards of manliness. The contest between rival models of masculinity has profound consequences for women; each rival form of masculinity requires for its validation the acceptance of a particular form of femininity. If a form of masculinity which has as its conforming complement a passive, demure, domesticated model of femininity gains public credibility, then genuine democratization is almost certain to be derailed. Militarized masculinity is a model of masculinity that is especially likely to be imagined as requiring a feminine complement that excludes women from full and assertive participation in postwar public life.

For the past two centuries this rivalry between gendered meanings has been played out in both national and international political arenas. How exactly those rivalries between forms of masculinity that politically marginalize women and those (more rare) forms of masculinity which are confirmed, rather than threatened, by women's vibrant, autonomous public participation actually evolve is determined in no small part by the trends in militarization. The rise or fall in levels of militarization is not caused by lunar orbits. Whether the process of militarization is stalled, reversed or propelled forward in any society is determined by the political processes that bolster certain notions of masculinity and certain presumptions about femininity over their gendered alternatives.

During recent years I have become convinced that it is not enough for us to talk about militarism. We must talk about – monitor, explain, challenge – those multi-layered processes by which militarism gains legitimacy and popular and elite acceptance; that is, we must learn how to track militarization. So let's look at each – militarism and militarization – and then at their interaction.

Like any ideology, militarism is a package of ideas. It is a compilation of assumptions, values and beliefs. When any person – or institution or community – embraces militarism it is thus embracing particular value assertions about what is good, right, proper and about what is bad, wrong and improper. By embracing the ideology of militarism, a person, institution or community is also accepting a distinctive package of beliefs – about how the world works, about what makes human nature tick.

Among those distinctively militaristic core beliefs are: a) that armed force is the ultimate resolver of tensions; b) that human nature is prone to conflict; c) that having enemies is a natural condition; d) that hierarchical relations produce effective action; e) that a state without a military is naïve, scarcely modern and barely legitimate; f) that in times of crisis those who are feminine need armed protection; and g) that in times of crisis any man who refuses to engage in armed violent action is jeopardizing his own status as a manly man.

Occasionally these beliefs are put under public scrutiny and examined; often, though, they are left unproblematized, as if they were 'natural'. Whatever one treats as 'natural' is close to the core of one's own ideology.

Now let's look at militarization. It is not itself an ideology. It is a socio-political process. Militarization is the multi-stranded process by which the roots of militarism are driven deep down into the soil of a society – or of a non-governmental organization, a governmental department, an ethnic group or an international agency. There is nothing automatic or inevitable about the militarizing process. Militarization can be stalled by exposure, critique and resistance at an early stage; occasionally it may be reversed. It also, however, can be propelled forward after years of apparent stagnation. Most militarizing processes occur during what is misleadingly labeled 'peacetime'. Thus the 1980s can now, with hindsight, be seen as an era in Yugoslav society during which militarizing processes were deliberately nurtured.

Interesting questions to raise today include the following. Has the end of the fighting in Bosnia-Herzegovina, the arrival of myriad international organizations and the onset of peace-building and reconstruction resulted in demilitarization. Or has militarization on the contrary been stubbornly sustained there? And when, as in the Netherlands, the way the purpose of a national army is imagined gradually shifts from war-fighting to peacekeeping, does that mean that militarization has gone into reverse? These questions are in the minds of the authors of several of the chapters in this book.

To chart and explain militarization in any place at any time, we need to equip ourselves with the analytical skills to monitor the transformation of assumptions, reassessment of priorities, evolution of values. This is, admittedly, a tall order. I have become convinced that it is an order that can be filled only by wielding an explicitly feminist curiosity. The observer does not have to be – at least at the outset – a self-identified feminist. One just has to start asking very specific sorts of questions. A 'feminist curiosity' is a curiosity that provokes serious questioning about the workings of masculinized and femininized meanings. It is the sort of curiosity that prompts one to pay attention to things that conventionally are treated as if they were either 'natural' or, even if acknowledged to be artificial, are imagined to be ' trivial', that is, imagined to be without explanatory significance.

What follows here is just the start of a set of necessary questions to which answers must be sought if militarization – and its complementary marginalization of women in public life – is to be accurately monitored and, perhaps, rolled back.

Feminist Monitoring Question Number One: Do people who can claim to have been 'combatants' in either the insurgents' or state's armed forces carry extra weight when they speak to officials or to the public, *and* does that differential weighting privilege certain sorts of manliness and marginalize most women, regardless of their presumed femininity?

The special objects of feminist curiosity here are the listeners. Pursuing this first feminist question sends one to quite mundane sites. In a postwar Bosnian town meeting, are most residents reluctant to interrupt a male speaker who claims to be a current or past army or militia combatant? Are veterans' claims most likely to receive an elite hearing – by either a civilian Bosnian or UN official in Sarajevo – or a politician in Amsterdam? In informal social gatherings, whose 'war stories' are listened to most attentively? In a policy meeting about the return of refugees to their homes in Bosnia, whose view is considered the most authoritative, that of the humanitarian NGO – or the battalion commander of SFOR, the international peacekeeper whose guns and armoured cars will wield the necessary threat of force?

There are serious implications for leaving any of these militarized dynamics unnamed and unchallenged. It matters for the long-term inclusiveness of the democratizing process who is listened to by harried, short-handed officials and staff, who is presumed to have the 'credentials' to speak, who is deemed to possess the pertinent experience, the relevant skills, the most acute stake to make their words worthy of attention when so many are vying for attention. *Insofar* as armed combatants in the recent conflict have been mostly male, and *insofar* as it is masculinized combatants who are presumed by their influential civilian listeners to have things to say that (even if unpleasant) must be addressed publicly, the immediate post-conflict political process will be on the road to *remilitarization* without a warning shot being fired. Listening can be militarized. Listening can be masculinized.

Feminist Monitoring Question Number Two: To what extent do those people who wield militarized power (whether or not they wear camouflage or gold braid) become, in everyone else's eyes, the people to whom one must gain access if one is going to have an impact on public affairs? People in positions of militarized authority can threaten to use coercive force. They can label some places and groups 'allies' and others 'public security threats'. They can deploy armed troops here but not there. They can assign armed escorts to some aid convoys but not to others. They can claim 'urgency' in tones that others rarely can invoke. They can resort to secrecy with less challenge than their non-militarized counterparts. One frequently hears militarized decision-makers fret over the consequences of these common perceptions, even if they, by their own actions, have helped create them. These fretful officials express frustration: so many people come to them for resources and solutions; they 'expect us to be social workers'.

Insofar as those officials wielding militarized resources and militarized authority perceive their missions to have primacy over all other missions, those officials are fostering a militarized political culture in the post-conflict society. *Insofar* as many others (inside and outside decision-making institutions) come to share that belief, the perpetuation of militarization will be fuelled further. Moreover, *insofar* as it is widely imagined to be unproblematic for those militarized posts to be assigned to manly men, it will be tempting for everyone in the society to couch their explanations and their needs in the sorts of terms understood by masculinized officials with militarized agendas. This, in turn, is likely to marginalize those officials less willing or less able to speak in these masculinized, militarized terms, and those civic groups who are actively seeking to civilianize postwar society. Some men thereby will be shut out of serious public conversation. Most women will be.

Feminist Monitoring Question Number Three: To what extent does a given officialdom or a general public assume that security – especially if used in the English phrase 'national security' – refers to militarized security? For years now, women active in creating peace groups – the Women in Black in Jerusalem and Belgrade, the protesters camping at the gates of missile bases at Greenham Common, England and Seneca Falls, New York, as well as members of the world-wide organization, The Women's International League for Peace and Freedom, or of Women Monitoring the Peace in the Southern Sudan – have been developing feminist analyses that reveal first, that security is gendered and, second, that to be realistic about what security entails one has to break down the ideological walls separating 'public' life from 'private' life.

For many women, the home and neighbourhood (and temporary 'home', a refugee camp) can be as insecure as a battlefield. In fact, a home or a neighbourhood street can *be* a battlefield. When postwar local and international authorities treat violence against women as a non-priority, as an issue to be put off until 'later', as a matter not falling within their own mandate, those same authorities perpetuate a crucial dynamic of militarization in a time of alleged peace.

Through the collection of evidence and its careful analysis, feminist peace activists have demonstrated that men and women, despite their sometimes shared conditions, do not experience identical threats. Their research has revealed that wartime violence translates into quite distinct forms of displacement, intimidation and privation for women and men, that whatever rewards wartime may generate – and, for some, wartime does generate rewards in security, status, power and material wealth – they are not equally distributed among the society's women and men. These women peace activists have found that the sorts of insecurity many women experience in the midst of openly armed conflict are surprisingly akin to the forms of insecurity that women experience when the guns are silent: the lack of those resources that can be used to insure their own physical integrity.

Yet all of this insightful observing and theorizing about security has only just begun to make a modest dent in the orthodox presumption that 'security studies' are the studies of militarized decision-making and that a 'national security' deliberation is a discussion devoted to the maintenance of a state's militarized well-being.

Domestic violence prevention and prosecution, consequently, are not deemed worthy of urgent attention by 'security' officials coping with the demands of post-conflict reconstruction. Those engaged in training a new police force, building a new judiciary, or drafting a new legal code, thereby leave the serious strategizing about domestic violence to the handful of feminists inside international agencies and their under-resourced allies active in over-worked local women's groups. (We shall see something of this in Madeleine Rees' Chapter 4 in this volume.) By their neglect, they perpetuate in peacetime one core propellant of militarization: the presumption that masculinized violence is natural.

Trafficking in women, likewise, is rarely treated by conventional 'security' officials – international and local – as an urgent concern inside their own bureaucratic bailiwicks. Those officials, instead, more often see only a shrunken list of security issues as appropriate to their fine-honed skills and as demanding their scarce attention. A commercialized violation of women's physical integrity – such as organized international trafficking – typically only achieves the conventionally lofty status of a 'security' issue when commercialized sex appears to have become a threat to male soldiers' health and discipline. It may be deliberately swept under the policy-makers' rug if police or military personnel are suspected of being directly engaged in the trafficking operations (see Rees, Chapter 4).

To gain an attentive hearing from officials imbued with this conventional notion of security is very difficult. It leaves 'security' deliberations not only militarized, but also highly masculinized, with most women working in NGOs and in international agencies cooling their heels outside the meeting room. This masculinized exclusion is made all the more intense by the typical shroud of secrecy draped over any discussions presumed to be about 'security'. Given these exclusionary dynamics, it becomes tempting for advocates of urgent action against domestic violence and trafficking in women to adopt a militarized discourse strategy of their own. That is, they may try to pry open the closed door to the security deliberations room by defining violence against local women as a matter of military discipline or as a question of militiamen's intimidation – when these advocates themselves really believe the issue to be a matter of economic justice, public health, democratization and human rights. If, using this tempting tactical ploy, they succeed in getting their toe in the door to security deliberations, they may well discover that, once inside, they have lost control of the original issue. As a result, women's well-being in the reconstructed post-conflict society will still be left on the proverbial back burner.

Feminist Monitoring Question Number Four: To what extent does the new (internationally mentored) government's budget allocate disproportionate public funds to that nascent government's security forces? It is true that police forces and military forces do not usually foster identical constructions of masculinity. They also are apt, in post-conflict times as in pre-conflict times, to be recruited disproportionately from rather different social classes and ethnic or racialized communities. Yet, these important dissimilarities notwithstanding, police forces and militaries each conventionally are overwhelmingly male in their composition, and more often than not, they are deeply masculinized in their institutional cultures. In some post-conflict countries – for instance, post-1994 South Africa – there has been an organized lobby created specifically to keep watch on the new military, to insure that it recruits a sizeable proportion of women into its reorganized ranks. The same is happening in some countries whose armies contribute to international peacekeeping forces – the Netherlands for instance (see the account in Chapter 8 of this volume by Jolanda Bosch and Desiree Verweij). 'Success', however, may come in the form of a small percentage of women in the new military. The upper reaches of the command structure, while now less mono-ethnic, may, nonetheless, be, just as before, reliant on a stubbornly persistent masculinized culture.

If the postwar military and the police forces are rebuilt by local and international officials who shy away from questioning these comfortable masculinized 'esprit' traditions and *if* those two institutions are awarded disproportionate slices of the new state's budgetary pie, then the result will be that a disproportionate share of scarce public monies will be invested in the salaries, equipment, morale and prestige of those parts of the larger state that are least invested in women's voices being heard inside the state. This deeply gendered – that is, masculinized – outcome will be produced even while the élites of the military and police force are routinely pitted against one another in funding contests.

Rivalries between men, whether personal or bureaucratic, do not roll back either masculinization or militarization. Most often, those rivalries merely turn women into silent bystanders. Or, and this is less noticed, they turn women and ideas about proper femininity into cannon fodder for the waging of those masculinized rivalries for political turf or material resources. Being turned into someone else's cannon fodder is not a promising formula for achieving first class citizenship.

Feminist Monitoring Question Number Five: To what extent is the status of a local woman, any woman, in the postwar setting, defined by influential decision-makers chiefly in terms of what they were during the recent war? That is, a feminist curiosity prompts one to keep track of whether certain women's wartime experiences (or the experiences to which anyone paid attention) continue to be deemed to be the principal basis for defining their present socio-political role. For instance, which women are seen by public figures as 'heroic mothers'? Which women are talked about in public almost exclusively as 'victims of sexual assault'? Which women are seen as the enemies of the newly established state, or of the nation emerging from war?

Employing categories helps us think. Some categories are useful in the making of policies and the nurturing of cultures that foster genuine democratization and demilitarization. But narrow, war-referenced categories into which many women are placed by journalists and decision-makers – even categories that seem to valorize some women – can become the basis for crafting patriarchal and militarized public policies. To act out of a feminist curiosity means conducting an examination of public policy discourse (memos, television news scripts, campaign speeches, legislative records) to see which categories are imposed to make sense of women's lives in the post-conflict societies. A feminist curiosity leads one to be suspicious of a dependence only on those categories that acknowledge women either as silently symbolic or as silently victimized.

Feminist Monitoring Question Number Six: Which organizations active in the post-conflict society's reconstruction are the most patriarchal? What area of authority, what resources for the remaking of the society do these organizations control? Whose senses of inclusion and well-being do these organizations' operations most perpetuate? By 'patriarchal' here I mean something quite specific. Any organization is patriarchal: insofar as its internal culture privileges masculinity; insofar as its decision-making is *un*informed by a concern for the actual lives of women as full citizens; and insofar as its policies and actual practices serve to re-entrench privileged masculinity in the wider society. One might take this questioning further, turn a feminist curiosity onto specific influential organizations, peer inside and ask which of its several departments is the most patriarchal and how does that shape the culture and resource allocation of the organization as a whole.

Take all the international and local organizations operating in Bosnia-Herzegovina during 1995 – 2001 (we see many of them at work in Chapters 5 and 7 of this volume). One could launch a comparative study of their relative patriarchal inclinations and impacts. Where, then, on the scale of institutional patriarchy would one place:

The Office of the High Representative of the Peace
  Implementation Council;
The World Bank;
The Dutch battalion of SFOR, the UN Peacekeeping Office;
The international NGO, 'Doctors Without Borders';
The UN High Commission for Refugees;
'Kvinna till Kvinna', the Swedish women's NGO;
The Office of the UN High Commissioner for Human Rights;
'Women of Mostar', Bosnian NGO;
OSCE, the Organization of Security and Co-operation in Europe;
The US Agency for International Development;
The International Police Task Force;
Catholic Relief Services;
The Bosnian Ministry of Labour;
The Bosnian Ministry of Health;
Each of the several Bosnian political parties.

In conducting this investigation one should not leave out this last set of organizations on our initial list, Bosnia's fledgling political parties.

One of the lessons we have learned from feminists in Chile, Nicaragua and other post-conflict and militarized societies is that the creation of new competitive political parties in the name of the establishment of democracy can perpetuate a subtle form of militaristic thinking and update old forms of masculinized privilege. Women active in electoral politics in countries as different as Sweden, Britain, France, India and Japan have been revealing through their analyses of their parties just how stubborn patriarchal ways of behaving and thinking can be inside allegedly democratic electoral political parties – of the ideological left as well as of the centre and right. Thus, promoting multi-party electoral politics in Bosnia is no guarantee that some of the beliefs and values which are essential to the perpetuation of militarization – especially the belief in the allegedly natural masculine proficiency in public arena competitions – will not be legitimized yet again.

Conclusion

We are only beginning to chart the multiple paths which militarization can follow. It is a subtle process. What fuels militarization can be disparate and hard to pin-point. It can move forward before the guns start firing and continue to do so after they have fallen (mostly) silent. Without a determined curiosity, informed by feminist analysis, militarization's causes and consequences will remain below the surface of public discussion and formal decision-making until they are almost impossible to reverse. None of these causes and consequences of militarization are more significant than the entrenchments of ideas about 'manly men' and 'real women'.

If the experiences of women in Bosnia – local Bosnian women of all classes and communities, as well as non-Bosnian women working with governmental, international, and independent organizations – are taken seriously, we have a far better chance of detecting how militarization and its complementary privileging of masculinity is perpetuated and perhaps how it might be put into reverse. But taking all of these diverse women's experiences seriously entails asking some pretty awkward questions. Feminist questions are always awkward precisely because they make problematic what is conventionally taken as 'logical' or 'natural'.

Then, there is the question of what to do with the answers. Sandbagging, or even reversing, the current subterranean flows of militarization in Bosnia today will require (as Cynthia Cockburn argues in Chapter 5 of this volume) a far more profound commitment to genuinely inclusive democratization than is often called for by bankers, health experts, security officials, lawyers and electoral strategists. Many of the players in contemporary Bosnia may have to surrender an advantage they have been loathe even to admit: the privileging of their own status as masculine.

For tutoring me on the subtle genderings of political life and the ongoing processes of militarization in post-conflict societies, I am especially grateful to Dyan Mazurana, Suzanne Williams, Cynthia Cockburn, Venessa Farr, Angela Raven-Roberts, Sandra Whitworth, Wenona Giles, and Maja Korac.

Masculinities, the reduction of violence and the pursuit of peace

R.W. CONNELL

Though women have often manufactured weapons and serviced armies – and in an age of nuclear weapons are equally targeted – it is historically rare for women to be in combat. The twenty million members of the world's armed forces today are overwhelmingly men. In many countries all soldiers are men; and even in those countries which admit women to the military, commanders are almost exclusively men. Men also dominate other branches of enforcement, both in the public sector as police officers and prison guards, and in the private sector as security agents.

In private life too, men are more likely to be armed and violent. In the United States, careful research by criminologists establishes that private gun ownership runs four times as high among men as among women, even after a campaign by the gun industry to persuade women to buy guns. (The average percentage of US men owning guns, in surveys from 1980 to 1994, was 49 per cent (Smith and Smith 1994)). In the same country, official statistics for 1996 show men accounting for 90 per cent of those arrested for aggravated assault and 90 per cent of those arrested for murder and manslaughter (US Bureau of the Census 1998).These figures are not exceptional.

There is a debate about the gender balance of violence within households, and it is clear that many women are capable of violence (for instance in punishing children). The weight of evidence, however, indicates that major domestic violence is overwhelmingly by husbands towards wives (Dobash et al 1992). Rape is overwhelmingly by men on women. Criminal rape shades into sexual intercourse under pressure. The major national survey of sexual behaviour in the United States finds women six times as likely as men to have an experience of forced sex, almost always being forced by a man (Laumann et al 1994).

Further, men predominate in warlike conduct in other spheres of life. Body-contact sports, such as boxing and football, involve ritualized combat and often physical injury. These sports are almost exclusively practised by men. Dangerous driving is increasingly recognized as a form of violence. It is mainly done by men. Young men die on the roads at a rate four times that of young women, and kill at an even higher ratio (Walker et al 2000). Older men, as corporate executives, make the decisions that result in injury or death from the actions of their businesses – industrial injuries to their workers, pollution injury to neighbours, and environmental destruction.

So men predominate across the spectrum of violence. A strategy for demilitarization and peace must concern itself with this fact, with the reasons for it, and with its implications for work to reduce violence.

There is a widespread belief that it is natural for men to be violent. Males are inherently more aggressive than women, the argument goes. 'Boys will be boys' and cannot be trained otherwise; rape and combat – however regrettable – are part of the unchanging order of nature. There is often an appeal to biology, with testosterone in particular, the so-called 'male hormone', as a catch-all explanation for men's aggression.

Careful examination of the evidence shows that this biological essentialism is not credible. Testosterone levels for instance, far from being a clear-cut *source* of dominance and aggression in society, are as likely to be the *consequence* of social relations. Cross-cultural studies of masculinities reveal a diversity that is impossible to reconcile with a biologically-fixed master pattern of masculinity (Connell 2000).

When we speak statistically of 'men' having higher rates of violence than women, we must not slide to the inference that therefore all men are violent. Almost all soldiers are men, but most men are not soldiers. Though most killers are men, most men never kill or even commit assault. Though an appalling number of men do rape, most men do not. It is a fact of great importance, both theoretically and practically, that there are many non-violent men in the world. This too needs explanation, and must be considered in a strategy for the reduction of violence and for peace.

Further, when we note that most soldiers, sports professionals, or executives are men, we are not just talking about individuals. We are speaking of masculinized institutions. The organizational culture of armies, for instance, is heavily gendered. Recent social research inside armed forces reveals an energetic effort to produce a narrowly-defined hegemonic masculinity (Breines et al 2000). Similarly, organized sport does not just reflect, but actively produces, particular versions of masculinity (Messner and Sabo 1994).

We may reason, then, that it is in *social masculinities* rather than biological differences that we must seek the main causes of gendered violence, and the main answers to it. How are social masculinities to be understood? In grappling with this question, we are able to draw on a new generation of research, to which I now turn.

Understanding masculinities

In recent years there has been a great flowering of research on the nature and forms of social masculinities. This research, and accompanying debate, is now world-wide (Connell 2000). It has moved decisively beyond the old concept of a unitary 'male sex role' or a fixed 'masculine' character structure. Empirical studies of the details of social life are necessarily complex, but some important general conclusions do seem to be emerging from this research as a whole. I will condense them into seven points, noting in each case some implications for peace strategy.

Multiple masculinities Different cultures, and different periods of history, construct gender differently. In multicultural societies there are likely to be multiple definitions of masculinity. Equally important, more than one kind of masculinity can be found within a given culture, even within a single institution such as a school or workplace. The implication is that violent, aggressive masculinity will rarely be the only form of masculinity present, in any cultural setting. The variety of masculinities that are documented in research can provide examples and materials for peace education. Education programmes must recognize diversity in gender patterns, and deal with the tensions that can result from social diversity.

Hierarchy and hegemony Different masculinities exist in definite relations with each other, often relations of hierarchy and exclusion. There is generally a dominant or 'hegemonic' form of masculinity, the centre of the system of gendered power. It may be the masculinity of a class elite, or of a military hierarchy or an ethnic-national leadership. The hegemonic form need not be the most common form of masculinity. This too has implications. Large numbers of men and boys have a divided, tense, or oppositional relationship to hegemonic masculinity. Clear-cut alternatives, however, are often culturally discredited or despised.

The most powerful groups of men usually have few personal incentives for gender change. Other groups may have stronger motives for change.

Collective masculinities Masculinities are sustained and enacted not only by individuals, but also by groups, institutions, and cultural forms like mass media. Multiple masculinities may be produced and sustained by the same institution. What are the implications here? The institutionalization of masculinity is a major problem for peace strategy. Corporations, armed forces, workplaces, voluntary organizations, and the state are important sites of action. Collective struggle, and the re-shaping of institutions, including military and police forces, are as necessary as the reform of individual life.

Bodies as arenas Men's bodies do not fix patterns of masculinity, but they are still very important in the expression of masculinity. Men's enactment of gender constantly involves bodily experience, bodily pleasures, and the vulnerabilities of bodies. It follows from this that peace education may often be too much 'in the head'. Health, sport and sexuality are issues which must be addressed in changing masculinity.

Active construction Masculinities do not exist prior to social interaction, but come into existence as people act. Masculinities are actively produced, using the resources available in a given milieu. It is an important principle that the process of constructing masculinity, rather than the end state, may be the source of violence. In rape, in homophobic violence, and in war men may be violent in order to assert (or defend) masculinity. But it also follows that no pattern of masculine violence is fixed, beyond all hope of social reform. Equally, no reform is final. It is possible that gender reforms will be overthrown and more violent patterns of masculinity re-introduced.

Division Masculinities are not homogeneous, but are likely to be internally divided. Men's lives often embody tensions between contradictory desires or practices. Thus, any pattern of masculinity has potentials for change. Any group of men is likely to have complex and conflicting interests, some of which will support change towards more peaceable gender patterns.

Dynamics Masculinities are created in specific historical circumstances. They are liable to be contested, reconstructed, or displaced. The forces producing change include contradictions within gender relations, as well as the interplay of gender with other social forces. Therefore, masculinities are always changing, and this creates motives for learning. However, as any agenda for change is likely to be against some groups' interests, controversy and conflict is to be expected.

These lessons are mainly drawn from research on local patterns of gender (some of which I cited above). In thinking about a strategy for peace, however, we must go beyond local contexts, and think at a global level too. The colonial empires from which the modern global economy developed were gendered institutions, which disrupted indigenous gender orders, and installed violent, often militarized, masculinities in the hegemonic position. This process was the beginning of a global gender order, and the colonisers' masculinities were the first global masculinities. In turn, the process of decolonization disrupted the gender hierarchies of the colonial order. Where armed struggle was involved, the use of western military technology also involved some adoption of western military masculinity, and further disruption of community-based gender orders.

World politics today is increasingly organized around the needs of transnational capital and the creation of global markets. Neo-liberalism speaks a gender-neutral language of 'markets', 'individuals', and 'choice', but has an implicit view of masculinity. The 'individual' of neoliberal theory has the attributes and interests of a male entrepreneur. Institutionally, the strong emphasis on competition creates a particular kind of hierarchy among men. Meanwhile the increasingly unregulated world of transnational corporations places strategic social power in the hands of particular groups of men. Here is the basis of a new hegemonic masculinity on a world scale.

The hegemonic form of masculinity in the new world order, I would argue, is the masculinity of the business executives who operate in global markets, and the political executives and military leaderships who constantly deal with them. I call this 'transnational business masculinity'. It can be seen at work in a country like Bosnia, in transition from war, where power resides with a cluster of leaders of institutions such as United Nations agencies, foreign governments, international bankers and business investors, global humanitarian organizations and peacekeeping militaries. I think that understanding the institutional masculinity of transnational organizations will be important for the future of peace strategies.

Peace strategies and masculinities

There are many causes of violence, including dispossession, poverty, greed, nationalism, racism, and other forms of inequality, bigotry and desire. Gender dynamics are by no means the whole story. Yet given the concentration of weapons and the practices of violence among men, gender patterns appear to be strategic. Masculinities are the forms in which many dynamics of violence take shape.

Evidently, then, a strategy for demilitarization and peace must include a strategy of change in masculinities. This is the new dimension in peace work which studies of men suggest: contesting the hegemony of masculinities which emphasize violence, confrontation and domination, and replacing them with patterns of masculinity more open to negotiation, cooperation and equality.

The relationship of masculinity to violence is more complex than appears at first sight, so there is not just one pattern of change required. Institutionalized violence (eg by armies) requires more than one kind of masculinity. The masculinity of the general is different from the masculinity of the front-line soldier, and armies acknowledge this by training them separately. The differing masculinities that are hegemonic in different cultures may lead to qualitatively different patterns of violence.

Some violent patterns of masculinity develop in response to violence; they do not simply cause it. An important example is the 'protest masculinity' that emerges in contexts of poverty and ethnic oppression. On the other hand, some patterns of masculinity are not personally violent, but their ascendancy creates conditions for violence, such as inequality and dispossession. The case of transnational business masculinity has already been mentioned.

A gender-informed strategy for peace must, therefore, be sophisticated about patterns of masculinity. It must also be designed to operate across a broad front, broader than most agendas of sex role reform would suggest. The arenas for action to reduce masculine violence are several. One is clearly child rearing, schooling and adult/child relationships in families, classrooms and play groups (including the issues commonly thought of as 'sex role modelling'). Personal life is equally significant. Marital relations and sexuality, family relationships, friendship are relevant arenas (including the role of sexual and domestic violence in constructions of masculinity).

Community life is another arena for action: peer groups, neighbourhood life, leisure, including sports (including youth subcultures as bearers of violent masculinities). Cultural institutions too: higher education, science and technology, mass media, the arts and popular entertainment (including exemplary masculinities in broadcast sports). Workplace and occupational cultures are very significant, including industrial relations, corporations, unions and bureaucracies; the state and its enforcement apparatuses (armies, police etc). Finally there are the dimensions of the economy – the labour market and the effects of unemployment; capital and commodity markets both international and local; management practices and ideologies.

What principles might link action across this very broad spectrum? I do not think we should follow the model of gender reform that demands men must adopt a new character, that they must instantly become 'the new man'. Such hero-making agendas deny what we already know about the multiplicity and the internal complexity of masculinities. Rather, strategy for peace needs to be embedded in a practicable strategy of change in gender relations. The goal should be to develop gender practices for men which shift gender relations in a democratic direction. Democratic gender relations are those that move towards equality, nonviolence, and mutual respect between people of different genders, sexualities, ethnicities, and generations.

A peace strategy concerned with masculinities, then, does not demand a complete rupture with patterns of conduct men are now familiar with. Some of the qualities in 'traditional' definitions of masculinity (eg courage, steadfastness, ambition) are certainly needed in the cause of peace. Active models of engagement are needed for boys and men, especially when peace is understood not just as the absence of violence, but as a positive form of life.

The task is not to abolish gender, but to re-shape it; to disconnect (for instance) courage from violence, steadfastness from prejudice, ambition from exploitation. In the course of that re-shaping, diversity will grow. Making boys and men aware of the diversity of masculinities that already exist in the world, beyond the narrow models they are commonly offered, is an important task for education.

Though the hierarchy of masculinities is part of the problem in gender relations, the fact that there are different masculinities is in itself an asset. At the lowest level, it establishes that masculinity is not a single fixed pattern. More positively, multiple masculinities represent complexity of interests and purposes, which open possibilities for change. Finally the plurality of gender patterns prefigures the creativity of a democratic social order.

For men, the democratic remaking of gender practices requires persistent engagement with women, not the separatism-for-men which is strong in current masculinity politics. The 'gender-relevant' programmes now attempted in schools, which do not necessarily segregate boys and girls but attempt to identify gender issues and make them the subject of conscious debate, are important examples. Educational and social action must be inclusive in another sense too, responding to the differing cultural meanings of gender and the different socioeconomic circumstances in which students live. A programme apt for suburban middle-class students may be very inappropriate for ethnically diverse inner-city children in poverty, or rural children living in villages.

No one with experience of struggles for peace, or of attempts at gender reform, will imagine these are easy tasks. Recognizing the interplay of masculinities with strategies for violence reduction and ultimately for peace is not a magic key. In some ways, indeed, it makes familiar strategies seem more complex and difficult. But it also, I believe, opens ways of moving past obstacles which both peace movements and the movement for gender democracy have encountered.

This paper is abbreviated and revised from a paper prepared for the UNESCO expert group meeting on 'Male roles and masculinities in the perspective of a culture of peace', Oslo, 1997. In its longer form it was published as 'Arms and the man: using the new research on masculinity to understand violence and promote peace in the contemporary world', in Ingeborg Breines, R.W. Connell and Ingrid Eide (eds), Male Roles, Masculinities and Violence: A Culture of Peace Perspective, *Paris, UNESCO Publishing, 2000. A short version appeared as 'Masculinities, violence and peacemaking' in* Peace News, *No. 2443, June–August 2001.*

International peacekeeping operations: to neglect gender is to risk peacekeeping failure

DYAN MAZURANA

In 2000/2001 a number of positive initiatives occurred that indicated a resolve within the United Nations to take account of the significance of gender in armed conflict and post-conflict environments. They included, and this is my concern in the present chapter, a commitment to *addressing gender issues in the planning and implementation of international peacekeeping operations*. These measures respond, belatedly, to years of activism and advocacy by women who have argued that war itself is profoundly gendered, and peacekeeping needs therefore to be acutely gender conscious. They have been saying that peacekeepers have not only neglected women's needs, but played into masculinist and militarist cultures, in some cases contributing to the exploitation and abuse of local women and girls.

The causes of armed conflict lie deeper, occur earlier, and are more complex and transnational than the majority of us acknowledge. Many contemporary wars are the legacies of colonialism and Cold War rivalries, and global shifts in economic and political power relations (Duffield 2001). When governments in marginalized and impoverished countries are weakened, their societies may experience armed conflict. When external and internal forces combine to destabilize markets and formal economies collapse, adaptive economies come into being that are often extra-legal and exceedingly violent.

In such structures, power lies in the hands of men, often militarized men, who govern through non-representative bureaucracies, often consisting of family relatives, mafiosi, local élites and heads of armed factions, including the military, paramilitaries, militias, police and secret police. Power is maintained through various levels and applications of violence. Genocide, mass displacement and attacks on civilian populations, torture, rape, enforced prostitution and custodial violence – these are not incidental to the conflict but are its goals and its tools (Macrae et al 1994; Reno 1998). These tools are fashioned with minute attention to gender: the gender of the victim, the gender of the perpetrator, and gender relations in the society and its cultures.

The purpose of many of today's post-modern wars is not necessarily to 'win' but to prolong opportunities for looting and accumulation. The spoils with which leaders pay for fighters' services include not only stolen goods and resources but human bodies, including women and girls used as sexual slaves and domestic servants, boys and girls used as porters and fighters by armed groups, and individuals of both sexes put to forced labour.

If peacekeeping operations are to have any level of long-term success in building peace in post-conflict societies, those involved in them have to become curious about such things. Moreover, they have to gain the skills to make responsible interventions into the social, economic and political dynamics that fuel conflicts and frustrate peace making and peacekeeping operations.

Peacekeeping operations predominantly masculine

Peacekeeping operations are dominated by defence departments and debates about national and international security – arenas where men, and masculine and militarized values and priorities, dominate and where feminist analyses and the use of gender perspectives are rare to nonexistent. Recently, however, women's advocates at local, national, and international levels have had varying degrees of success in influencing the policies and programmes of some civilian and humanitarian agencies that participate in peacekeeping operations and in branches of state governments responsible for humanitarian assistance. It is because of these efforts that the issues of gender and peacekeeping are now being raised at the highest levels of intergovernmental and governmental organizations, such as the UN Security Council and member government foreign affairs departments.

Of senior international officials involved in peacekeeping, UN Secretary-General Kofi Annan is among the few who repeatedly call for attention to the gender dimensions of armed conflict, post-conflict reconstruction, and peacekeeping (United Nations 2000a and b). But individual attentiveness, even at this level, does not appear to compensate for a lack of gender mandates, expertise, policy, and accountability throughout the upper levels of peacekeeping operations.

Tardiness in evolving a gender policy is not unrelated to the low presence of women among those responsible for designing or carrying out peacekeeping operations. It is of course ultimately member states that decide who to send on police, military and government assignments, and the percentage of women contributed by member governments to peacekeeping is routinely lower than the percentage of women in their national militaries. But the UN, that could have taken a lead, did not issue specific requests for women peacekeepers until 1994 – a peak year, it so happened, in the demand for peacekeeping personnel.

At the end of 2000, the number of international peacekeepers stood at around 38,500 (Kaufholz 2001). Women comprised 25 per cent of professional staff, 51 per cent of general service staff, 15 per cent of field staff and 26 per cent local staff (United Nations 2001a). Percentages of women are lowest on the military side of operations. Between 1957 and 1989, women represented less then 0.1 per cent of military personnel in UN peacekeeping (Beilstein 1995). By 2000, the figure had crept up – but only to 2.6 per cent of military personnel, 4 per cent of civilian police peacekeepers (United Nations 2001a).

Comparable data for civilian personnel contributed by intergovernmental, international, regional and national organizations are not available. Nor do we know what is the proportion of women among the numerous foreign government representatives or private contract personnel in a given host nation at any one time. We need much better identification and analyses of all these groups, and their roles and interactions with local populations, before we can feel confident of having a clear picture of the gender dynamics of 'post-conflict reconstruction'.

One thing we do know – peacekeeping operations with more civilians and less militaries, and those with strong human rights monitoring mandates, have tended to have more women personnel (35-37 per cent) and also to have been the most successful. They have included the UN operations in Haiti (MICIVIH), Guatemala (MINUGUA), and South Africa (UNMOSA) (Helland et al 1999; Olsson 1999). By 'success' is meant here the ability of the operation to meet its mandate, contribute to peaceful resolutions of external disputes, promote rights education, provide assistance in enabling civil society to develop, and empower the local community in ways that help them reconstruct their lives and society. Successful operations also include those in which local populations reported positive interaction with peacekeepers and were (largely) not subject to abuses by peacekeepers (Hudson 2000). In MICIVIH and MINUGUA, many of the women in the peacekeeping operation were lawyers who had extensive knowledge of indigenous issues and worked well with the human rights organizations in those countries, the majority of which were created and staffed by local women (Helland et al. 1999).

Since 1997, the humanitarian component of peacekeeping operations has been administered by the UN Office on the Co-ordination of Humanitarian Affairs (OCHA) where, in 1998, women held approximately 35 per cent of the decision-making positions (Olsson 1999). Under OCHA's supervision, the civilian side of peacekeeping currently has four women in senior decision-making positions. At the same time, the majority of senior staff in the emergency or humanitarian divisions is male and there is a distinctly masculinised culture in the sections within these divisions that deal with interventions in emergency situations, most notably those covering transport, communications, logistics, water, electricity, and supply. (A similar process is described in Oxfam, by Williams, in Chapter 6 of this volume.)

Within the UN, it is DPKO that is charged with implementing and overseeing peacekeeping operations. The Department currently has one military woman in an upper-level decision-making position, Colonel Annette Leijenaar. It is under her guidance that DPKO has been undertaking its current gender and peacekeeping initiative. But it is an institution shaped and informed by particular types of masculinities and militarization and, as she herself reports, no military woman has ever held a senior command post in a DPKO field operation (Leijanaar 2000).

Gender initiatives in peacekeeping operations

International humanitarian and human rights law provides the legal foundation for all peacekeeping operations. And a solid basis exists within this body of laws and instruments for mandating a gender perspective into those operations. The premier international treaty on the rights of women is the Convention on the Elimination of All Forms of Discrimination against Women (1979), and its Article 1 is often cited in this connection.

More precisely, however, the precedent for mainstreaming gender into peacekeeping operations is established in *The Beijing Declaration and Platform for Action* that followed from the United Nations Fourth World Conference on Women in 1995. The *Platform*'s section on 'Women and Armed Conflict' set out the gender-specific bearing of armed conflict on girls and women and, among other things, called for a greater involvement of women in decision-making after war and in international peacekeeping interventions (United Nations 1996a).

'Gender mainstreaming' subsequently became a policy of the UN itself, following Economic and Social Council Resolution 1996/310, in which a commitment was made to achieving gender balance in all professional posts of UN bodies, not excluding peacekeeping operations (United Nations 1996b).

Gender issues have since impacted on peacekeeping policy more directly. Responding to pressure from women and men, human rights and other non-governmental organizations and some governments, the Security Council mounted a debate on 'Women and Peace and Security'. As a result, a new Security Council Resolution, No 1325, was adopted. It called on all actors involved in conflict and post-conflict situations to incorporate gender perspectives into their work. What is more, it called for 'a gender component' in UN field-based operations (point 5) and an expansion of the role and contribution of women in the field, especially among military observers, civilian police, human rights and humanitarian personnel (point 4). It committed the Security Council to work in consultation with local and international women's organizations for these purposes (United Nations 2000c).

Formal incorporation of gender perspectives into peacekeeping operations is thus an emerging phenomenon. Notable examples (although they have produced mixed results) include the creation of civilian Gender Affairs offices in the UN peacekeeping operations in Afghanistan, Kosova/o and East Timor, with the most recent office in the MONUC mission in the Democratic Republic of Congo. Another positive (if late) development is described in Chapter 4 of this book, by Madeleine Rees, one of its initiators: the creation of a Gender Co-ordination Group within the international community involved in Bosnia-Herzegovina to counter the gender-blind Dayton Peace Accords.

The latest most influential international document shaping responses to peacekeeping is the *Report of the Panel on United Nations Peace Operations* (United Nations 2001). It recommends the establishment of a Gender Unit in DPKO and a fair gender distribution in peacekeeping positions. But these, it has to be said, are the report's only recommendations on gender.

Building on them, UN Under Secretary-General for Peacekeeping, Jean-Marie Guéhenno, prioritized the creation of a Gender Unit to 'mainstream gender perspectives systematically into peacekeeping operations and to recruit women candidates for positions at all levels' (UN General Assembly 2001b, p1). DPKO followed by putting forward a request for a Gender Unit in their 2000-1 budget proposal

(UN 24 January 2001c). Disappointingly, in spring 2001, lacking the fanfare of the previous announcements, DPKO quietly dropped the Gender Unit and its budget request.

Inadequate funding and staffing and a low priority for mainstreaming gender into the departments that must implement these measures, remain serious obstacles. There is currently only one person, who serves as a Gender Focal Point, with responsibilities in many departments, whom DPKO can sometimes call on for assistance in this field. Now the proposal for a Gender Unit has been halted. Given the department's leading role in peacekeeping, its resistance to adequately funded gender initiatives urgently needs to be addressed. Otherwise, the commitments made by the UN at the highest levels, including recent pledges by Kofi Annan and the Security Council, will not be fulfilled.

The challenge and potential of mainstreaming gender throughout peacekeeping operations is clearly demonstrated by the case of the Gender Affairs Bureau for UNTAET, East Timor (Whittington 2001). At the beginning of the operation in East Timor, the Gender Affairs Bureau was 'mainstreamed' out of existence by senior male UNTAET staff. Then its Director arrived in East Timor and reinstated it. Operating without a budget at first, she spent several months successfully raising funds for the Bureau. In less than a year, the Bureau added several part-time staff, with individuals responsible for statistical analyses of the operation and all new appointments; legal advocacy and analyses; networking and capacity building with local women's organizations throughout East Timor; promotion of women's rights and human rights; and women's empowerment. For example, in preparation for the elections in August 2001, the Bureau ran a series of workshops for potential women political candidates, a necessary step in building a sustainable, equitable democracy within East Timor.

The Bureau also works in close co-ordination with and provides gender training for the office that orients all new UNTAET personnel. It runs gender training for UNTAET's military and police peacekeeping forces and the new national Timor Loro Sae Police Service. Significantly, the Special Representative to the Secretary-General for UNTAET stresses the importance of mainstreaming gender throughout UNTAET at public speaking engagements, political parties, consultative bodies, and high-level meetings. This message is also carried through articles in UNTAET's newspaper, radio and television programmes, and posters. By working in close collaboration with East

Timorese women activists, the UNTAET Gender Affairs Bureau has pioneered from scratch the first effectively functioning gender office in the history of peacekeeping. As such, it could well serve as a model for other operations.

Providing adequate support for gender offices, bureaus and advisors within UN peacekeeping operations should be a priority for UN Headquarters. Local, governmental, and international women's advocates and organizations need to be at the forefront of monitoring and evaluating these developments to ensure that the proper commitments and funds are made available for implementation and evaluation of gender mainstreaming initiatives, that gender initiatives actively involve and consult with local organizations working for sustainable peace and development, and that such initiatives achieve their objectives.

The politics of training peacekeepers

Intensive training for peacekeepers in issues of gender and women's rights under international humanitarian law and international human rights law is in its initial stages. When the majority of peacekeepers first arrive in the field, most rely on the only training they receive before deployment, which is military training. Yet, as feminist scholar Fetherston notes, 'if we only train people for war it is far more likely that is what we will get' (Fetherston 1998, p172). Instead of grounding peacekeeping training largely on militarized force, training programmes should reflect the broader context of the causes and consequences of the armed conflict, and the experiences, needs, and rights of men, women, boys and girls within particular conflict zones.

Recently, some peacekeeping training centres and countries have adopted the latter approach. To introduce and strengthen gender perspectives within peacekeeping operations, the Canadian Department of Foreign Affairs and International Trade (DFAIT) and the United Kingdom Department for International Development (DFID) produced an intensive training course 'Gender and Peace Support Operations' (DFAIT/DFID 2000). The first of its kind, it is designed to assist military, police, and civilian personnel and institutions involved in peacekeeping to acquire a deeper understanding of the gender dimensions of armed conflict and post-conflict peacebuilding, thereby improving their ability to uphold international humanitarian and human rights law, recognize and promote women's human rights, and carry out their missions.

Under the leadership of Colonel Leijenaar, DPKO has drawn on and significantly adapted the Canadian/British material for use in training military personnel and police before and during UN peace-keeping operations (DPKO does not offer training for civilians). Although they cannot require them to be applied, the DPKO will also make the training materials available to member states, whose military and police authorities have primary responsibility for training the personnel they contribute to peacekeeping operations.

In spring 2001, DPKO field-tested the gender material in UNTAET, East Timor and UNMEE, Eritrea/Ethiopia, the Democratic Republic of Congo and Sierra Leone. Angela Mackay headed the programme. Finding she was unable to obtain enough current, context-specific information on the conflicts in those countries or on the unfolding of the peacekeeping operations, she decided to open the gender training sessions to both the military peacekeepers and the local populations, as a means of having the local men and women provide their analyses and stories. In UNMEE, several community leaders attended the training, including the mayor, as well as local women and men. Mackay found that the most profound learning came about when local civilians partic-ipated in the training sessions with the military peacekeepers, as it gave all participants an idea of how the conflict and peacekeeping operation had affected them, and the role of gender within those experiences and structures. She found that often this was the first time that military peacekeepers had actually spoken with the local people or heard their perspectives (Mackay 2001).

While Member States such as Canada and the United Kingdom have taken the lead in developing training for peacekeepers in gender issues and perspectives, and countries such as Bangladesh, Denmark, Norway, and Sweden repeatedly demonstrate more gender-aware actions, other countries have shown much less enthusiasm for gender-informed peacekeeping initiatives. The United States, a top contributor of peacekeepers, is a case in point.

Unlike their counterparts in the United Kingdom that have devised advertising campaigns to use peacekeeping as a means of attracting more women into their military forces, or the Canadians who are recruiting more women police officers into peacekeeping, strategists and recruiters for the United States military believe that peacekeeping threatens their ability to fill their already difficult-to-meet quotas by not permitting the kind of environment where male soldiers can be 'real soldiers' (Enloe 2000). When they do participate in peacekeeping, traditionalists within the United States Army still see their role primar-ily relating to combat force, and they consider detrimental anything that might threaten that masculinised military function. According to retired Colonel Robert Helvey:

> The purpose of the Army is to kill people, and the purpose of the Army is to always be alert. You take the edge off our military guys when you tell them: 'Hey, don't shoot. You're not permitted to fire first.' Or, 'You can't put ammunition into your weapon ... ' That's not good for our troops (Keeler 2000).

After the murder of 11-year old Merita Shabiu by United States Army Staff Sgt Frank Ronghi while on peacekeeping duties in Kosova/o in December 2000, the Pentagon and United States Army ordered all of its fighting units to undergo specialized rights training. The 'new' training, however, will not focus on human rights, international humanitarian law, or the rights of women and girls. According to Army officials 'the new training' will include 'confrontations with angry civilians, demonstrators, and feuding ethnic groups'. Such exercises use mock villages and role-playing, last several days and can be as stressful as combat training (Dao 2000). How such training will prevent further abuses of local women and children is unclear.

Nonetheless, the United States military is exporting its brand of peacekeeping internationally. Recently, United States Special Forces went to train Nigerian peacekeepers. Nigeria has the most powerful army in West Africa and is a top contributor of peacekeepers. They are among those most criticized for participating in the violent adaptive political economies and for permitting the abuse and endangerment of civilians (Briscoe 2000; The Perspective 2000). Such a move enables the United States military to reduce the number of soldiers it might have to commit for peacekeeping duties in Africa, export its theories and practices on military security and combat, potentially increase United States weapons sales, and transmit its version of masculinized, militarized peacekeeping.

Reports from observers of the training of the Nigerian troops, who afterwards joined the UNMISL peacekeeping operation in Sierra Leone, said they were not aware of any training relating to human rights, gender, or women's human rights. However, they noted that the Nigerians felt they were combat-ready (Mark Malan, electronic communication with author, 30.01.01). At the same time, it is increasingly clear that the 'American relationship between masculinity, soldiering, and military peacekeeping does not have global applicability', with military officials and recruiters from Bangladesh, Canada,

Fiji, Finland, Ghana, and Ireland taking very different approaches (Enloe 2000, p241).

* * *

Because many officials within peacekeeping operations miss the centrality of masculinity and femininity in both the conflict and post-conflict periods, believing that issues regarding women, gender, and human rights are 'soft issues' and therefore less important, they also fail to fully understand the centrality of civil society to any democratic society. In particular, their biases against women and 'women's issues' prevent them from understanding that women's groups are among the savviest and most active groups within civil society (as Cynthia Cockburn and Meliha Hubic show to be the case in Bosnia, Chapters 5 and 7 of this volume). They cannot have all the answers because many of the causes of violent conflicts are transnational and must be addressed transnationally. But many of the women's groups operating in the post-conflict period operated throughout the conflict, assessing and addressing the causes and consequences of the conflict as they could, and thus have a much clearer understanding of the dynamics of the conflict than the majority of peacekeeping officials sent to build peace in their societies.

At a fundamental level, leadership within peacekeeping operations must refrain from a pattern of undermining local efforts to build peace and strengthen civil society, especially when those efforts come from women's groups. If they are able to do these things, their peacekeeping operations stand a greater chance of helping to build the conditions necessary for sustainable peace and democracy.

Deepest thanks to Angela Raven-Roberts, Cynthia Enloe, Shelley Anderson, Cynthia Cockburn, Ariane Brunet, Sherrill Whittington, Angela Mackay, Martina Vandenberg, and Sanam Anderlini for continuing to help me make better sense of the interweaving of masculinity, femininity, gender, and peacekeeping. My gratitude to Khristopher Carlson, Cynthia Cockburn, and Dubravka Zarkov for their encouragement, reviews, and editorial assistance.

PART 2:
GENDERED INSTITUTIONS, GENDERED INTERVENTIONS

International intervention in Bosnia-Herzegovina: the cost of ignoring gender

MADELEINE REES

The engagement of 'the international community' (IC) in Bosnia-Herzegovina (B-H), during, immediately after, and now for six years since the end of the 1992-95 war, is an experience from which many lessons can be drawn for future peace brokering, peacekeeping and peace sustaining operations. It has been the subject of a good deal of criticism, not only from ordinary citizens of Bosnia and some Bosnian politicians but also from some individuals within the operation itself.

In this chapter I write from the perspective of someone who works for the United Nations and who is therefore an insider to the workings of the international community, reviewing a single aspect of the engagement: the slow start and difficult course of measures concerning women and gender in postwar B-H.[1] First, I address some of the provisions of the 'Dayton' peace agreement and the huge international presence it conferred on postwar Bosnia. I describe the absence of thinking, policy-making and strategy on women and gender both in the Agreement itself and in 'post-Dayton' Bosnia. Second, I describe how a gender intervention into the work of the international community is belatedly being attempted – though it lags well behind what Bosnian women's groups, and even the Bosnian government, are now thinking and doing. I conclude with a discussion of one particular abuse of women's human rights – the trafficking of women for purposes of forced prostitution – an abuse to which the international intervention in Bosnia must be seen as having contributed, both actively and passively.

Dayton, human rights and women's rights

The General Framework Agreement for Peace in Bosnia and Herzegovina (GFAP) was negotiated in proximity talks at the US Airforce Base in Dayton, Ohio, and signed in Paris on 14 December, 1995. It brought to an end four years of death and destruction, confirming the cease-fire, providing for the withdrawal of foreign combatants and establishing a zone of separation between the warring forces. But 'Dayton' contained more than an agreement between the belligerents to end the fighting. The accords were going to be influential for the lives of Bosnian people far beyond the immediate postwar moment. Annex 4 of the Agreement was nothing less than a Constitution for a new country. Annex 3 established the framework of an electoral system of politics. The Preamble provided for 'the protection of private property and the promotion of a market economy'. Dayton was clearly intended to lay the groundwork for a new state and a new society.

The Constitution with which B-H was endowed by the Dayton Agreement has proved problematic in several ways. First, by structuring the country into two entities, the 'Federation of Bosnia and Herzegovina' and the 'Republika Srpska', it seemed to confirm the strong impression created by the preceding weeks of negotiation (as Noel Malcolm reported) 'that the negotiators were thinking in terms of potentially separate statelets rather than mere administrative divisions within a single state' (Malcolm 1996, p269). The accords did not reverse but rather reinforced ethnic identifications by establishing ethnic criteria of citizenship in the entities. Second, to the two levels of state and entity the Constitution added ten cantons (in the Federation) and a lower tier of local, municipal authorities on both sides of the Inter-Entity Border Line. Later the disputed area of Brcko was constituted as a district, yet another kind of authority. So the Dayton Agreement created a cumbersome governmental and administrative machinery, and what were effectively fourteen different legal systems.

In the context of this chapter however what concerns me most is another outcome of the Dayton decisions: the massive involvement in postwar Bosnia of inter-governmental/international institutions. This has been very much more than a peacekeeping operation. It has been a peace-*making* exercise in which international bodies have acquired a quasi-colonial role, running what is widely acknowledged to be a protectorate or trustee-ship, in the shade of which the native Bosnian political system and civil society are supposed to grow to maturity. History may prove this degree of intervention to have been an error. What is clear at the time of writing, and should have been obvious at the signing of Dayton, is that particular responsibilities were being placed on the international community for the observation of human rights, democracy and gender equity in its own operation.

The entry onto Bosnian terrain of the international community, including the armed United Nations Protection Force, UNPROFOR, began while the war was still at its height. But it was nothing to the influx of internationals once a peace deal was signed. Responsibility for implementing the military aspects of Dayton (embodied in Annex 1a of the Agreement) was conferred on the North Atlantic Treaty Organization (NATO) which was responsible for deploying (from SHAPE, its headquarters in Brussels) the 32,000 military personnel of the Implementation Force (IFOR). In a later phase this was scaled down and renamed the Stabilisation Force (SFOR). (For an account of SFOR's operation in Bosnia and its relationship with Bosnian women's organizations, see Cynthia Cockburn and Meliha Hubic, Chapter 7 of this volume.)

At the political level, the international body responsible for implementing Dayton was the Peace Implementation Council (PIC), involving the governments of those states attending the London Peace Implementation Conference of December 1995.[2] The PIC's 'man on the spot' is the High Representative, sited in the Office of the High Representative (OHR) in Sarajevo. The High Representative was given extraordinary powers to implement Dayton, which allow him to remove or replace officials perceived as opposed to the Agreement's provisions or hindering their implementation. The essential problem with this institution is that it is neither transparent nor accountable to the people of B-H, who have no mechanism for voicing their disapproval of policies or their opposition to legislation. Only recently has the possibility of judicial review of OHR decisions been raised.[3]

Because of the powers given to the OHR, the United Nations does not play in B-H the central role it has done elsewhere. But it is present in the form of the United Nations Mission to Bosnia-Herzegovina (UNMIBiH), which is part of the United Nations Department of Peacekeeping Operations based in New York. Its main operation is fielding the International Police Task Force, staffed by police personnel from over forty different countries. IPTF is responsible for the restructuring, monitoring and training of local police forces.

There are also several major United Nations agencies with a considerable number of staff in B-H. The United Nations High Commissioner for Refugees (UNHCR) and the United Nations Children's Fund (UNICEF) already had a presence in the country during the fighting, when the priority was emergency relief. Their role continues, but as the humanitarian crisis of war gave way to postwar reconstruction and development (a very slow process in B-H) the UN Development Programme (UNDP) has taken on greater importance. Also involved were the World Health Organization (WHO), the International Labour Organization (ILO), the Food and Agriculture Organization (FAO) and the Fund for Population (UNFPA).

The Office of the United Nations High Commissioner for Human Rights (OHCHR) has also had a presence in Bosnia since 1993, essentially to service the Special Rapporteur appointed by the Human Rights Commission and tasked with reporting on the human rights situation in Bosnia to that Commission in Geneva. It too continued to maintain an office in Sarajevo in the postwar period. I became the head of that office in November 1998. Its activity will be discussed further below.

To the UN bodies must be added the Organization for Security and Cooperation in Europe. OSCE was given the mandate to supervise and run elections and monitor human rights. Also present are the international financial institutions, concerned with the conversion of the B-H economy to a full market system. The World Bank, the International Monetary Fund, the European Bank for Reconstruction and Development all have staffs and operations in B-H. And, of course, there are many large international non-governmental organizations (NGOs) working in the region (such as Oxfam, see Suzanne Williams, Chapter 6 this volume).

An absence of gender awareness in the peace process

The extraordinary influence of the international community in B-H in the postwar period might be thought to have placed a special obligation on them to take account of women, and of the prevailing relations between women and men, in the society to which they came. The groundwork for a gendered international intervention should have been laid at the peace negotiating table. It was not. Gender issues never surfaced in the drafting process.

One of the reasons for this neglect was that the negotiators of the

GFAP were almost all men. The main actors were the Presidents of Bosnia-Herzegovina, Croatia and the Federal Republic of Yugoslavia and the principal mediators were Richard Holbrooke (USA), Carl Bildt (EU) and Igor Ivanov (Russia). As a retrospective report by the Swedish women's NGO Kvinna till Kvinna, titled *Engendering the Peace Process*, puts it:

> Basically, the Dayton peace negotiations were a dialogue of men, often with purely militaristic overtones. No women were present around the negotiation table, and there was only one woman represented among the signatories. There were a few women among the international delegates but none in the regional delegations (Kvinna till Kvinna 2000, p20).

On the day of the official signing of the Dayton accords a number of international NGOs addressed a letter to Madeleine Albright calling her attention to the lack of sensitivity to women's interests in the peace negotiations – but it had no result (Kvinna till Kvinna 2000, p20).

This absence of women and gender awareness in the GFAP ought, I would argue, to be thought extraordinary for several reasons. One we have already discussed: this was not just about a cession of hostilities – it was about state-building and society-building, with a 'how-to' element and a 'who's going to do it' element. It should have been unthinkable to omit any definition and allocation of responsibility for women's needs and gender issues. But there are two other reasons that make the absence of women and gender awareness remarkable.

First, the war itself had been a highly gendered affair. Of those who took up arms and fought, the great majority were men. The war in B-H, like many contemporary wars, was specifically aimed at uprooting large numbers of civilians, and, through the destruction of houses, gardens, farms and local economies, making it appear impossible that they could ever return home. This war against the domestic environment was experienced by many women as a war against all they stood for. Women were also the majority of those subjected to rape, and other forms of sexual torture and humiliation at the hands of soldiers and paramilitaries – something for which this war was particularly notorious. A high proportion of those who experienced first expulsion and flight, and then life in temporary centres for refugees and internally displaced people, were women and children.

After the cease fire, when the death toll could be reckoned, it became clear even without a formal census that around two-thirds of the population now was female. Large numbers of women found them-selves single parents. Even those whose partner did return from the war were characteristically responsible for re-establishing home life, assur-ing the wellbeing of children, the sick, disabled and elderly. Meanwhile, the health and welfare services needed to support them in this respon-sibility had collapsed (UNICEF 1998). Women were disproportionately active during the war (and would continue to be after the war) in forming and running the small local organizations involved in both humanitarian and advocacy work that would be the foundation of a postwar civil society (Walsh 1999; see also Cockburn, Chapter 5, this volume).

Finding a new source of livelihood was particularly hard for women. This was not only a postwar moment, it was and still is a period of transition from a mixed economy with a large element of state intervention to a radically privatized market economy. The legal protections for workers that existed in the former Yugoslavia had been swept away. Women would have to compete amid all the discrimina-tions and exclusions of a capitalist economy. The highly masculinized and militarized society, characterized by a significant growth in organ-ised criminal activity, increased the marginalization of women. Experience in other war zones showed that there was likely to be more (or more severe and more visible) domestic violence against women after the war than before.[4] Because of all these factors and many more it should have been considered imperative that the peace agreement reflect the gender realities on the ground. Without that, women were bound to continue to be disadvantaged in the future society the GFAP was intended to create.

Second, gender awareness had already entered inter-governmental and governmental policy processes worldwide. There was no excuse, this time, for neglecting gender and women's rights in the shaping of a peace agreement. Major initiatives had included the UN Decade for Women, 1975-85, and the adoption in 1979 of the UN Convention on the Elimination of All Forms of Discrimination against Women (CEDAW). The UN World Conference on Human Rights, held in Vienna, had been specially important because in the resulting *Declaration and Programme of Action*, women's rights had, for the first time, been articulated as human rights (United Nations 1993).

Two years later, in the very year the Dayton Agreement was drafted, a World Conference on women had been held in Beijing. The resulting *Platform for Action* stated what governments should do, what interna-tional agencies should do and what NGOs could contribute to women's development and the assertion of women's rights. The document has a section on 'Women and Armed Conflict' which draws attention to the sex-specific impact of armed conflict on women and girls, and notes the under-representation of women in decision-making in peace processes and postwar reconstruction. A key recommendation in this section was the insertion of a gender analysis and gender perspectives into national and international interventions in conflict and post-conflict situations, including peacekeeping operations (United Nations 1996).

None of this thinking, activism and advocacy by women worldwide, and the proclamations, resolutions and ratifications with which the UN and member governments responded to it, visibly influenced the Bosnian peace process or the wording of the General Framework Agreement for Peace. In their detailed study of the gender significance of Dayton, Christine Chinkin and Kate Paradine write: 'the Dayton Peace Accords presented the West with an opportunity to structure a model for women's empowerment that could benefit women elsewhere, including within Western Europe'. But the Agreement failed 'to re-imagine gender relations and to provide a contemporary model of citizenship and democracy for women' (Chinkin and Paradine 2001, p112). More than a lost opportunity, I believe, from first hand experience of the outcome, this omission was frankly appalling.

The Dayton Agreement did (in Annex 6) commit the state of Bosnia-Herzegovina to adherence to all the major international human rights conventions including the Convention on the Elimination of All Forms of Discrimination against Women (United Nations 1979). Many of these (including CEDAW) had in fact already been adopted by the former Yugoslav state. It put in place the European Convention on Human Rights and its Protocols, giving it priority over other law. Those who would defend the Dayton Agreement in relation to gender would argue that these provisions were sufficient to ensure women's equality. In fact, while Annex 6 provided a legal framework through which women could theoretically assert their rights, it was insufficiently articulated. The legislation the new state had inherited from the former Yugoslavia now needed additions and revisions under the new constitutional structure. How were human rights to be incorporated in fresh legislation, and in the interpretation of the old? The majority of the population who were to live under these laws were given minimal opportunity to shape their content or even to express an opinion.

As well as these structural deficiencies in the legal arrangements under which the reconstruction of Bosnia would begin, there were individual and institutional factors at work in the international community that contributed to a lack of gender-awareness and gender-sensitive policy and practice in the postwar moment. The international institutions entering the country were mainly staffed, particularly in senior positions, by men. Although many of the organizations involved may be expected to have sex-equality policies and commitments, at least in principle, to gender-awareness, at home, at headquarters or at base, these did not noticeably translate into their practices once they were operating in B-H.

Besides, the incomers often found themselves dealing with situations which appeared to have the qualities of 'emergencies'; the circumstances did not appear to offer the latitude to think about 'mere' sex equality or women's rights issues, either as they affected the country or their own institutions and operations. The influential officers were even less disposed to consider the effects on their work of the dominance of men and of masculine cultures. As a result the now-official formula that a gender analysis should be incorporated in all programmes and policies was practically ignored.

Gender as an afterthought: mobilizing action in the international institutions

It was only in 1998, three years after the end of the war, that change began to occur on the gender front. As I mentioned above, the Office of the United Nations High Commissioner for Human Rights (OHCHR) had retained a presence in postwar Bosnia. Early in 1998 an expert was brought to Sarajevo to evaluate the future role of the office. He was given the task of identifying any areas being inadequately addressed by the international community, so that OHCHR might supply the missing expertise. Among other shortcomings the report voiced concern about a deficiency in expertise on gender issues. As a result, in 1998 the mandate of OHCHR was altered. In addition to continuing the obligation to support the Special Rapporteur, the Office would now concentrate on gender, discrimination, social and economic rights, the protection of minorities and the rule of law. Given the small size of our office this would prove a very broad and challenging brief.

This is how OHCHR became the first international organization in B-H with a mandate to address the issue of gender. When I was appointed Head of Office in November 1998, it was specifically because of my background in discrimination and human rights law, particularly as it concerns women's rights. I thus became in effect the only 'gender expert' employed by any of the international institutions present in B-H.

There had been informal discussions with women in several agencies about the need to join forces in facilitating co-operation and driving forward a gender programme. These informal discussions resulted in the creation in April 1999 of a 'Gender Co-ordinating Group' (GCG). The main push for this came from three individual women, Heike Alefson, of the Council of Europe Office in Sarajevo; Elisabeth Rasmussen, head of the Democratization Branch of the OSCE; and myself. We invited each international institution to nominate an officer as 'gender focal point' and commit their attendance at monthly meetings.

Terms of reference were drawn up. We decided to make our benchmark the *Platform for Action* document that resulted from the World Conference on Women, Beijing 1995 (United Nations 1996). We adopted the twelve 'areas of concern' that the drafters of the Platform had believed to be critical. There would be an annual evaluation of the Gender Co-ordinating Group's progress on each of them. Phase 1 would focus on the deficiencies apparent in the international community itself. The aim was to ensure that institutions introduce a gender analysis of all their programmes and policies, exchanging information about them, and co-ordinating their gender initiatives. Phase 2 would draw in representatives of the Bosnian Government and of the NGO community, international but also local. This would ensure two important qualities: accountability, and progress towards sustainability of gender initiatives.

An immediate problem the GCG encountered was a lack of gender expertise within the group itself. While some of the individuals nominated as 'gender focal points' by the various institutions volunteered out of interest for the work, others were merely nominated to participate. Few had experience in equality programmes or gender analysis.[5] Another problem was the lack of seniority of the participants. Most were women and most were relatively junior in status (the two things are related of course). Most of them lacked the access to decision-making levels they needed if they were to take gender issues back and get them addressed by their agencies. Thus, with the exception of some international NGOs, such as Kvinna till Kvinna and the International Human Rights Law Group, the gender awareness stayed with the 'focal points' and was seldom translated into institutional action.

All this took many months. Every initiative in B-H is frustratingly slow, partly because of the rapid turnover of personnel in the international community which has the effect of a failure of institutional memory. Nonetheless the meetings of the GCG were often informative and even dynamic. The initiative can be said to have had a degree of success.

For instance, once the initiative was up and running we were able to affect laws as they were being created. A revision of the Federation's criminal code was carried out before we came into existence, and without consulting NGOs. (There was a somewhat disrespectful attitude among some members of the IC towards those who would actually have to live under the laws being brokered on their behalf. Indeed it was their, very reasonable, suspicion that we would involve local NGOs that inhibited some of the international institutions from sharing information with the GCG.) As a result so called 'minor acts' of domestic violence were allowed to remain outside the scope of criminal law and the law that was adopted was of much less use to women than it might have been. By contrast, we were able to have an input on the Labour Law. With cost in mind, the OHR had wanted to drastically reduce the maternity rights and benefits that women had had in the former Yugoslavia. We were able to add our weight to the actions of local NGOs to prevent this happening.

But perhaps the most significant achievements of the GCG have been not inside but outside B-H. One was the organization of a three-day round table on 'Lessons learned about gender from Bosnia-Herzegovina for Kosovo', attended by staff of the international institutions that were going to be involved in the postwar intervention in Kosovo, including representatives from their head offices in New York and Geneva. A second achievement was forcing gender onto the agenda of the Stability Pact for South-Eastern Europe. In the Gender Co-ordinating Group we drafted a series of arguments as to why gender must be incorporated into the work of the Stability Pact. The Bosnian non-governmental organizations also drafted similar arguments. Both were formally transmitted to the 'Working Tables' of the Stability Pact. Overall, I believe the GCG has brought about a noticeable improvement in the gender thinking and gender practice of the international community in B-H. At the very least the issue can no longer be evaded or ignored.

Trafficking in women:
the impact of the international community
The main lesson that can be learned from our experience in Bosnia is that it is absolutely vital that there be a gender analysis at the very beginning of a peacekeeping or postwar reconstruction operation. The Dayton negotiators, and the international community as it entered B-

H, should have fulfilled their human rights obligations. International programmes and policies should have addressed the sex-specific needs of both women and men from the outset. As it was, we were engaged in a firefighting exercise, trying to salvage what was possible after the years of neglect. And it has to be said that the greater part of our efforts was addressed to changing the practices not of the Bosnian government but of the international institutions themselves.

Trafficking in human beings – mainly women and children for purposes of enforced prostitution – is a distressing example of a human rights abuse that the international institutions in B-H failed for too long to identify and address. This failure is partly due to a lack of gender consciousness and partly to the more general refusal to acknowledge that there can be negative consequences of international intervention.

There has always been a small local sex industry in the countries of the former Yugoslavia. But this is entirely different to the phenomenon of trafficking. It is really only since 1995 that women have been brought into Bosnia from other countries as commodities. The UN Convention against Transnational Organized Crime, in its Protocol to Prevent, Suppress, and Punish Trafficking in Persons, Especially Women and Children, defines trafficking in persons as follows:

> ... the recruitment, transportation, transfer, harbour or receipt of persons, by means of force, other forms of coercion, of abduction, of fraud, of deception, of the abuse of power or of a position of vulnerability or of the giving or receiving of payments or benefits to achieve the consent of a person having control over another person, for the purpose of exploitation. Exploitation shall include, at a minimum, the exploitation of the prostitution of others or other forms of sexual exploitation ... (United Nations 2000).

It is largely understood that trafficking emerges with the creation of a potential market for sexual services. The Dayton Peace Agreement brought to Bosnia-Herzegovina over 50,000 international personnel, the vast majority of them males. They constituted such a market. In the immediate postwar period of 1995 and 1996 the clients of those women brought into B-H to work in the sex industry were almost exclusively from the international community. Local men at this time simply did not have the money to frequent these brothels. The situation gradually changed and more locals today are involved in using not only local prostitutes but also trafficked women. This is acknowledged in the existence of different charging rates for locals and internationals.

The supply side of the market is mainly Moldova, Romania and Ukraine where the transition from a communist to a capitalist economy has deprived women of employment opportunities and reduced many to extremes of poverty. As a result many women seek opportunities to migrate. They will answer advertisements that appear to offer jobs as waitresses, hairdressers, *au pairs*, dancers or models in Western countries. Having no independent access to passports, visas or money for fares, these women – many of them very young, some little more than children[6] – find themselves in the hands of traffickers, who transport them with false papers from one country into another. The women who eventually end up in Bosnia have usually been driven overland by their recruiters via Belgrade. There they are sold to local dealers, and then to pimps. Unable to speak the local language and without a valid passport or visa, often physically detained, and tricked into debt, they are coerced into providing sexual services, caught up in a system that is equivalent to slavery. The exact numbers are still not known. The Bosnian NGOs have identified over 700 sites in Bosnia in which foreign women are known to be involved in prostitution. And there are characteristically between four and twenty-five women in each site.

The first time trafficking was formally discussed in B-H was December 1998, when OHCHR, together with the Council of Europe, held a conference in the Bosnian town of Tuzla to discuss with the government ministries, international agencies and NGOs what we knew on the problem. From the knowledge brought together there it became clear that trafficking was one of the most serious human rights issues in contemporary Bosnia. From that moment on, the OHCHR office took the lead in pressing for coherent strategies to deal with it. When the GCG formed, the following spring, it set up a 'trafficking subgroup'. Its objectives were: first to devise mechanisms for assisting women who had been trafficked; second, to try to prevent the prosecution and deportation of the women themselves; and third, to devise a proper strategy for dealing with the problem on a long term basis, with a focus on protecting the human rights of the women themselves.

OHCHR, the International Organization for Migration (IOM) and UNMIBiH collaborated in temporary rescue assistance to women, so that when trafficked women came to the attention of the police the International Police Task Force could bring them to Sarajevo where they would be accommodated and cared for, before being flown home.

This was always seen as a transitional emergency measure. There are fundamental flaws in such a strategy, of course. The first is that it can only help those women who can show they have been trafficked – and this is always a matter of the subjective interpretation of an IPTF officer or staff member of the IOM. Second, it is only justifiable to repatriate a woman if that is what she wishes. In fact, for more than understandable reasons, only about 30 per cent of the women want to return to their country of origin.

The GCG understood that for action against trafficking to be effective it must involve a partnership between the international institutions, the Bosnian government and local non-governmental organizations. The trafficking subgroup from the start centrally involved NGOs. As regards the Bosnian government, the GCG made several unsuccessful attempts to stir a response on the trafficking issue, but it was not until October 2000 that Bosnian ministers and officials began to take the issue seriously. We convened a meeting at the OHR with representatives of all the relevant ministries. Helga Konrad, who had been appointed as the chair of a Trafficking Task Force established by the Stability Pact, came to address them and to insist on action. As a result of this meeting the Council of Ministers passed a resolution giving the Bosnian Ministry of European Integration and Stability Pact the role of co-ordinating a governmental working group to draw up a national plan of action (NPA) to combat trafficking.

The working group is comprised of all the ministries that have some form of responsibility in relation to trafficking, both at State and Entity level. The NPA is comprehensive and addresses the needs for prevention, awareness, training, legal reform, and direct assistance to victims. It involves the local NGOs and uses the international community in a consultative capacity. At the time of writing the NPA is in its final format awaiting adoption. The difficult task of implementation will then commence.

By contrast, a major problem we faced, and continue to face, was a reluctance in the international community to accept that *we ourselves contribute significantly to the problem of trafficking*. There is a deep reluctance to acknowledge that international men are significant clients, users of the sexual services of foreign women who do not provide those services freely but are coerced.[7] An approximate calculation by human rights officers in the IPTF is that the international community constitutes 30 per cent of the customers of the foreign women, numerically, but accounts for 80 per cent of the revenue accruing to the men who manage them. The IOM believe this is an underestimate of the involvement of international men. The women themselves, in interviews IOM have conducted, say 50 per cent of their customers are internationals.

In B-H, prostitution itself is illegal – although a minor misdemeanour, a public order offence. Any member of the international community buying sexual services is therefore breaking the law. It is continually broken, yet the international community turns a blind eye. OHR drafted a code of conduct prohibiting its staff from engaging in commercial sex only in 2001. UNMIBiH has a code for its personnel but despite a policy of zero tolerance, it is rarely applied. OSCE have a code – but it is in draft form only. There is the inevitable confusion between prostitution and trafficking for the purpose of sexual exploitation. The testimonies taken from those women who have come through the IOM programme graphically describe the violence, the abuse, their inability to leave or seek help and their financial indebtedness to their trafficker, all of which make them the equivalent of slaves. The men who frequent the brothels where they are held are doing more than infringing a minor law (for which in any case they are not held accountable, since the law is only ever applied to the woman providing the 'service'). They are participating in serious crime. They are violating fundamental human rights. It is frankly dishonourable that the international institutions have failed to take responsibility for their part in the exploitation of women, and to investigate the practices of their personnel.

UNMIBiH I believe calls for special mention. Its role, as part of the United Nations CIVPOL (civilian police) function, is to field the International Police Task Force. The IPTF, having the role of restructuring and training the local Bosnian police, were from the start ideally placed to take practical action to deal with the crime of trafficking. But for far too long (as an UNMIBiH/OHCHR report put it) not only local police but also the IPTF would 'characterize the women as prostitutes, whether or not the women have been forced/trafficked. They tend to have a great deal of difficulty with the distinction between voluntary sex workers and victims of procurers'. At the beginning it was standard practice 'to prosecute victims, not to protect their rights or go after the true culprits – the traffickers and pimps'. Our report stressed that these men were part of the very criminal fraternity the police were there to root out. We challenged the IPTF with 'naivete', for ignoring that the high profits realized from trafficking were funding 'other criminal enterprises many of which are traditionally viewed as more "serious" societal ills than the "victimless" crime of prostitution' (UNMIBiH and OHCHR 2000).

It is fair to say there have been a number of very committed IPTF officers who have tried to address the problem, initiating programmes with the local police; and at the time of writing a major new initiative has been launched by UNMIBiH to address the issue. But IPTF personnel themselves, like SFOR soldiers and international personnel more generally, frequent the brothels where trafficked women are held. More than this, there have been suggestions that a few individual officers have been implicated in the activities of this organized crime. However, when challenged from within or without on the practices of its own personnel, UNMIBiH has chosen denial and a refusal to investigate rather than dealing openly and transparently with any allegation.

Meanwhile, every year more women are being trafficked into Bosnia. The nightclubs and bars in which they are put to work are more evident. All involved in the trade act, for the most part, with impunity. We can only hope this will change when the national plan of action is actually implemented.

The abuse of women: parallels between war and postwar

Where there is militarization, including peacekeeping operations, there is an even chance that those who seek to exploit the sex market will start trafficking women into the area. This could have been anticipated in Bosnia. Preventative measures could have been taken right from the start – education and training of international personnel before they are sent and after they arrive, strictly enforceable codes of conduct, repatriation of offenders to their home states, with prosecution to follow. None of this happened.

A more gendered understanding of the war could have given us premonitions and warnings about the postwar moment. Among the acts of war in Bosnia one of the most serious and egregious violations of international law was the rape of women. Many women were held in conditions of slavery in rape 'camps' or in houses or apartments for the use of the various militaries. The International Criminal Tribunal for Yugoslavia in the Hague has adjudicated that these actions were a crime against humanity, and torture under the Geneva Conventions. There is a striking continuity between what happened to Bosnian women then, and what is happening today to trafficked women in these postwar years. The parallels include the imprisonment of women, their brutalization and sexual enslavement, and their lack of access to outside assistance.

The other striking parallel, of course, is the nature of their abusers. The more militarized a state, the more do men, both military and civilian, have the possibility of abusing women with impunity (see Cynthia Enloe, Chapter 1 of this volume). And Bosnia-Herzegovina today, even if the uniforms seen in the barracks and on the streets are those of international peacekeepers rather than local armies and militias, is nothing if not militarized.

I have tried to show that a cost has been paid in B-H for the neglect of gender in the drafting of the Dayton peace agreement and the international action that flowed from it. But a further cost may be paid in other conflict-damaged countries. International peacekeeping interventions can only learn from each other. There are hopeful signs of a new alertness in the United Nations to gender issues in conflict and peacekeeping operations. UN Security Council Resolution 1325 of 31 October 2000, on 'Women, Peace and Security', and subsequent moves in the UN Department of Peacekeeping operations testify to this (see Dyan Mazurana, Chapter 3 this volume). These developments are encouraging. But resolutions and policies emanating from New York and Geneva are no use unless they are accompanied by training for peacekeeping personnel, military and civilian alike, implementation in the field, and rigorous evaluation of its effectiveness.

One thing the Bosnian experience teaches, is that the incomers must be ready to listen to and to learn from: first, local women's NGOs, and second, feminist international NGOs such as the Swedish Kvinna till Kkvinna, whose role and work in Bosnia has been exemplary. But for men to be willing to listen to women they must first respect them. This means a fundamental change of attitude. If, as in Bosnia, it does not come about, the masculine cultures of militarized societies will be amplified and exaggerated, instead of counteracted, by the intervention. And women will be the ones to pay the price.

I would like to thank and pay tribute to Cynthia Cockburn, whose work on behalf of women, and in particular for those in B-H, commands the highest respect, and without whose expertise and enthusiasm this chapter would not have been possible.

Notes

1. The position I hold has given me the insight into the workings of the international community. The opinions I express, however, are personal and are not necessarily the position of the OHCHR.
2. To give a flavour of the extraordinary range of countries and institutions involved in postwar Bosnia – the Peace Implementation Council's Steering

Board comprises representatives of the USA, Russia, France, Germany, Japan, Canada, Italy, the EU and Turkey. The Office of its High Representative in Bosnia-Herzegovina coordinates the activity of the 'Main Implementation Agencies' (MIA) of the Dayton agreement. Its meetings in Brussels are attended by, among others, representatives of the Council of Europe, the European Commission Monitoring Mission, the International Committee of the Red Cross, the International Criminal Tribunal for the Former Yugoslavia, the International Organization for Migration, and the United Nations.

3. A recent decision of the Consitutional court in respect of the State Border Service found that as the decisions of OHR are in the official Gazette then the court does have a right to review them for their compliance with the constitution.

4. Women's postwar situation is described in numerous reports, of which see: Prism Research 1998; UNICEF 1998; Walsh 1998 and Independent Human Rights Law Group 1999.

5. This deficit in relevant knowledge and skills is not, of course, confined to the issue of gender. It has been a problem in many of the other international community working groups in B-H – for instance in social and economic rights.

6. Article 1 of the United Nations Convention on the Rights of the Child, deems a person to be a child until the age of eighteen years, United Nations 1989.

7. The evidence from the courts and NGOs is that local prostitution has been driven onto the sides of highways and into public toilets. The majority of local prostitutes work for pimps. There is still insufficient evidence as to the extent.

Women's organization in the rebuilding of Bosnia-Herzegovina

CYNTHIA COCKBURN

The 'postwar moment' in Bosnia-Herzegovina has been a turbulent time in which Bosnians have found themselves travelling along on not one but several trajectories of change. The journey from war to peace comes first to mind. But in some ways this transit has been the least clearly achieved. In 1999 and 2000, when we were doing the research on which this chapter is based,[1] there was still much tension between nationalist groups and parties, with outbreaks of violence deterring refugees from returning to re-establish Bosnia's pre-war ethnic mixity.

More clearly irreversible, but still unfinished, was the transformation of the political system. The General Framework Agreement for Peace (the Dayton agreement) had affirmed the shift made in Yugoslavia in the late eighties from single-party rule to a multi-party electoral system and had furnished the new state with a constitution, and a structure involving two 'entities' (the Republika Srpska and the Federation of Bosnia-Herzegovina) under a weak state government. But the country remained under the tutelage of the international institutions placed in authority by Dayton. A third change had been economic: a rapid conversion of the state-led economy of the former Yugoslavia, characterized by a combination of social ownership and market, to the thorough-going neo-liberal free market made a condition of foreign aid.

This chapter is however concerned with yet another dimension of potential change, one that is normally far from the minds of those fostering post-Communist 'transition' and postwar 'reconstruction'. *What was happening to Bosnia's gender order in the postwar moment?*[2] The militarization of a country during war, and the differential impact of armed conflict on women and men, in some ways deepens traditional gender complementarity and inequality, while in others it can be observed to disturb old patterns, forcing new roles and capabilities in women. In the postwar moment, does a society revert to the *status quo ante*? Or does the hegemony of militarized masculinity perpetuate the gender relations of wartime? Or, in the social turmoil of the postwar moment, is an opportunity seized to transform gender power relations in the interests of women?

As a socialist society, the former Yugoslavia had legislated for equality between the sexes. Women's 'emancipation' was officially held to have been achieved, mainly through the access of women to education and paid employment on equal terms with men. There were many social provisions (such as generous maternity benefits – see Rees, Chapter 4 in this volume) envied by women in Western European countries. On the other hand, the sex equality had been more formal than real. Research showed women's initial equality in education and the early years of work did not translate into equal careers. Men and male cultures dominated in the political system and the large enterprises of the socialist economy (Milic 1994). Family relations had been particularly resistant to change, especially in rural society. Mirjana Morokvasic had written in 1986:

> Women in Yugoslavia can be economically independent, socially active, recognized and respected at work and yet remain mere servants at home, where the man retains authority ... In the private sphere, legislation was unable to resist the old values and replace them with something new (Morokvasic 1986, p122).

This patriarchal power and ideology that Yugoslav socialism had failed to shift in the nineteen fifties, sixties and seventies contributed directly to the rise of nationalism and militarism, and to the legitimation of violence, in the eighties and nineties (Milic 1993; Morokvasic 1997; Zarkov 1999). So a question underlying our research was this. Is the flux of the postwar moment, this time of turmoil in all social structures and relationships, generating a gender order different from both socialist patriarchy and militarized nationalism?[3] And if so, is it one in which men do not dominate, in which women are no longer marginal but central to the social, political and economic order? The answers would establish the odds for and against progressive change in all the other dimensions of Bosnian life.

Something might depend, we felt, on women's agency. How active were women, as women and for gender transformation, in the postwar moment? One of the dimensions of change experienced by Bosnians between the late eighties and the late nineties had been a transformation of the 'civil' aspect of society, the area of free association independent of the state.[4] In the former Yugoslavia there had been a multitude of clubs and societies, mostly concerned with hobbies or charity. During the war these had fallen into abeyance, but many new associations had formed in response to the devastation, providing emergency humanitarian relief to specially needy groups. After the war the number of non-profit, non-governmental organizations soared.

Women were noticeably active in this expanded sphere of voluntary organization. When we analyzed a 1999 directory of associations we found about half to be led by a woman, a far greater female presence than in business or what remained of the state (International Council of Voluntary Agencies 1999). Of this half, around one-third are associations in which the activists and beneficiaries are entirely women. A few of these are of national scope. Many are monocultural, some even religious, and concerned primarily with humanitarian work. Often their focus is 'the family'. But a number of listed organizations were of special interest to us as being (a) women-only; (b) addressed to women's rather than family needs; (c) locality-based; and (d) clearly committed to integrative working.[5]

We chose seven of these organizations for closer study, partly guided by their location in towns or cities interesting for their ethnic structure, war history and current tensions. Two are in Banja Luka, now the capital of the Republika Srpska and a heartland of Bosnian Serb political life. All eighteen mosques and two Catholic monasteries were destroyed in the war, and the city had become almost monocultural, with Bosniaks (Muslims) and Croats, now much reduced and vulnerable minorities, keeping a low profile. The other two towns are in the Federation: the celebrated southern city of Mostar and the West Bosnian town of Gornji Vakuf – that its Croat inhabitants now call 'Uskoplje'. These are alike in being towns cut into two halves, either side of a border slashed through them by the fighting between Croat and Bosniak forces. Most Serbs fled or were driven from these localities when Serb nationalist forces were attacking earlier in the war. Our seventh organization was in fact formed by Serb women refugees from Mostar, now living in Nevesinje, a small rural town only a short drive from the city but now lying across the border in the Republika Srpska.

Organizing as women, for women, on women's issues

We went out as researchers to meet the seven women's organizations, spend time with them and interview some of their activists.[6] What we wanted to learn, at a basic empirical level was: who were the women, how were they organized, what was their activity, how successful and unsuccessful were they, what difficulties did they encounter, what support did they get, what were their prospects? But at a more conceptual level we were interested in exploring what kind of relational world they aspired to shape. What did they want their town or city to become? And what did that say about the future of gender relations, and the future of democracy?

The groups are all formally registered as civil associations under Bosnian law. Typically they centre on a small core of women of conflicted national identities, who trust each other because of pre-war friendships. They tend to have one dynamic founder, who contributes vision and drive. Around the core members are concentric circles of belonging – groups of regular contributors, of users, of occasional contacts, of beneficiaries.

All the organizations we chose to examine have a principle of inclusiveness. They minimize the importance of national name. They are working for a re-integrated society. Most of the core members are not affiliated to political parties, but those that are favour the non-nationalist opposition parties. In actual membership some of the organizations are more ethnically mixed than others. Much depends on locality. The town of Gornji Vakuf/Uskoplje for instance is comprised almost entirely of Bosniaks and Bosnian Croats – and membership of the two women's organizations there reflects this. Two of the organizations in the Republika Srpska are principally comprised of Bosnian Serbs. But it is valuable to have such groups, actively contradicting dominant Serb nationalist politics, open to and co-operating with women of all identities. The organizations differ in size. All of them have ups and downs. Up means: projects funded, offices, salaries to pay two or three staff. Down means: running on empty, paid workers reduced to volunteering, many dropping out.

In their choice of activity we found five important themes, differently emphasized in the individual projects. First and foremost is getting women back to the *economic independence* to which they had been accustomed. At the war's end, unemployment was 90 per cent. How were women to survive and maintain their dependents? Most of the organizations began by setting up simple income-generating projects such as knitting and sewing workshops, or the gathering and drying of medicinal herbs for sale. They went on to provide skills training – in computer use for instance, or hairdressing, or elementary business management. Some administer micro-credit schemes.

Secondly, several of the organizations take action *against violence against women*. The publicity given to rape in the war, and the activity of women's projects for survivors, had sensitized women to male sexual violence. They saw now it had been endemic in pre-war society and knew it would be prevalent after war. So some organizations set up SOS phone lines for traumatized women and children, survivors of rape and domestic violence. Two organizations have shelter projects in hand. Third, some organizations offer *legal advice*. Their lawyers help women resolve housing disputes – half the population moved home in the war and the housing situation is chaotic – and advise on things like divorce, alimony, inheritance and other perennial problems made more urgent and more complex by war. In some cases this legal work leads to campaigning round women's human rights.

Fourth, there are projects to get women more *involved in politics* – educational seminars about the representative system and the various political parties; encouraging women to register and use their vote in elections; calling politicians to account. Finally, and most important, there is *reconciliation work*. Of course the organizations are doing this internally by co-operating across national lines and organizing mixed activities. But most importantly several of them are supporting 'returners'. A future integrated society in Bosnia depends on the return of displaced people to their homes. People fled these towns for many reasons: some were expelled, others went because of fear of reprisal for what was being done in their name. But return, especially to areas where the returnee will be an unwanted minority, is very hard both practically and psychologically. So the women's organizations give moral support and material aid – a cow, perhaps, and tools, candles, a few kilos of flour.

The women's motivations in being active and organized seem to be, first, to *quell their own fear* (they experienced being afraid as terrible and are simply refusing to go on feeling afraid.) Secondly, to *escape confinement*. During the war it was a shock to be pinned in a basement under shellfire and, afterwards, not to have a job to go out to every day. Hate-filled towns are riddled with borders you can observe or defy – in either case at a cost. One is the threshold of your own front door. A third motivation is *regaining agency* after the victimhood of war. It is mainly men who have become the new entrepreneurs. 'Doing NGO' on the other hand is something women seem to be good at. It offers a chance to move forward, to effect something.

So far this account may sound ultra positive. But there is a down side to the picture. At a workshop we organized, attended by representatives of six of the seven organizations, the women were candid about many weaknesses that we too had observed in them. Management structures are often incoherent or illogical. There is a lack of conscious reasoning and choice concerning the procedure of decision-making, and relations between paid and unpaid personnel. There are problems of leadership. Most of the organizations centre on a single, rather well educated, 'leader'. Some leaders are criticized for egoism, but in turn they criticize their followers for passivity. Skills, roles and opportunities are not always well shared. Information and process are not always transparent. There is lack of contact and co-operation between groups – which must compete for the favour of funders. Such failings are acknowledged to be widespread among NGOs, and give rise to a certain cynicism about 'civil society' (Chandler 1999).

The feelings with which we emerged from the fieldwork were therefore profoundly ambivalent. On the one hand we felt these seven integrative, local women's organizations – even if you add a dozen others like them in other parts of Bosnia – added up to disappointingly little. They are such a tiny phenomenon, we said to ourselves, so fallible, and so ephemeral. On the other hand, you could not help but admire the women for the risks they were taking. We were continually surprised and heartened by the projects, saw the urgency of the problems they are addressing and how minimal their resources. We felt both things at the same time. But we came away believing such organizations should be fostered, less for what they are today than for the significance they may have for tomorrow.

Towards a women's movement?

Much depends on whether they may realistically be seen as foundation stones for a *women's movement*. So, one of the questions we asked the women was: why do you organize as women? why not an organization that includes men too? The answers we got were various, but they all pointed to a sense that the events of the past decade (1989 -1999), war and postwar, had challenged and even strengthened women but had not shifted male dominance.

At one level the women were responding to their feelings. It was a matter of *compassion and solidarity*, a supportive engagement with certain sex-specific experiences of women in the war. Bosnian women and Bosnian men had in some ways shared the experience of war. Both men and women left, or lost, or were driven from their homes – a shocking and entirely unanticipated occurrence. How, in the routine of their modern, domestic lives, could they have imagined such a thing happening to them? Women and men alike had sometimes found themselves on epic journeys on foot through forests and mountains – risking death in places they might have visited in an earlier life on weekend picnics in the family car.

But in other ways the sexes had lived rather different wars. Men of fighting age had carried arms and engaged in combat, willingly or unwillingly. For many the fighting had involved brutalization and trauma. Or they had escaped the country, by expedience or by principle. A few women did serve in the military, but mostly women had the experience, in a way men did not, of helping the young and the old to live through this uprooting, and of maintaining their own and others' nutrition and health in very challenging circumstances. Typically unarmed, they had found themselves ascribed surprising new identities, at odds with their sense of self – that of 'victim', 'refugee' or 'war survivor'. Some had turned to prostitution to survive. If, that is, they did survive. Many did not. And many lived at such cost in trauma and loss that they would have preferred not to.

Gender differences persisted as war receded. Men experienced abrupt demobilisation into a world in which their role was uncertain, while women struggled to re-establish domestic normality in a population that was 50 per cent uprooted from home, was mourning the death of 6 per cent of its people, had a radically changed age and sex structure, and had experienced a massive reduction of resources in terms of habitable housing and the basic social and health support systems on which women as primary carers had formerly relied.

A second reason the women had for organizing as women was a refusal of *the inequality and marginalization of women* in the economy, in politics and more generally in public life. They remembered the inequalities that had persisted within the 'emancipation' of women in the former Yugoslavia. But they resented much more the loss of rights during and since the cataclysm of 1991-95. One woman told us:

> The war hasn't changed much family relations. Men's mentality in B-H is just 'give me a job and a social life', or 'I want a car, I want a house, I want money'. And they don't understand women's wish to work in women's organizations. But we organized a survey and found out that 80 per cent of families are only

surviving thanks to the woman's income. So women have to have power and organize together.

The renewal of currents of nationalism and religious fundamentalism has had dramatic implications for gender relations. Deniz Kandiyoti writes of nationalisms in other countries in terms that have resonance for B-H. She says:

> on the one hand, nationalist movements invite women to partici-
> pate more fully in collective life by interpellating them as
> 'national' actors: mothers, educators, workers and even fighters.
> On the other hand, they reaffirm the boundaries of culturally
> acceptable feminine conduct and exert pressure on women to
> articulate their gender interests within the terms of reference set
> by nationalist discourse (Kandiyoti 1993, p432).

In recent Yugoslav history, gender and the family have indeed been fearsomely manipulated by nationalists. Silva Meznaric has analyzed the way a fabricated scare over the rape of Serb women by Albanian men in Kosovo in the late 1980s was a key moment in the resurgence of nationalism. Both Kosovan Albanian and Serb leaders at the time of this incident 'spent enormous amounts of money, energy and ideas on defining tradition and continuity', using women's bodies and men's familial honour as 'markers' of ethnic difference (Meznaric 1994, p82.). Women in B-H have responded in polarized ways to this kind of pressure. More than before have a confessional belonging, Christian women attending church, Muslim women going covered. But others feel more alienated, resenting the way religion is intruding into politics, and politics into everyday life. Women say they have never had the respect and trust accorded to men in this region. One woman told us, 'There's a basic lack of confidence in women'. Now, with conservative patriarchal ideologues attempting to control women's dress, behaviour and role, women were even less likely to be treated as equals.

A third reason that emerged for women choosing to organize as women was a sense that it made possible certain *ways of working*. If an organization is known to be a women's organization, ordinary women are more likely to feel comfortable stepping in the door. Through women you have a good chance of helping family members. Being a women-only organization was a way of avoiding the ascendancy of men. Several women told us how, as well-qualified and even profes- sional employees in large enterprises in the former Yugoslavia, they had remained in the shadow of men. 'Men were the directors, the bosses. It was difficult to realize any idea of our own, however good it might be.'

Now the women's organizations were surrounded by bureaucracies – party political, state institutional, international. Even the NGO sector can produce authoritarian cultures. Men in NGOs, one woman told us, can be 'very powerful, possessive and individualistic'. As we have seen, the women's organizations have not yet made the most of the potential for democratic process. But we were told nonetheless that women found a women's environment more congenial.

Most important, women saw women as the best hope for integrative working in these divided and embittered towns. One woman said, 'Between men here, there is this wall'. And another explained, 'It was the men who carried guns in the war, they were the ones directly involved in the fighting'. The impulse to rethink enmity and recover friendships seemed to wake in women before men.

We asked the women we interviewed, as we asked ourselves, whether this self-organizing we were observing amounted to a 'women's movement'. In the eighties there had been a small but radical women's movement in Yugoslavia. It had involved mainly women with higher education and its groups and activities had been mainly in Belgrade, Zagreb and Ljubljana (Jancar 1985; Papic 1994). There had been some interaction with women's movements in Western European countries and the USA.

Sarajevo, less cosmopolitan than the other republican capitals, had been more or less bypassed by the pre-war women's movement. During and immediately after the war in B-H, however, a handful of women's organizations, opposing the ethno-national principle, sprang up to undertake social and psychological care of war-traumatized women (Walsh 1999). Medica Women's Association was important among them. Women's organizations in Belgrade and Zagreb that were opposed to what was being done in their national name by extremists in Bosnia quickly rallied to the support of the Bosnian women. As soon as the dust of war settled, organized women from all parts of the region quickly re-connected with each other at workshops and conferences. Supportive women also came from the USA and countries of Western Europe, bringing feminist experience.

Contact was now also possible between women of the former Yugoslavia and women from East Central Europe and the former Soviet Union. From them it became clear that the adverse circumstances encountered by women in B-H were not due to war alone.

Peggy Watson writes that the transition to liberal capitalism in all these formerly state socialist countries 'offers men the opportunity of putting a greatly increased social distance between themselves and women. It is the rise of masculinism which is the primary characteristic of gender relations in Eastern Europe today'. With the new ascendancy of neo-liberal economics, the primacy of competition and the loss of socialism's welfare safety-nets, has come 'the enactment of masculinity on a grand scale' (Watson 1996, p216, see also Molyneux 1996).

Organized resistance to this process, in Bosnia as elsewhere in the region, is clearly needed. We've seen that B-H has no shortage of women's NGOs. But many of them, far from furnishing resistance to masculinism, play into it, promoting conventional gender roles and family values. The smaller number that, like our seven organizations, do address women's rights and seek change in gender relations are scattered and poorly connected. Can they be said to add up to a movement? The women we interviewed were divided on this. Some felt part of a movement, others would have liked to do so but doubted such a thing existed as yet. Sevima Sali-Terzic, legal advisor of the International Human Rights Law Group in Sarajevo, who has worked closely with Bosnian women's organizations said, 'We have lots of groups but I wouldn't say we have a women's movement.'

Theorists of social movements have generated certain criteria by which to identify them. We checked out what we found against, for example, those of John Wilson (1973).[7] He notes that some movements are *reformative*, some prefigure *alternatives* and some have *transformative* goals. And the Bosnian women's organizations we studied were indeed trying to reform the existing gender order, they were establishing their own alternative gender regimes within their little organizations, and they clearly wanted to rid society of patriarchal power relationships between men and women. Wilson also stresses the *non-institutional* nature of movements, and we have seen how Bosnian women's NGOs have flowered in the voluntarist space of civil society. He suggests too that we may *reshape ourselves* within movements. Many women in Bosnia told us how they had acquired a new sense of self through being active on women's issues. 'We're not the same people we were at the start', as one woman put it. In these terms, then, it seems to us there is potentially a women's movement in B-H, within and around women's organizations of the kind we are studying.

But certain factors point the other way. Wilson sees a social movement as 'a conscious, collective, organized attempt to bring about or resist large-scale change in the social order by non-institutionalized means' (Wilson 1973, p8). But our organizations cannot really be said to emerge from and reflect a growing of radicalized *consciousness* among Bosnian women about disadvantage and oppression. It is understandable that women are unready to criticize the patriarchal relations of the family – they are still grieving and honouring husbands and sons killed in the war. There is as yet little in the way of subversive women's culture, no women activist groups in the professions, no women comedians, novelists, singers or artists dramatizing the inequities of gender relations. One woman told us:

> To say 'I'm a feminist' is very dangerous here. Only to say it. To *be* it is more dangerous. You have very many male, conservative and retrograde tendencies expressed in all the regions in transition, especially in B-H, especially in those parts where nationalists are in power. This ideology is very unfriendly to any feminist way of thinking. Nationalism, sexism and xenophobia intersect. They support each other. I think it is a kind of totalitarian way of thinking. It is very hard to be a feminist in these cultural circumstances.

There are, of course, misperceptions and differing interpretations of the word 'feminist' in Bosnia, as elsewhere.[8] But even if one uses the less controversial term 'women's movement', her point stands: the social environment in Bosnia is sexist, and there is little open anger at the sexism.

It is also doubtful whether there is sufficient *militancy* – Wilson for instance speaks of the element of 'crusade' in an effective social movement (Wilson 1973, p5). To be transformative, or even reformative, a movement requires its activists to enter public space and challenge the system. For example, the word 'campaigning' was never much used in Bosnia. More common has been the weaker alternative 'advocacy' – and even for this the English is retained. The lack of a word reflects the historical lack of a practice. There was a certain 'activism', yes. At the end of the Second World War two million women belonged to the Anti-Fascist Front of Women, the mass organization supporting Tito's Partisan resistance. After the war the Front was bound in to the party structure of the League of Communists, first as the Union of Women's Associations, then as the Conference for the Social Activity of Women. But these mass mobilizations of women did not subject the patriarchalism of Yugoslav socialism to critique – something that was beginning to happen only in the women's movement of the eighties, interrupted by war (Mladjenovic and Litricin 1993; Bozinovic 1994; Papic 1994).

Today, although the organizations are taking practical measures in their own localities to meet women's needs, they are not as yet greatly involved in exposing to public view the causes of women's disadvantage and who gains from it. They are not on the whole lodging demands. One reason of course, is that they feel too vulnerable to take risks with the authorities. Another is that the funding regime supports service projects rather than campaigning. So we have come to feel that the women's organizations we were studying are *tendentially* elements of a progressive social movement. They have many characteristics that fit the criteria. But they do not yet add up to an autonomous women's movement. While there are many reasons such a thing is unlikely in postwar Bosnia, we would argue that it is, for all that, greatly needed – and not only for the sake of women. It is also needed if democracy is to be established in the country.

Towards democracy?

The first elections to the several levels of government established by the Dayton agreement were held in 1996. Nationalist parties emerged as the dominant force. Disappointed by this result, and hoping thereby to diversify politics, the international institutions began to give greater emphasis to the promotion of 'civil society' (for instance United Nations Development Programme 1998). This was criticized by some as deflecting energy and resources from the state (Chandler 1999).

It is true that democracy cannot thrive without effective state institutions and a strong political society. And those things are direly lacking in Bosnia-Herzegovina, even six years into the 'peace'. Its sovereignty as a state is compromised by the continuation of an international protectorate. The constitutional arrangements encourage nationalist instincts in party politics and voting patterns. The anti-nationalist parties with democratic potential are fragmented and weak. More hangs on personalities than on structures. There are frequent corruption scandals. Lack of transparency, for instance in the process of drafting legislation, inhibits confidence.

At the same time, an effective state is not all that is needed. Democracy cannot come into being and be sustainable unless and until it is also valued and practised at the grassroots (Held 1987). Juan Linz and Alfred Stepan, for instance, in their study of societies in transition to 'consolidated democracy', propose that statehood and free elections must be accompanied by five other conditions (Linz and Stepan 1996). One of them is a thriving civil society, the area of free association in the space between the family, the state, the market and political society. Of course, social movements and voluntary associations are not necessarily all progressive. Civil society can as easily generate non-democratic as democratic movements. Democracy by its very nature is always wreckable (Keane 1998, p50). But elements of a democratically-tending civil society are visibly developing in B-H.

We found ourselves, then, arguing the case (see Cockburn 2001) for supporting the growth of specifically *inclusive and democratic grassroots women's organizations* in B-H – not at the expense of, but in tandem with, effective state structures and responsible political society. And on this basis we believe, especially if they are an expression of a wider women's movement, women's NGOs, such as the seven we studied, tendentially contribute to the configuration of democratic society in a future B-H. They do so in three ways – by promoting inclusive democracy, local democracy and gender democracy.

Inclusive democracy. The dominant experience of the post-Dayton world has been the fixing of ethnic difference and separation. Those who launched the wars of separation in Bosnia largely succeeded in their aims. Those who stood for co-existence and inclusivity lost. Some Bosnians, depending on circumstances, felt safer for this new separation. But the pre-war republic of Bosnia-Herzegovina had a higher 'tolerance index' than other republics (United Nations Development Programme 19989) and many when they awoke to the new demography felt bereft by the loss of the old companionship. These women's organizations, on however modest a scale, are modelling and promoting ethnic inclusion and integration. They are not the only forces for re-integration in B-H. Generous individuals are now privately trying to re-establish cross-ethnic friendships. The international institutions and some political parties are striving to de-ethnicize politics. But what is lacking, and what these women's organizations can contribute, is public activity at the mid-level of collectivities and institutions.

Local democracy. These women have a clear vision for their town or city. They tell us they want it to be a place where old friendships can be affirmed and renewed despite intervening experiences; where people are judged by what they do and say, not by the name they carry; where political divergences are dealt with non-violently and democratically; where religion is a question of private belief not of politics; where economic competition is lively but humanized; and where there are no extremes of wealth and poverty. They believe in an integration of the three ethnicities honed in war, but also want their town or city to be inclusive of refugees and returners. The municipal authorities within whose domains the women's NGOs operate are, by contrast, separatist and nationalist. They have no sense of participatory governance. On the contrary, they resent community organizations, reading all critique as opposition. As manifestations of local activism, women's organizations could help draw into existence worthy protagonists in the shape of responsive and responsible local authorities.

Gender democracy. Anne Phillips writes, 'With the odd exception, the entire debate on democracy has proceeded for centuries as if women were not there ... ' As a result, a 'relentless privileging, not just of real living men, but of the very category of the male itself, has formed and deformed political theory and practice'. Politics – this is the message of her book *Engendering Democracy* – has to be reconceptualized with both sexes written in (Phillips 1991, pp2, 3). Despite attempts through 'quotas' to redress the dominance men quickly established in the new political system, women remain marginal to organized politics in Bosnia. Since the days of Yugoslavia, there has been, as Martha Walsh put it, 'massive retrenchment of women from public life' (Walsh 1999, p18). Activity by local women's organizations informing women about politics, encouraging them to vote and stand for election, showing them ways to intervene and giving them the skills to do so, can make a significant contribution to shifting an emergent Bosnian democracy towards gender democracy.

At a more general level too, women like these, stepping into public space, expecting more of a contribution from men in the home, taking initiatives that conflict with the norm – are all part of a reshaping of entrenched patriarchal gender relations. Full democracy means a democratic *society* as well as a democratic state (Held 1987). Gender democracy therefore means not only a fair share of parliamentary seats and executive posts but also democracy in marriage, in the family, in the street and in every workplace from the soup kitchen to the 'dot.com' enterprise.

Three problems are liable to prevent women's organizations from growing into a women's movement and playing a full part in the democratizing of Bosnia. First, they are still a long way from either effective self-management or effective organizational democracy. If they are to survive and gain an impact, new skills and practices have to be developed within them. Second, opportunities for realistic engagement with political power are lacking to the women's organizations. John Keane suggests that an important condition for civil society is 'the

cultivation of public spheres of controversy in which the violent exercise of power over others can be monitored and resisted non-violently'
(Keane 1998, p156). The public spheres available to Bosnian women in
which to question power – contested urban governance, a practice of
political lobbying, campaigning and advocacy, a responsive media,
accessible courts – are still seriously under-developed. The result is that
women are muttering to themselves, rather than shaking the pillars.

Third, Bosnian women's NGOs lack security of funding. They
scratch a living as 'hunter gatherers' in a primitive world. They are
crucially dependent on international NGOs and the international institutions, both governmental and inter-governmental, for survival.
Funding is very much on donors' terms. It is on a stop-start basis,
always short term, seldom covers overheads. Now, many donors are
pulling out of Bosnia and moving to the sites of more recent wars and
catastrophes. There are strong arguments for an improved legal framework and a thought-through, responsible, long-term international
funding policy for progressive NGOs (Independent Bureau for
Humanitarian Issues 1998).

Gender orders are not static, and the Yugoslav region is no exception. The Second World War marked a transition from a largely rural
and traditional form of patriarchal society to a brutalizing period of
armed conflict in which two kinds of political ideology entailed opposing forms of gender order. Nationalism, which would emerge again to
foment war half a century later, entailed a deep divergence of masculine
and feminine identities, and pronounced inequality between the sexes.
An emphatically militarized form of masculinity was hegemonic. The
anti-fascist resistance movement, under the leadership of Josip Brod
Tito, needed the massive cooperation of women. It furnished the ideology for Yugoslavia's half-century experiment with an anti-Stalinist
form of socialism, establishing a gender order that was more egalitar-
ian, inclusive of women in economy and administration, but ultimately
male dominated. Throughout the Cold War, Yugoslavia remained a
militarized country with a large standing army. But the hegemonic
masculinity defined male leadership in a mode that was less individual,
less overtly violent, more collective, bureaucratic and statist. That
gender order died with Yugoslavia itself.

Today, in the postwar moment in Bosnia, we found women feeling
marginalized within a catastrophically male-dominated society in
which they were up against a confusing amalgam of assertive masculinities – generated variously by religious authorities of renewed
influence, nationalist movements, militaries both national and interna-

tional, and frankly criminal fraternities. They were also experiencing an emergent capitalism with new exclusions, new class structures – an entrepreneurial culture in which men were again in the ascendant. It is against great odds therefore that women are struggling to clarify the causes and dimensions of their disadvantage, to find each other, to imagine change and to assemble the resources to act for it. The fact that, here and there, they are succeeding in carving out little spaces in which to invent a localized woman-centred gender regime is a source of hope.

Notes

1. The research involved a partnership between the author, based in the School of Social and Human Sciences, City University London, where she is a Research Professor in Sociology, and Rada Stakic-Domuz and Meliha Hubic, of Medica Women's Association, Zenica, Bosnia-Herzegovina. It was funded by the Ajahma Charitable Trust, the Lipman-Miliband Trust, the Network for Social Change and the Open Society Institute. She would like most warmly to thank all of the above, and in addition the women of the Bosnian women's organizations who participated in the study – giving most generously of their time and sharing their wisdom. The author is indebted to the University for Humanist Studies, Utrecht, Netherlands, for the visiting position of Ribbius Peletier Professor of Feminism, Humanism and Emancipation in 2000, which provided a supportive academic environment in which to write up the research.

2. In this chapter I use the terms 'gender order', 'gender regime' and 'hegemonic masculinity' as developed by R.W. Connell 1987. The usage is discussed in the Introduction to this book and evident in Connell's own contribution, Chapter 2.

3. The usage of the term 'patriarchy' has been keenly debated in the context of the feminist movement since the late 1960s (Eisenstein 1979; Sargent 1981). A particularly useful formulation has been that of Pateman 1988, stressing its historical variations. Here, as elsewhere, I use it to mean a long-lived, but adaptive, form of gender order characterized by a hierarchy among men, and of men over women, that structures and is structured by other hierarchical systems, notably those of class and ethnicity.

4. The term 'civil society' has been used in many ways, at different periods and with different political intentions. See discussions in Fine and Rai 1997, and Keane 1998. I choose here to exclude from its scope the family, business organizations and political parties. The latter, following Linz and Stepan 1996, I term 'political society'.

5. Note that I use 'integrative' here, not in the sense made current by Angela Miles in her *Integrative Feminisms*, 1996, but to mean tending to diminish

differentiation of ethno-national identities and the distance between them.

6. We were a team of three. Our approach was qualitative, involving documentary research, observation and thematic (tape recorded and transcribed) interviews with 36 women inside the seven organizations and ten other, more centrally placed, informants over a period of three months in the autumn of 1999. Opportunities for data gathering were augmented by the fact that the project was not designed to be research alone. Our agreement with the women's organizations was that, as well as seeking information from them, we would support their development in certain practical ways and facilitate networking between them. We are thus engaging in sustained interaction with all seven organizations over an eighteen month period.

7. Wilson's among other definitions of social movement is usefully discussed in Cohen and Rai 2000.

8. We explore further the plurality of feminisms, and different emphases in and interpretations of feminism, in connection with Bosnia-Herzegovina in Cockburn 2001.

9. This UNDP report cites a survey by the Consortium of Yugoslav Sociological Institutes.

Conflicts of interest: gender in Oxfam's emergency response

SUZANNE WILLIAMS

It is now widely recognized amongst international non-governmental organizations (INGOs) that working in the context of conflict and turbulence presents them with specific challenges in relation to delivering gender equity in both their humanitarian and development aid programmes. INGOs in general accept the need for gender-desegregated data, the fact that women and men have different needs and interests and that conflict and upheaval present women with opportunities as well as threats, and the chance to re-negotiate gender roles following *de facto* assumption of male responsibilities in the absence of men. However, the analysis is rarely taken further, or deepened. Gender is not identified by INGOs as a key defining factor of identity in relation to how war begins, what it is about, how groups are mobilized to fight, how cease-fires and peace agreements are reached, and what kind of peace can be said to have been achieved. For women, the end of war rarely brings peace, and can in fact bring new levels of violence into their lives.

The power relations which define gender identity, the allegiances, the beliefs and behaviours which are gender-based, are seldom regarded as important for, and even more rarely built into, the analysis of most INGOs of war and non-international conflict, or the planning of interventions to address its consequences. The failure to do this can sometimes be attributed to lack of expertise or experience in gender analysis, and sometimes to a profound, often unformulated, resistance to incorporating it into the analytic framework, for a number of reasons which will be examined later in this paper. To address gender relations in the context of conflict entails entering the highly contested terrain of conflicts of interest, not only within the war-torn society, but within all the institutions intervening in the situation, including the INGOs.

In this chapter I will explore the mission of a large British-based

INGO – Oxfam – and some of its experience in addressing gender inequalities in the institutional structures and policies which govern its activities in conflict and its aftermath.[1] I present some of the contradictions and dichotomies within Oxfam's organizational culture which have held this work back and continue to provide obstacles to it, in spite of substantial work on the issues within the organization over the years. I also examine some of the recent developments within Oxfam which are beginning to seek new solutions to the problem of gender-blindness in its interventions, and look at some positive examples of gender-sensitive practice.

My perspective is that of a Policy Adviser in Oxfam's Policy Department, with a brief to work on gender, human rights and conflict. My principal role is to offer advice and support to Oxfam's programmes at regional or country level, and to contribute to the development of Oxfam's global programme policy on conflict, gender and human rights, within which violence against women is a key priority. While here I present my own views and not those of Oxfam as a whole, I draw upon the experiences and concerns of many staff around the organization – indeed, all of us who believe in and work for the consistent delivery of gender equity by every intervention of Oxfam's.

Having looked at some of Oxfam's 'institutional imperatives', in other words its goals and aims, the mandates, policies and guidelines, which govern its work during conflict and its aftermath, I will discuss some of the problems inherent in several conceptual and programmatic divides which make programme implementation in this area complicated and difficult. These divides, which overlap each other, are those that separate *relief* and *development* responses, and *technical* and *social* approaches, and which represent institutional conflicts of interest. Interwoven with them are different perceptions within Oxfam of the division between the *public* and *private* domains, and indeed different perceptions of these amongst those, in the North and the South, with whom Oxfam works. The critical feminist insight that the private/public divide has to be broken down, and the personal made political, to end discrimination against women and build gender equality, is taking a long time to percolate through Oxfam. There still remain both perceptual and actual obstacles to making the connections between gender relations in the private and public spheres. However, there is a growing area of work, on violence against women in war and in 'peacetime', which has the potential to encourage new ways of thinking beyond these divides, and I look at some of the implications of this work at the end of the chapter.

I will consider selected examples from Oxfam's programme in Kosovo, Central America, South Africa and Cambodia, in particular at some of Oxfam's experience in relation to integrating gender equity into its programme goals for work in the aftermath of war. Both direct operational interventions, especially in Kosovo, and work with counterpart organizations are considered. While Oxfam's work is increasingly concerned with campaigning and advocacy, these areas are beyond the scope of this chapter. Nonetheless it is true that many of the contradictions and conflicts which make it so difficult for gender equity to be at the heart of Oxfam's direct interventions are equally problematic in its campaigning and advocacy initiatives.

Oxfam's institutional imperatives

Founded in 1942, Oxfam is based in Oxford in the UK, with a decentralized structure of nine offices in regions around the world. Oxfam's mandate is to relieve poverty, distress and suffering, and to educate the public about the nature, causes and effects of these. It describes itself as a 'development, relief, and campaigning organization dedicated to finding lasting solutions to poverty and suffering around the world'. Oxfam works principally with partner or counterpart organizations, international, national and community-based, supporting them to achieve goals common to both. In the fields of emergency response and campaigning, Oxfam is also operational, employing its own staff to deliver relief in the field, or to lobby and campaign for changes in policy and public awareness, and working in conjunction with other INGOs and international agencies.

In recent years, Oxfam has defined its purpose in terms of helping people to achieve their basic rights, loosely in line with articles related principally to social and economic rights within the Universal Declaration of Human Rights, and the two International Covenants. Thus Oxfam aligns its programmes according to a range of basic rights, including health, education, freedom from violence, and a sustainable livelihood. Additionally, a political and civil right is phrased by Oxfam as the 'right to be heard', related to governance and democratic representation, and the 'right to an identity', referring to gender equity and discrimination.

Oxfam has had an institutional Gender Policy since 1993, but the implementation of this policy throughout the organization has been patchy, dependent upon the efforts of committed individuals, and limited to only its international programme. This has meant that the profound transformations envisaged by the Gender Policy in human

87

resources policy and the structure and culture of Oxfam as a whole have not taken place. The progress of implementation of the Gender Policy within the international programme was mapped in 1997, and pointed to several important lessons. These included that in the absence of clear criteria for measuring progress in implementing gender policies and practices, managers used very different standards, and there was no overall consistency in the integration of gender equity throughout Oxfam. One of the strengths revealed by the study was that Oxfam could demonstrate considerable success in working at grassroots level with women's organizations, and in its gender titles publishing programme. There has been less success in relation to mainstreaming gender in large-scale emergency or development programmes, and little to point to in relation to gender-sensitive advocacy and campaigning work (Oxfam 1998). The mainstreaming of gender throughout Oxfam and its programme thus remains a challenge, but it is a challenge that the organization has prioritized, and is beginning to take up in a systematic way through its new framework of objectives and account-ability, related to basic rights and gender equity.

Oxfam has developed a number of sets of guidelines and standards relating to gender for its emergency programming over the years, and these have been implemented successfully in some instances, but are not routinely applied. In the last few years, Oxfam was a key collabo-rator in an interagency project known as the Sphere Project, which aims to 'improve the quality of assistance provided to people affected by disasters, and to enhance accountability of the humanitarian system in disaster response' (Sphere Project 2000). The Sphere Project has produced a field handbook which sets out a Humanitarian Charter, and a set of minimum standards for the various technical sectors in disaster response – water and sanitation, nutrition, food aid, shelter and site planning and health services. The first trial edition produced in 1998 was gender-blind. A gender review was called for, and Oxfam, amongst other agencies, submitted a detailed revision of Sphere from a gender perspective. The second edition, published in 2000, has incorporated some of these revisions. The Charter itself, however, makes no specific reference to gender or any specific commitment to gender equity in the delivery of emergency relief, and there is still room for improvement in the guidelines themselves. Given these shortcomings, Oxfam GB is currently developing a set of organizational minimum standards for gender-sensitive response in humanitarian aid, including protection.

Oxfam is also developing the concept of 'net impact' or 'net benefit' in relation to humanitarian relief. This has arisen as a result of the work

– and the challenge – of Mary Anderson's 'Building Local Capacities for Peace' project. The question addressed by Anderson's work is:

> How can international and local aid agencies provide assistance to people in areas of violent conflict in ways that help those people disengage from the conflict and develop alternative systems for overcoming the problems they face? How can aid agencies and aid workers encourage local capacities for peace? (Anderson 1996, p3).

Oxfam, along with other international humanitarian agencies, has to ask difficult questions. When does our presence do more harm than good, by exacerbating the conflict through diversion of aid, or by an inadvertent support to perpetrators of human rights violations in conflict? When do we contribute to the perpetuation of the war through provision of humanitarian relief thus enabling national resources to be allocated to arms and the war itself? David Bryer, Oxfam's former Director writes:

> The future of humanitarian aid is now perhaps more in question than at any time since 1945. The providers question whether the abuse of their aid outweighs its benefits; while the donors, at least the official ones, reduce their funding. Yet the need for aid continues; the number of people who suffer needlessly for lack of it rises. Here, we consider some of the practical difficulties and ethical choices involved in judging the 'net impact' of aid that is provided in armed conflicts, where its abuse has become a certainty (Bryer and Cairns 1997, p363).

Such questions apply equally to gender. When do our interventions bring more harm than good to women? Are we inadvertently exacerbating male violence against women by acting without a clear analysis of gender power relations? Are we making it easier for male oppression to continue by focusing on women's projects that do not disturb the *status quo*? Are there times when we should be making a judgement and deciding to pull out of a direct intervention, and focus on high profile lobbying and campaigning for women's rights? Is some predictable risk better than doing nothing? In the context of conflict, and in highly militarized societies, which can have extreme consequences for women, these dilemmas are particularly acute. Such issues arose in acute form for Oxfam in Afghanistan, when the Taliban took control of Kabul in 1996, and the organization's local female staff were prevented from coming to work. Oxfam had to scale down its operation, and find a way to balance its presence in the country with a principled stance on the abuse of the rights of women under the Taliban regime.

This judgement – are we doing more harm than good? – is not routinely applied to Oxfam's work, and the analytical tools to help staff make such a judgement are not yet developed. But the issue is regularly debated, and current work on impact reporting and the development of standards within Oxfam is beginning to address it in relation to development, humanitarian and advocacy work.

Programming in conflict-prone areas: dilemmas and dichotomies

'The thing about this programme,' one of the water engineers said to me in Kosovo in 1999, 'is that it's the soft side of the programme that is the hardest to do'. This kind of categorising and opposing of different forms of action into the 'hard' and the 'soft' is symptomatic of a dichotomized thinking about conflict and poverty, and responses to them, that powerfully impacts on Oxfam programmes.

Actions and interventions that are characterized by urgency, that show fast, quantifiable results, that are predominantly technical in nature – are 'hard'. The inputs, in humanitarian relief work, are 'hardware', quantifiable, and largely material. On the other hand, those interventions which are associated with more subtle, and cautious approaches, whose inputs are less quantifiable (such as awareness-raising, informal education work, or group formation) and the results of which are more difficult to measure and take longer to manifest, and which are predominantly social and cultural in nature – are 'soft'.

This dichotomy is closely associated with stereotypical categories of the masculine and the feminine, and runs through not only the ways actions and achievements are perceived in Oxfam – and indeed, in most institutions – but the ways they are valued and rewarded. The 'hard', masculinized, interventions, whether in policy and advocacy work, or humanitarian relief, are generally more visible, and perceived as urgent. The supply lines of the 'hardware' and the context of much policy work, is male-dominated and masculinized. Visible results and high profile carry a premium in NGOs which are struggling in the marketplace for funds and which are under pressure to show concrete and quantifiable results to their donors – many of whom, in their institutional structures and cultures, are subject to the same kinds of masculinized and feminized dichotomies in values. The less visible, 'soft', feminized interventions do not thus attract the same attention nor the same amounts of money, and are not valued as highly, both inside and outside the organization. This of course becomes a self-perpetuating cycle of highly gendered systems of value and reward, which affects not only the nature of interventions, but the staff responsible for them.

Gender equity programming in conflict-prone areas is thus itself prone to conflict in quite complex ways – linked to the opposing categories of the 'hard' and the 'soft'. Other divides intersect or run parallel with this broad dichotomy, as outlined above. For although organizations like Oxfam have theorized the end of the 'development-relief' divide, the division still persists institutionally, and in field policy and practice.[2] The technical ('hard') and social ('soft') approaches to programme planning and implementation are also strongly associated with short-term relief and longer-term developmental approaches within the humanitarian intervention. Threading in and out of these issues, as was mentioned above, is the divide between the public and the private, and the implications for perceptions of violence against women in war, and in 'peace'. Rape as a war crime is perceived as 'hard', a public crime, associated with military strategy; rape as a domestic crime is 'soft', a private crime, associated with social issues and intimate relationships.

The short-term/long-term divide is gradually narrowing, but its persistence in both policy and practice means that the nature of the immediate relief effort is only peripherally influenced by the longer-term social and economic prospects for the victims of the conflict. The focus is on life-saving, principally through the provision of clean water, sanitation and hygiene promotion – and this aim, and its achievements, cannot be underestimated or undervalued. However, longer-term goals such as improving women's prospects through education, empowerment or training, or strategies to prevent further conflict, are secondary to the provision of immediate relief.

Often, given limited resources, the aims of relief and recovery can seem to be counterposed, one at the expense of the other. Moral claims raise the temperature. Staff saving lives through a quick, large-scale response, accuse those emphasizing the social complexities of the emergency of 'fiddling while Rome burns'. Worse still, they may be seen as exacerbating social and political tensions they do not fully understand. Social development staff, on the other hand, accuse the technical staff of rushing in blindly, treating people like numbers and objects, potentially doing more harm than good by ignoring social and gender differences in the population, creating dependencies, and paying little attention to the long-term consequences of the relief aid itself.

Add gender equity to the mix and the environment may become explosive. It is common to find strong resistance to building in gender equity goals to emergency response on the grounds that (a) lives have to be saved quickly, information is not available and there is no time for social surveys; (b) there is immense pressure from donors and the media to show that measures are in place rapidly and having an immediate impact and gender issues lack the necessary visibility; (c) while we know distribution is more effective through women, there is often not time to organize it that way, or local resistance to it which Oxfam should not challenge; (d) an emergency is not the right time to challenge gender power relations; and (e) why should special attention be paid to women when everyone is suffering?

I have heard all these arguments in the field. They are arguments which frustrate practitioners on both sides of the debate, all trying to get the job done as best they can. These are complex issues which are not easily resolved in the clash between speed of response and the social, cultural and political composition of groups which will determine the quality of that response.

Dichotomies in practise: the example of Kosovo

Oxfam's response to the Kosovo crisis brought these issues out quite clearly. Managers of the programmes made real efforts to work across the relief/development and technical/social divides, and integrate the 'hard' and 'soft' elements into a single programme. The process seemed to get off to a good start.

Oxfam had been in Kosovo since 1995, working closely with women's groups and associations in several regions in the country. Oxfam-Pristina had strong relationships with partner organizations, many of them women's organizations, and a strong local team. The focus was on long-term development initiatives aimed at the social and political empowerment of women, through capacity building of women activists. With the intensification of the conflict in 1998, Oxfam's focus shifted to the needs of displaced women and children. Women's Centres were funded in Viti, Pristina, Obiliq and Gjilan as relief distribution points as well as meeting places for psychosocial support. The programme also included substantial work on water and sanitation and public health.

In March 1999 with the onset of the NATO campaign, Oxfam evacuated with other International NGOs, setting up an office in Skopje, Macedonia, with several of its staff from Pristina. The existing Albania programme was rapidly expanded to take on the humanitarian relief of the refugees flooding into Albania. During the period of exile and displacement, Oxfam continued to work in Macedonia with its highly committed ex-Pristina staff, and some of its Kosovar counterparts, principally in the refugee camps. With this continuity, and programme experience from several years in Kosovo, the chances of a well-integrated programme, building the relief response within longer-term strategies for recovery and return, with gender equity goals at its core, seemed to be high, if not optimal.

However, this integration did not happen, for a number of reasons. A large-scale humanitarian relief programme was mounted, with an enormous budget raised by emergency appeals in the UK, and in the limelight of the high media interest in the crisis. The pressure was on Oxfam to spend the money, and spend it quickly. A large number of expatriate staff, mostly water technicians and engineers, flew into Macedonia to set up Oxfam's water programme in the camps. Money flowed freely for the emergency response. But the dynamic between the social and technical responses, when I arrived to look at gender, human rights and protection issues in April 1999, was difficult and competitive. Kosovar staff, refugees themselves, were dealing with their own personal and family trauma, and with loss and uncertainty, as a result of the war. The problem was heightened by the fact that the newcomers who arrived en masse to run the emergency relief response were all expatriates, some with no previous experience of the region. The ex-Pristina Kosovar staff felt overrun by the new technical 'expats', misunderstood, and alienated from a programme that had been theirs, and now had inflated beyond recognition.

Kosovar refugees – mostly educated young men and women – were taken on by the technical and social programmes to carry out the work in the camps. There was a heated debate about payment of the young workforce. In the old Pristina-based programme, much of the work was based on voluntarism. But in the refugee situation, many of the other international agencies were paying their local recruits. Initially, the debate was played out in gendered terms – the young men working with the water engineers were paid, and the young women were not. This was subsequently adjusted.

The technical staff, running the water programme (the 'hard' side of the programme), were almost exclusively male, and were perceived by the almost exclusively female staff working on gender, disability, social development and hygiene promotion (the 'soft' side of the programme) to have privileged access to the emergency resources. The technical aspects of the programme were thus perceived by those working on the other parts of the programme to be valued more highly than the social aspects. In fact, as in any emergency, all staff were clamouring for more resources, whether logisticians, engineers, managers, or social development staff. Where all eyes are on the crisis, urgency defines the response. The pressure is there externally as well as from the desperate plight of the refugee population; competition over resources is inevitable and, where other divisions exist, very diffi-cult to manage.

As is often the case, strong feelings became focused on access to vehicles, as key and desirable programme resources. I travelled with staff from all three parts of the programme, and observed that the water programme staff in each camp had access to their own, new four-wheel drive vehicles, while the hygiene promotion, disability and social development staff had to share older vehicles, one of which was quite unsafe, with a cracked windscreen and a field radio which did not work. I vividly recall sitting on the dusty roadside at the exit from one of the Stankovic camps for some time, trying to hitch a lift back to Skopje because the Social Development programme did not have its own vehicle. This put extra pressure on the social development, disabil-ity and hygiene promotion teams, and made it harder for them to accomplish all they had to do in the dispersed camps where they worked. There were other specific and more general problems around access to programme resources that were not adequately resolved, and this exacerbated the divisions between teams responsible for different responses. This in turn militated against the integration of the social and technical aspects of the programme.

In a report at the time I described Oxfam's programme as a three-pronged effort, comprising community development, with special emphasis on women and disabled people; hygiene and public health promotion; and the provision of clean water,

> and recommended that its three elements needed to be built into a single integrated programme, based on a clear analysis of the needs and rights of women, men and children. Assessment meth-ods sensitive to gender and age were would provide the necessary information for programme planning in order for Oxfam to make a significant contribution in both the immediate crisis and the future in Kosovo (Williams 1999, p10).

The importance of technical/social programme integration was re-emphasized in an Oxfam Gender Workshop in September 2000.

Nonetheless Oxfam's programme in Macedonia did address some of the key issues. Specific needs related to gender and disability were taken into account by the technical team in, for example, the design of washing facilities in the camps. The work of the Social Development and Gender team in providing separate tents for social spaces for women and men set the context for beginning to address the gender-related violence experienced by women and girls, and Oxfam lobbied UNHCR to fulfil their protection mandate and provide better protection measures for women and girls in the camps.

A difficulty common to all humanitarian response was the tension between the pace and style of work of quick-impact emergency relief, and longer-term social processes, and the substantial differences in scale and funding levels of these programmes. Staffing patterns in humanitarian relief are based on rapid scaling-up of numbers, high turnover, and short-term contracts. Induction processes for these staff members are usually sketchy, and the culture of 'hitting the ground running' is not favourable to training in social and gender awareness in the field. In the Kosovo crisis the result was the running of parallel, rather than integrated, programmes in Macedonia. This split was carried forward into the post-conflict work of reconstruction and recovery after the refugees returned.

The nature of the funding environment during a crisis and in its aftermath is relevant to the style and content of programming. 'Red' money is tied to specific donor-defined goals; 'green' money is Oxfam core money – and thus offers more flexibility. When the 'red' appeal money that sustained the Kosovo humanitarian programme ran out, Oxfam had to fund its development and gender work under the US-funded Kosovo Women's Initiative (KWI), managed by UNHCR. Although this $10,000,000 fund set long-term empowerment goals, the spending requirement was short-term. This put considerable pressure on both the Kosovar and international NGOs involved to get new projects up and running and spending money, often beyond the organizational capacity of the partner groups, many of them women's groups set up specifically in response to the KWI. The KWI was in itself an example of the tension between short-term emergency funding demanding quick and visible returns, and developmental goals whose benefits are only achievable and measurable in the longer term. When the emergency money moves on to the next crisis, the gap left can be devastating to organizations which were mobilized, or created, in the plentiful funding climate, who subsequently find themselves without support (see also Cynthia Cockburn's comments on the funding of women's organizations in postwar Bosnia-Herzegovina, in Chapter 5 of this volume).

Gender assessments were carried out during the Kosovo crisis in both Macedonia and Albania. The Consolidated Recommendations drawn up by Gender Advisers for the response in both countries, which hold for Oxfam programming in general, include the following. First, gender and social development issues need to be fully integrated in the emergency response and future programme development, with every aspect based on a clear analysis of the needs and rights of women, men, and children, and disabled people. Second, the social and technical aspects of the programme should inform each other effectively for maximum impact. Social and community services must run hand-in-hand with distribution of non-food items, and water, sanitation and health/hygiene planning from the start; they must be as well resourced and should operate concurrently in Kosovo as soon as Oxfam has access to the designated sector. Third, unified programme aims and objectives for social and technical interventions need to be set for the region, within the framework of Oxfam's strategic change objectives, to which gender equity is central, and gender sensitive indicators for success should be set. And, fourth, baseline data and indicators for gender equity should be set at the earliest stage in programme planning for effective monitoring and impact assessment (Clifton and Williams 1999).

Working with counterparts in conflict

Oxfam's success in integrating gender equity into programming in conflict and its aftermath depends critically not only upon how Oxfam's institutional dichotomies are resolved (or as in the Kosovo case not resolved), but also on the relationships with partner organizations and local/national NGOs, and their analysis of the situation. In this section I will turn to Oxfam's experience in El Salvador, in Latin America – a region where Oxfam programmes have been notable for the quality of long-standing relationships with local counterpart organizations. Here I focus on the work with counterparts in the immediate aftermath of conflict, where Oxfam did not have the same level of operationality in its response, and thus the 'technical/social' dichotomy is less evident than in the Kosovo example. Here too, however, the 'hard' and 'soft' elements of the situation, and the programme response through counterpart organizations, had a key influence on the way gender equity was addressed.

From the 1960s and 1970s the country programmes were charac-terised by intense counterpart relationships, many of which were built around a strong sense of solidarity with the political struggles against brutal military dictatorships and the social injustice and poverty brought about by these regimes. The emphasis was on the long-term transformation of society. Because of the nature of the regimes, much of the work supported by Oxfam was initiated by the Catholic Church and took place under its umbrella. But the analysis of social injustice did not include an analysis of women's oppression by men.

In El Salvador, Oxfam's programme focused before and during the war on the strengthening of popular organizations allied to the church and progressive Salvadorian NGOs. In common with many of the liberation struggles of the 1980s, however, gender equity was not seen as part of the liberation goal, and the analysis of gender oppression often regarded as a 'special interest' issue and potentially divisive to the aims of the movement. The liberation struggle was 'hard', armed, macho, political. Women's specific issues were 'soft', secondary, personal, and for women and men alike, diluted the toughness and authenticity of the armed struggle, whose goal was social justice for all. Moreover, despite the long history of popular feminism and women's struggles in Latin America, both counterparts and some of Oxfam staff saw the analysis of gender inequity as yet another example of cultural imperialism, particularly from the United States. Martha Thompson, Deputy Regional Representative in Central America at the time, writes, 'Most counterparts saw the inequalities based on gender rela-tions as a Northern concern, and not one of their priorities' (Thompson 1999, p48).

While Oxfam began to include elements of gender analysis into the El Salvador programme in the 1980s, the extent to which it pushed its gender work was greatly influenced by its counterpart organizations. By 1995 however, Oxfam's Gender Policy began to require field programmes to show evidence of pursuing gender equity in their work. Martha Thompson (1999) outlines four basic mistakes made by Oxfam in trying to incorporate gender analysis into the programme.

First, money was thrown at the issue. Counterparts could access funding if they attached 'gender' to a project. Without a gender analy-sis, counterparts included projects with women, such as training or micro-enterprises – some of which were effective, some of which were not. Funding agencies went along with this to gain the approval of Head Office. Second, rather than fully explore the tension between a class and a gender analysis, an uneasy compromise was reached, whereby Oxfam and counterpart agencies basically continued working as before, but with the addition of specific projects with women, and support to some women's organizations in the popular movement. A broad discussion with counterparts and local women's organizations on gender should have taken place, and would have avoided Oxfam contributing to the distortion of the concept of gender equity. Third, agencies did not recognize the gains that women had made during the war, gaining visibility in acts of courage, as combatants or resisting the fighting. Nor did agencies understand how transformation of gender roles could be integrated into social transformation. Fourth, Oxfam was unwilling to risk prejudicing its relationship with counterparts by raising gender power differences because of its perceived potential to cause divisions.

In El Salvador, the popular movement was dominated by men. A narrow political analysis, which did not take account of gender oppression and the value of internal democracy, held women back during the political struggle. During the war, women became stronger and were able to challenge their position after the fighting had ceased (Thompson 1999). The experience of Salvadorian women in the post-conflict arena is reflected in countries such as Nicaragua, Mozambique, Zimbabwe and South Africa. Once the war is over, women are sent back to be 'barefoot, pregnant and in the kitchen', while men make the political decisions about peace and reconstruction, and fill the political positions in the new government order. Women are less likely to accept their subordination once they have experienced relative autonomy and respect during the war, but the obstacles to their advancement are exacerbated by militaristic constructions of masculinity and femininity. The overall message to them is clear: both the war and peace will be dominated by men and masculinist priorities and interests; and this will be maintained as long as women do not have a formal role in peacemaking and reconstruction. The message to international NGOs is that they need to bring their global experience to bear on local and national politics and social relations, and to seek and strengthen counterparts locally, particularly amongst women's organizations and organizations working for gender equality.

The heart of the matter: gender violence and postwar peace

Peace does not come with the cessation of armed hostilities, and the signing of peace agreements. High levels of social and gender violence are a feature of postwar societies. South Africa has experienced spiralling levels of interpersonal violence, with shocking statistics of sexual abuse of women and children. As Thandi Modise, of the African National Congress Women's League, put it, 'In Africa there is not a universal definition of peace. It is not the cliched definition of not being at war. In South Africa today there is increasing domestic violence, an increase in child abuse. So we cannot say South Africa is at peace'.[3] Violence, like war, is gendered. Its expression is inseparable from female and male gender identities, and the relations between women and men. Gender identities constructed, promoted and sustained by armed conflict and the impact of militarization power-fully influence women's and men's attitudes and behaviours in the post-conflict environment.

I will end this chapter by looking specifically at the significance of gender violence and the meaning of peace, in the light of the dichotomies I have problematized here. To address gender violence means overcoming the private/public divide, and bringing together issues commonly categorized as 'hard' – those linked with war, arms and high-profile, militarized peacekeeping – and 'soft' – those linked to the personal experiences of violence of women, girls and boys during and after war. It means making the connections between the violence perpetrated in war, within the ambit of relief interventions, and the violence perpetrated out of war, addressed by development programmes. Policies for the construction of postwar peace must also embrace and ensure peace between women and men. In this sense, programming on gender violence goes right to the heart of the matter, bringing the issues described in this paper into stark relief.

The wars in Rwanda and Bosnia brought rape and sexual violence in wartime to the public gaze through intense media coverage. These crimes were in the public domain, and thus became a legitimate focus for the attention of human rights organizations, and for the interven-tions of development agencies – although in fact research in Bosnia showed that the majority of rapes and sexual crimes against women were committed by men known to them. The crimes of domestic violence and sexual abuse in societies not at war, or recovering from it, do not attract the same attention, and international organizations show greater ambivalence in addressing issues still widely perceived as too difficult, too complicated, and too private.

Nonetheless, Oxfam has supported work on violence against women for many years, and in line with the new programme objectives outlined earlier in this chapter a global programme on violence against women will be developed over the next few years. The programme seeks to overcome the analytic division between the public and the private, and to address violence within a framework of understanding gender relations and the construction of masculine and feminine identities in any sphere, in war and in peace. Oxfam's experience from all over the world – South Africa, Central and South America, the Great Lakes, Eastern Europe, Cambodia, Vietnam, South Asia – shows that gender violence after war carries on decades after the war is officially over; peace means different things for women and for men. A closer analysis of gender violence is beginning to inform Oxfam's work in post-conflict reconstruction and recovery, but gender violence has yet to be tackled strategically, and in an integrated way, as a central element of emergency response.

Oxfam has supported work by local and national NGOs which tackles violence against women in the aftermath of conflict, or where conflict is endemic, in many parts of the world – notably in South Africa, Rwanda, Bosnia, Indonesia, Cambodia, Guatemala and Colombia. In Cambodia, for example, the Alliance for Conflict Transformation, comprised of nineteen NGO and government workers, conducts training on conflict resolution for officials from the municipality of Phnom Penh, to be applied to disputes ranging from land issues to domestic violence. Domestic violence is widespread in Cambodia, the legacy of 30 years of war and brutalized relationships. The Project Against Domestic Violence in Cambodia (PADV) has been instrumental in raising awareness of violence against women through education and public campaigning, with government support. A national survey of the incidence of violence against women in 2,400 households gained national and international media attention. These organizations make the link clearly between the violence of war and continuing violence against women after the war is over. A victim of violence is quoted in PADV's survey of domestic violence in Cambodia as saying, 'After 1979 men changed. Nine out of ten men are broken, nasty ("Khoch"). During the Khmer Rouge period they had no happiness at all. So now that they are free, men do whatever they want' (Zimmerman 1994).

There are many examples of the brutalization of men by extreme nationalism and the experience of military action, and the implications for women of this violence. This has been well documented by women's NGOs and international organizations in Bosnia, Uganda, Sierra Leone and other parts of the world. A chilling case from South Africa shows how brutalized men transmit the violence to women. A township gang was formed to rape women as a way of bolstering or recovering male identity and status, while at the same time getting back at political leaders by whom gang members felt betrayed. These ex-combatants replicate militaristic patterns of discipline and punishment, and assert their dominance through acts of gendered violence – the sexual abuse and rape of women.[4] The leader of the organization was interviewed on television and stated:

> I was a comrade before I joined this organization. I joined it because we were no longer given political tasks. Most of the tasks were given to senior people. Myself and six other guys decided to form our own organization that will keep these senior comrades busy all the time. That is why we formed the South African Rapists Association (SARA). We rape women who need to be disciplined (those women who behave like snobs), they just do not want to talk to most people (L.Vetten cited in *Pickup*, Williams and Sweetman 2001, p198).

Addressing masculinities and the forces which lead to, promote and maintain male violence towards women as a defining feature of gender power relations, will be part of Oxfam's mission to have a significant impact on gender equity through all aspects of its programmes. To do this effectively, Oxfam – as any INGO or international agency – will have to examine closely its own gendered structures and cultures, and its own gendered conflicts of interest. I have identified some of the key areas of difficulty in relation to delivering on gender equity in the context of conflict and postwar programming. The tensions show up at all levels in the institution.

My core argument in this chapter has been that the ways Oxfam's organizational imperatives are both conceptualized and implemented are themselves simultaneously dichotomized and gendered. The 'hard' and the 'soft' run through Oxfam's structure and culture as metaphors for the masculine and the feminine, and can bump up against each other in the heat of the moment, in the highly-charged context of emergencies and post-conflict interventions, with the effect of generating tensions over priorities and resources, value and reward. It is only through a thorough and profound commitment to gender equity in all aspects of its structure, culture and programming that Oxfam – as any other organization – can begin to overcome these gendered conflicts of interests and strengthen its effectiveness in fulfilling its mission to relieve human suffering and address its root causes.

Notes

1. 'Oxfam' throughout this chapter refers to Oxfam Great Britain only, and not to the wider family of organizations known as Oxfam International.

2. Many writers have emphasized this. Oxfam's Regional Representative for the Great Lakes region from 1991-94, Anne Mackintosh, writes 'even agencies who recognize the inappropriateness of regarding "relief" and "development" as separate phenomena perpetuate this false dichotomy, through resourcing long-term and emergency programmes in different ways and having them managed by different departments and staff. This often leads to unhelpful tensions and rivalry', Mackintosh 1997, p468.

3. Cited in 'Women and the Aftermath', Report on a Conference held in Johannesburg in July 1999, 'The Aftermath: Women in Post-Conflict Reconstruction', *Agenda*, No.43, Durban, South Africa, 2000.

4. From an article in the South African *Sunday Independent*, during 1998, cited in *Pickup*, Williams and Sweetman 2001, p148.

Gender and the peacekeeping military: a view from Bosnian women's organizations

CYNTHIA COCKBURN AND MELIHA HUBIC

We have seen in the Introduction as well as in several chapters of this book how international institutions sent to bring humanitarian relief to a war-afflicted region, to pacify it and assist in postwar reconstruction, often fail to take account of gender inequities and the imbalance of power between women and men in the country on which they are billeted. They bring their own unreformed gender relations with them, fail to support women's struggle for change and, at worst, may even add to the oppression and exploitation of women.

There is a particular problem, in that regard, with armed international peacekeeping forces. They are overwhelmingly male in their personnel and masculine in culture. This has a particular bearing on women's organizations active in the country hosting a peacekeeping operation. This chapter draws on the experience of women's organizations in Bosnia-Herzegovina (B-H), where we have been involved in women's activism and research. We address three questions. What is the relationship between women's organizations and soldiers of the international peacekeeping military in Bosnia, NATO's Stabilization Force? What do the women want from SFOR? What gender changes are implied for the military, if these women's wishes are to be fulfilled?

SFOR: mission and structure

The fighting in Bosnia-Herzegovina that had begun in 1992 was halted by the General Framework Agreement for Peace, negotiated in talks at Dayton, Ohio and signed in Paris on December 14, 1995. A United Nations 'protection force' (UNPROFOR) had already been present in Bosnia from 1992, its numbers insubstantial and its role unclear. Now UN Security Council Resolution 1031 assigned a NATO-led multinational 'implementation force' (IFOR), the largest military operation ever undertaken by the North Atlantic Alliance. Its first task was to establish a zone of separation between the armed forces of the warring parties, move heavy weapons to approved sites and patrol the border drawn between the two 'entities' (the Bosnian-Croat Federation and the Republika Srpska) created by the Dayton accords. When the mandate of IFOR expired on 20 December 1996, the Alliance extended its mission in the interests of consolidating the peace, renaming it a 'stabilization force' (SFOR), and cutting the number of troops by half. SFOR has remained in Bosnia ever since – its numbers reduced, at the time of writing, to around 20,000.

SFOR is an army of extraordinary social diversity. Every NATO nation with armed forces has played a part, but non-NATO countries too, including Albania, Austria, Argentina, Bulgaria, Estonia, Finland, Ireland, Latvia and Russia, have participated. Representatives of these countries are also involved in deliberations with the North Atlantic Council and in the SFOR Coordination Centre at the Supreme Headquarters of NATO (SHAPE) in Brussels. The presence of so many ethnic and national identities has generated in SFOR a complex, and no doubt contradictory, international military gender regime.[1]

Since a revision of SFOR's structure in the winter of 1999/2000, SFOR's Bosnian headquarters are at Camp Butimir, outside Sarajevo. It has three regional multi-national divisions. Each division has four battle groups located in its districts. There are also dedicated Operational Reserve Forces capable of intervening anywhere in the country.

The civilian aspects of the Dayton agreement are being carried out by a raft of international institutions. Overall authority rests with the Office of the High Representative appointed by the Peace Implementation Council. Other important organizations include the UN High Commissioner for Refugees (UNHCR), the Office of the UN High Commissioner for Human Rights (UNOHCHR), the Organization for Security and Co-operation in Europe (OSCE) and the International Police Task Force (UNIPTF). SFOR is mandated with securing an environment in which their work of civil and political reconstruction can take place.

Gender concerns did not feature in the Dayton agreement, nor did the international institutions bring to their work in Bosnia any notable gender equity policies (Kvinna til Kvinna 2000; Chinkin and Paradine 2001). Only five years later, on the initiative of senior women in the UNOHCHR and OSCE, was a Gender Co-ordinating Group established at which representatives of the international institutions are supposed to consider their work in B-H in relation to women, sex equality and gender issues.[2] SFOR has not been a party to this Gender Co-ordinating Group. Indeed, being held to be quite distinct from the 'international community' (deemed civilian), it was not invited.

Yet the work of SFOR is not exclusively military. In addition to its military functions, it has a clearly defined mandate to assist reconstruction through co-operation with local civilian organizations, including municipal and cantonal political and administrative authorities, small business enterprises and non-governmental organizations (NGOs). Typical activities are the rebuilding and equipping of schools and clinics, donations of toys to kindergartens and playgrounds and the rehabilitation of houses for returners.[3] Co-ordination is effected by a combined joint Civil Military Co-operation task force in Sarajevo, but each division and battle group has its CIMIC unit.

We interviewed CIMIC officers in the Turkish battle group in Zenica, who gave us a highly professional video presentation of their activity. This includes maintaining comprehensive data files on every village in the area; extensive co-operation with local NGOs both sides of the Inter-Entity Border Line; support of new small enterprises (bee keeping, poultry farming etc.); and the giving of small grants (for instance to an SOS crisis line for women survivors of violence) and practical assistance (eg building repairs to a young women's hostel, reconstructing the Orthodox priest's house). The battle group opens its medical and dental clinic to the local population free of charge. Members of the battle group, apparently voluntarily, make donations from their wages to support such humanitarian work.

Women's NGOs in relation to SFOR

There are more than fifteen hundred non-governmental organizations in Bosnia-Herzegovina (International Council for Voluntary Associations 1999). NGO activism is a sphere in which women are particularly active (see Chapter 5 of this volume). About half of the listed NGOs appear to have women as co-ordinators. Of this half, around one-third are associations in which the activists and beneficiaries are entirely women. Many of these, like many of Bosnia's mixed-sex NGOs, are monocultural, some are religious, and the majority are concerned primarily with humanitarian work. But in the research reported here we selected for interview only organizations known to us as being women-only, as addressed to women's rather than to 'family' needs, as locality-based and clearly committed to ethnically integrative working.

We visited eight such women's associations in the course of October 2000, and questioned them specifically concerning their relations with SFOR. Five are in the Federation of Bosnia-Herzegovina and three in the Republika Srpska. The former are *Anima* (Gorazde), *Medica* (Zenica), and *Vrelo, Koraci Nade* and *Zena Mostara* (in Mostar). The latter are *DOM* (Nevesinje), *Buducnost* (Modrica), *Lara* (Bijeljina). The SFOR units currently stationed in these areas include Turkish, Spanish, French, Italian, German, Russian and US battle groups. The women's associations also had earlier experience of Portuguese, British and Norwegian battalions.

The typical activities of these eight women's organizations include: skills training and income generation projects for women; legal advice and advocacy; a concern with women's relation to the political system; support for women victims of violence, sexual abuse and trafficking; women's reproductive health; and reconciliation – including the return of refugees and displaced people to their homes. The organizations, similar to the cluster considered in Chapter 5, tend to be small, with few staff. Their funding, mainly from international donors, is inadequate and insecure.

Though the quality of their relationship with SFOR has clearly varied greatly from one unit, area and period to the next, the women we spoke with on balance value the presence of SFOR and wish them to remain in B-H for the foreseeable future. These are some of the positive accounts we heard.

Women individually, and women's organizations, had benefited from the *security* UNPROFOR, IFOR and SFOR have successively provided, protection against the ethnic aggression that characterized the war. 'The only peace I've felt has been due to SFOR's presence' (Devleta, *Zena Mostara*). *Medica* had held the valued 'blue card' during the siege of Central Bosnia, so that their vehicle had been able to travel in UNPROFOR convoys. In the still dangerous times that followed the cease-fire, IFOR soldiers would drop in on the women's groups to ensure they were safe and well. *Buducnost* had had IFOR protection when they took women from the Republika Srpska across the border to visit and tend Serb graves. SFOR's current work clearing landmines and collecting weapons was universally valued. It is appreciated that SFOR units sometimes stand guard over refugees when first they come back to their homes, and that they sometimes use their vehicles to distribute humanitarian aid.

Secondly, the women say they value the *economic and practical effect* of the presence of an international military. Soldiers' spending boosts the local economy. There are many jobs, with fair pay and conditions, created for women in the bases. Putting military men and equipment to work (graders levelling roads, bulldozers clearing garbage) speeds reconstruction. Although the various money grants, donations in kind and practical services given by the battle groups to local NGOs, schools, hospitals and kindergartens are not large, they are appreciated.

Thirdly, the women value the feeling of *connectedness* with a wider world that the international troops can sometimes give. They appreciate it when local battle groups supply them with information, bring foreign visitors to meet them and introduce their replacements when their tour of duty ends. They like it when soldiers accept invitations to parties, festivals and sports events in the community. They often remember individual soldiers who have formed a personal relationship with them, shown an interest in their problems, responded to requests, brought gifts.

It is clear that from SFOR's point of view too there are positive aspects in these relationships. Clearly a lot of their sociability, and the small services they render to women's organizations, can be seen as 'good public relations', increasing their acceptability to the native population. We heard of two instances where battle groups had recruited women's NGOs to mobilise local women for collection of illegally held weapons from ex-combatants in their families and villages, and to educate children on avoidance of landmines. The units clearly gather information about the local area from women. 'I think they come and see us so that they can fill in their reports to senior officers' (Marija, *DOM*). An article in *SFOR Informer*, describing the community activity of the Nord-Pol battle group, states:

> The personnel of CIMIC know that to be effective they have to maintain a dialogue with and between the people they are trying to assist. To this end, a CIMIC officer visits every village at least once a day and tries to get to know every single inhabitant.[4]

And Turk-bat officers have a slogan on their wall reading, 'every soldier is involved in CIMIC activity'. They explained, 'it means being courteous and kind to local people, that is CIMIC work'.

The interactions described above are however relatively superficial. We will describe two ways in which the women felt their organization's relations with SFOR could, had SFOR willed it, have been much more interactive and productive to both sides. One concerns *reconciliation*, *reconstruction and return*, the other issues of *prostitution and sexual health*. Both highlight the significance of gender relations and militarized masculinity in the context of peacekeeping. And both afford a potential for co-operation that would have been valued by the women and could have been helpful also to the military. They are opportunities that currently go to waste.

Reconciliation, reconstruction and return

The return of refugees and internally displaced people to their homes is a major challenge after any war. In Bosnia-Herzegovina the war of 1992-5 saw around one million Bosnians displaced within the country and a further million driven abroad. It is estimated that half the population moved from their home. One of the tasks of women's local organizations therefore has been assisting returns. The organization called *DOM* ('Dom' means home; and the initials stand for Dolina Ostaje Moja, which means 'The Valley Remains Mine') is a case in point. *DOM* has its office in the market town of Nevesinje in a rural area of East Herzegovina, now in the Republika Srpska. The key women in the organization are mainly Bosnian Serbs, displaced during the war from Mostar and the Neretva valley (now in the Federation). Although living in a predominantly Bosnian Serb community, they often feel victimized and vulnerable in Nevesinje, both because they are displaced persons and because they oppose the nationalism of local Serb authorities and the 'ethnic cleansing' to which they subjected non-Serbs here in the war.

Their project is bold however. Among the work they consider most important is fostering minority 'return', which they see as essential to the re-establishment of an integrated and inclusive society in B-H. They assist Serbs who found shelter in Nevesinje to go back to their homes in the Neretva valley. And they help Muslims who took refuge in Mostar to come back now to their villages around Nevesinje. While the authorities of the Republika Srpska have been obliged by international pressure to bow to this reversal of 'ethnic cleansing', they do little to encourage re-integration, knowing it could eventually threaten their numerical strength and political majority.

Working closely with UNHCR and other women's organizations in the region, *DOM* maintains lists of people who wish to attempt a return. They organize trial visits by returners, and sometimes accompany their journey. They mobilize material aid from various donor organizations for livestock, tools, or a temporary supply of food. Often the returners are elderly people, no longer able to rely on young family members many of whom have abandoned rural life, or even emigrated. If the returners are resettling nearby, often in totally devastated and deserted villages, surrounded by potentially unwelcoming local communities, *DOM* visit them, so that they know there is friendship not far away. In Nevesinje, they have opened a small cafe, serving drinks, cakes and pastries. It is the only place in the town where non-Serbs can be sure of a welcome.

Many exercises in return have proved a disappointing waste of time and money. People come back, but there are no houses for them. Or houses are built and there is nobody wanting to live in them. A lot gets spent with little to show for it. Successful return programmes require a great deal of accurate, up to date information, experience, efficiency and organizational skills. Sometimes it is SFOR that plans and implements a scheme of return. For example, an Italian CIMIC unit visited *DOM* to discuss a return project for one particular village. They brought an architect. Photos were taken of the ruined site.

DOM made them a proposal. Make us your partners in this project, they said. We won't cost you much money – just give us a contribution to salaries and operating costs. You build the houses – and be sure to build twenty or thirty in a single village so as to offer a viable community. We for our part can offer two things. Firstly, we'll put a woman in the field for a given period of time. We'll use our local contacts and knowledge to help you select building contractors whose honesty and competence we can guarantee, we'll help you organize the tendering and selection process, monitor the construction, ensure the building work is not shoddy, see that money is not wasted, that middlemen do not drain off the funds.

Secondly, we'll use our resources to organize and monitor the social side of this return. We'll check in the municipalities where the returners are temporarily living and select those who genuinely want to live in their homes – not just to establish their property rights, get the dwelling fixed and then sell it. We'll make sure they don't already own a flat or a house somewhere else. We'll try to include some younger people, so that the community has a future. We'll make sure you are aware of everything needed for sustainability – not just houses, roads, electricity and water supply, but also tractors and power tools.

The Italians listened to the women's proposal, went away to consider it. But they failed to take it up. Why? Marija Belovic, *DOM*'s coordinator, feels it was not ignorance. SFOR are in fact quite acute about the local situation. It may be that they are unable to distinguish Serbs of different political views, and so fail to see that *DOM* could be good allies for SFOR in the predominantly nationalist, unco-operative and resentful environment in which they are working. Perhaps they ascribe undue importance to the political authorities, too little to civil associations. But it is certain that also at work is a masculine under-valuing of women and the feminine. Politics and reconstruction, like soldiering, is 'men's work'. Can SFOR not see, Marija asks, that women, who were not in the main the ones who took up arms, can contribute to healing the rifts in postwar society?

What *DOM*, and other such women's organizations, are saying is: instead of this 'small change' you give us, these goodwill visits and Christmas presents for the children, offer us a genuine partnership for substantial projects on a basis of equality. Don't be so closed to us, behind your ugly barbed wire fences. We can help you do your job, and you can help us to do ours – because the partnership we have with you will give us credibility in the eyes of local politicians, local police, bureaucrats and donor organizations.

Soldiers, prostitution and sexual health

A second issue that often concerns women's organizations during and after war is prostitution. War generates both demand and supply factors in this market. There are more soldiers and paramilitaries. Predominantly these are men – men in groups detached from home, seeking commercial sex. More civilian women, many of whom are uprooted and have lost their employment, some responsible for main-taining dependants, are driven to prostitution as a livelihood. The troops are released from the restraints of community and embedded in a deeply militarized culture that accords little value or status to women.

The women's organizations we spoke with confirmed that prostitution is much more evident today than it was before the disintegration of Yugoslavia. Particularly worrying is the presence in Bosnian brothels of many 'trafficked' women, commonly from Ukraine, Moldova or Romania. Traded between foreign and local men, along with other ille-gally imported commodities, they are held in conditions of sexual servitude. There is evidence that pimps expose women to abuses of vari-ous kinds by clients, and sometimes require them to have unprotected sex.

Recently an alliance of international institutions and local women's NGOs, led by the Office of the High Commissioner for Human Rights, has been investigating and taking action against this traffic in human beings – in which it is believed that the local police (and even perhaps members of the International Police Task Force) are involved as dealers or facilitators.[5] Women have been interviewed, in some cases rescued, and helped to return to their countries.

Four of our organizations – *Anima* and *Koraci Nade* in the Federation, *Buducnost* and *Lara* in the Republika Srpska – had a working concern with trafficking, or prostitution or women's reproductive health, or all three. They told us they had observed a change in the nature of local prostitution as a result of the arrival of foreign women. Bosnian women now more commonly work from the roadside. There has also been an increase in the use of very young women (sought by clients as being less likely to be HIV positive). Often they are brought to town from rural areas, and put to work in small brothels disguised as cafes. There has been a parallel growth in video pornography, including the recruitment of children by misleading advertisements for 'auditioning'.

Brothels and cafes, we were told, had mushroomed in Bosnia. They are observed to cluster round the bases of SFOR battle groups, lending weight to the belief that SFOR is the main source of clientele for the industry.[6] 'Anyway, at first, foreign soldiers were the only men with the money' (Mara, *Lara*). In the course of our research we questioned the Public Information Officer at Supreme Headquarters Allied Powers Europe (the ultimate source of SFOR's mandate), an official spokesperson at SFOR HQ in Sarajevo, and CIMIC officers of the Turkish battle group about SFOR regulations on prostitution. The responses were consistent.

SFOR as a whole, they told us, has no regulations governing the use of prostitutes by its personnel, nor does the force have an overall concern with or policy on sexual health matters, including risk of HIV/AIDS. They said, succinctly, 'SFOR has no policy on these issues (and sees no need for one)'.[7] SFOR troops in Sarajevo 'have a walking out of camp restriction and a curfew is enforced'. We may suppose this to be indicative of concern, but not, of course, evidence that prostitutes are not used. SFOR HQ told us that the regulations extant in participating countries on prostitution and sexual health apply to their battalions in Bosnia, and they recognize that these vary.

Unusual among the international community, UNOHCHR in Sarajevo are concerned about a lack of responsibility shown by SFOR in these respects. On an SFOR radio programme recently the (woman) Head of Office appealed to SFOR to admit that their soldiers have recourse to prostitutes and instruct the men to observe rules. Any member of SFOR personnel, she said, before engaging in sex with a prostitute, should ensure that the woman involved is engaging in prostitution by her own will and that she is not under-age. He should pay the woman herself not the man who is exploiting her. And he should use a condom.[8]

Prostitution is of concern to women's organizations first because of the health and wellbeing of the women concerned. Some projects, like *Koraci Nade*, have a particular focus on women's reproductive health. They keep contact with doctors and hospitals, monitor abortions, provide contraception and do educational work on sexually transmitted diseases. 'We organized an HIV/AIDS day. We distributed free condoms all over town. We put them in cafes, toilets, police stations. We handed them out to soldiers. We even took them to SFOR barracks' (Vesna, *Anima*).

They are also concerned because prostitution is just one feature of a black economy in which criminal networks deal in drugs, weapons and other profitable commodities. The trade transcends rivalries between formerly warring ethnic groups: 'they are all getting rich together' (Mara, *Lara*). The gangs involved are growing in power and reach. The competition between them is expressed in extortion, threats and assassinations. 'It's warfare!' Some of the economic criminals are also wanted for war crimes. To concern themselves with the well-being of the women, women's organizations thus have to oppose the interests of very dangerous men. They cannot rely on the protection of the local police, some of whom are known to be in league with the criminals, and the IPTF have been disappointingly slow to step in.

What they would like, they told us, was an acknowledgement by SFOR that its personnel do use the services of prostitutes. They would welcome dialogue with responsible officers in the local battle groups with a view to minimizing the criminal aspects of the trade and risks to sexual and reproductive health of both women and men. The women point out also that there are, inevitably, in addition to prostitution, non-commercial relations between international soldiers and local women (and often both are quite young). Such relationships give rise to emotional and health problems that likewise should be recognised and addressed.

In short, in a similar way to *DOM* and other organizations working on postwar reconstruction and return, organizations like *Lara* and *Koraci Nade* are asking SFOR to recognize they have valid concerns, and collaborate with them in projects for women's human rights and the sexual/reproductive healthcare of soldiers and local women. Instead of this they are met with a vexing coyness in the international institutions and militaries, who are miserly in their official words about peacekeeping soldiers' recourse to prostitutes but let slip hints (such as references to the dangers of HIV/AIDS) that make it clear they know what goes on and, well, men can't do without sex.[9]

Female personnel in SFOR

The logic of SFOR's failure to validate the women's organizations role in social reconstruction, and their unwillingness to partner them in reducing sexual exploitation, resides to a considerable extent in its gender regime, the predominance of men in its ranks, its officer corps and its management structure, and the masculinity of its culture. Would it make a difference if there were more women in the peacekeeping military? We discussed this with women in our interviews. We also asked SFOR HQ about their policy on including women in the peacekeeping force, and in particular whether women were ever given responsibility for gender policy within the unit or for CIMIC work concerning women or with women's organizations.

SFOR did not know how many women they had on the payroll. 'For us' they e-mailed us, 'gender integration is not an issue for peacekeeping operations, and therefore the stats are not kept'. The inclusion of women in the peacekeeping forces, they wrote, is 'nation specific' and based 'on their own internal national policies, not those of SFOR'. 'As such NATO and SFOR do not have a policy on gender integration and certainly do not employ quotas for such'. They further told us that SFOR 'does not have any specific policy recognizing the significance of women's organizations in postwar peacebuilding and social reconstruction'. And finally, their e-mail read, 'there are no female officers with specific responsibility for gender policy ...'

By contrast to this negative picture, we learned of two events in SFOR that signalled an interest in the active participation of women. In the first, Italian soldiers of the Sassari Brigade received a seminar on the role of women in the Armed Forces. Nine female soldiers answered questions about their experience of serving in SFOR. Motivating factors for women enlisting in the army were discussed, maternity rights, and the issue of 'remaining feminine'. The second instance involved women officers and non-commissioned officers from the Bosnian Federation army. *SFOR Informer Online* commented 'Six thousand women took up arms in support of the Federation in 1992 and 650 of them received officer and NCO appointments after the war ... They've had no formal training. Consequently, they cannot compete for additional training courses essential for their positions or advancement'.[10] Now twelve women would attend a gender-specific course of training and professional development to be conducted by women soldiers of SFOR. They would receive training on discipline, logistics, communications, and on 'dress, behaviour and female hygiene in the field'.

The Bosnian women's organizations had all noticed women serving among the soldiers of the various battle groups. In some cases they were few – for instance Turk-bat had females only in nursing roles. In some cases, such as the Norwegian unit, there seemed to be a sizeable proportion of women and even a woman commanding officer. 'Not that we ever managed to get her attention on women's issues' (Gordana, *Buducnost*). A larger presence of women does not, it seems, necessarily lead to more officially-sanctioned contact with women in the community. Instances were reported to us, however, of individual women soldiers who had stepped from behind their military anonymity to befriend a women's organization on a woman-to-woman basis. One woman soldier had brought cooked dinners from the SFOR canteen for returners on their first days back. Such gestures of friendship were greatly valued.

Majority opinion among the women of these NGOs, we concluded, would favour four developments. First, they would like to see more women present among the soldiers. Second, they wished women to be present at all levels of seniority. (This point is important, for if women are not respected inside the military they unlikely to be respected in the community.) Third, on entering the army, women should retain their 'women's colouring', bringing with them their interests and concerns as women. They should avoid adopting the masculine military culture. Fourth, and finally, they wished some woman or women to be given a specific CIMIC brief and responsibility for liaison with women's organizations.[11]

Women's 'wish list' and its gender implications

We asked women what demands they would like to make of policy-makers for military peacekeeping operations. Taking their comments and grouping them under themes, we conclude as follows.

Military assertiveness. They would like to see SFOR pursue, even more energetically, its military work of pacification, demilitarization, weapons collection, landmine clearance and protection. Peacekeepers should have had more power during the war to intervene to save lives. Now, postwar, women emphatically wished SFOR would 'do their real job' and speed up the arrest of war criminals. This would help draw the teeth of the criminal gangs that beleaguer their towns – 'It would make our lives safer' (Duska, *Medica*).

But the women's organizations would also like to see a development of SFOR's CIMIC role. As organizations within civil society, they would like a more gender conscious policy from Headquarters, and a more policy-driven, productive relationship, as women's organizations, with their local battle groups. Effectively, they are asking for the following...

Recognition and respect. They wish SFOR, both HQ and territorial units, to understand the democratic values of integrative women's organizations, regardless of the ethnic identity of their members, and to differentiate them from their (mainly nationalistic) political contexts. They want the usefulness of their local knowledge and the effectiveness of their work in re-integrating Bosnian society to be recognized and acknowledged. They want to be respected as women.

Accessibility and communication. They want SFOR to realize just how intimidating their military uniform, weaponry and defences can be, and to make it easier for civilians such as themselves to approach officers and go into the bases. They want systematic data on the area that only SFOR has, and in turn are willing to provide useful information. They want much more candour and honesty from SFOR in addressing problems, such as criminality, prostitution and sexual transmitted diseases, in which SFOR is implicated.

Co-operation and partnership. The women's organizations would like SFOR to be more co-operative and to enter working partnerships with them on a basis of respect and equality. For instance, as illustrated above, they would welcome joint local projects on 'return' and on soldiers' and women's sexual health.

Sensitivity to local culture. Women said they would like peacekeeping troops to be well-educated, before they arrive, in the history and culture of Bosnia, the distinctiveness of Bosnian expectations and needs. The soldiers of SFOR themselves come from a wide range of cultures and religions. They should be wary of misperceptions and imposing their own values. In particular they wished that Western European and US militaries would recognize the modern European identity of former Yugoslav society, avoid patronage, 'treat us as equals'.

Humanity and warmth. Women said they would like SFOR soldiers to show their human nature, ' be a human being first and a professional second' (Vesna, *Anima*). They are saying, effectively, 'Come out from behind your defences, look around for us, hear us, relate to us and trust us. See us as people, don't just use us.'

At first sight the wishes in this list appear contradictory. On the one hand the women are urging the military to do quite traditionally militaristic things: to 'protect them' and to perform violent acts. The arrest of war criminals can be a frightening, bloody process. While we were in Biljelina SFOR arrested a wanted man in a neighbouring town. He blew himself up with a hand grenade, wounding, and no doubt badly traumatizing, four German soldiers. The women are clearly not saying 'feminize the military'. On the other hand, they are just as clearly not admirers of Rambo. They are not saying 'we love your macho ways'. They are rather, asking the military to 'act strong' but simultaneously lower their defences and be open and responsive.

Taking account of the wish expressed by many women to see more women in SFOR, and having regard to popular gender stereotypes and expectations, we might extrapolate from these two sets of wishes to suppose that they are asking for a force comprising 'men' acting 'manly', alongside 'women' acting 'womanly'. But to introduce more women to SFOR, or to any peacekeeping military, in order to strengthen the fulfilment of its 'soft' functions, would be both ineffective and wrong. It would be ineffective because there is no guarantee that women will identify feminine and act 'womanly'. On the contrary, they may well adapt to masculine military cultures. It would be wrong, because if we wish to change male cultures for the better we should not exempt women from, and load exclusively onto men, responsibility for wielding just and necessary violence. (No more, of course, should we load onto women the stereotypically womanly tasks.)

Rather, we would suggest, the women are implicitly asking for a *regendered* notion of the soldier. This of course also means a regendered military culture, since this is where soldierly identities are formed. It means a regendered army. We will conclude by thinking what these things might involve.

A new kind of soldier, a new kind of military

Let us think back, first, to the situation a peacekeeping army enters. The violence in Bosnia-Herzegovina that UNPROFOR, IFOR and SFOR were sent to subdue and the postwar society they encountered there were emphatically gendered. Furthermore, the violence of both the ethnic aggression and the postwar criminality in Bosnia were not merely gendered, they were markedly *sexualized*.

Militarized culture took a particular form in which sexual abuse and torture could be seen as legitimate practices. Bosnia shows us how nationalist war culture not only gives rise to dangerously gendered militias, but also dangerously gendered markets. The exploitation of women in enterprises of prostitution and sexual slavery began in the war and has become an increasingly important element of (highly masculinized) criminal business since it ended. The Bosnian women's associations we are working with told us their experience matches the above analysis. They are women's organizations for this very reason. They say women had sex-specific experiences in the war, they have sex-specific experiences now in relation to the violence and criminality, and they believe they can make a sex-specific contribution to pacification and reconstruction. They want SFOR's help in doing this.

To respond to their hopes, what does SFOR need to do? It needs to be much more wised up than it is about gender: sex distributions, sex stereotypes, gendered cultures, gendered identities, gendering as a social process and gender as a relation of power. It needs to learn and speak a language that can express concepts of this kind. It needs to redesign its structures and strategies in gender-intelligent and gender-constructive ways. If peacekeeping forces are not rethought along these lines, they will step into postwar situations, as SFOR has stepped into Bosnia-Herzegovina, and risk contributing directly to the malign gender relations operating locally. They will aggravate them, and fail to contribute what they could to the transit to peace, legality and equality.

So this research exposes a serious contradiction. SFOR, and other peacekeeping armies, are a military force sent to a country to demilitarize it. They are a masculine force cast in a mode not dissimilar to the masculinity that has been implicated in the war. How can one militarized masculinity defuse and neutralise another, rather than playing into it, 'man to man'? Let us end by breaking down this question into some smaller, more approachable ones.

- First about *soldier identities*: Can we create a new soldier identity that is available to both women and men? A soldier who is seen as, is expected to be, and feels, on the one hand assertive, competent and courageous; and on the other relational, responsive and caring? Can a peacekeeping soldier, in other words, embody some good 'feminine' qualities, without sullying or exploiting them? Can s/he keep desirable 'masculine' traits, while throwing out some of the less desirable ones that have often been associated with militarism? And can s/he do these things without losing operational effectiveness?

- Second, some questions about *military cultures*: Can we create a military culture in which democratic equality between individuals is valued, in which authority does not mean tyranny, orders may sometimes be questioned – but one that nonetheless produces soldiers who are effective in facing danger and disarming violence? Can we create a military culture that is respectful of women as people – but (even more difficult) respectful also of things usually associated with femininity, such as domestic life and the nurturing of relationship? Can this military culture respond creatively to soldiers' distress and trauma, not require the suppression of feelings of weakness and fear, allow for the exploration of values and choices? Can it allow for bonding between men that is not based on the rejection, diminishing and abuse of women and femininity? or predicated on the despising of less militarized forms of masculinity? And indeed can it allow for non-sexualized friendship and bonding between men and women?

- Third, some final questions about *regendered armies*: What would it take to build an army in which men as a sex, and traditionally male ways of thinking, do not overwhelmingly dominate the decision-making and authority structures? What would it take to build an army in which gender has an expected place on the agenda at policy-making level, and in which there are units and staff with special responsibility for monitoring and adjusting gender relations within army structures? What would it take for an army to bring sexuality out of the closet, acknowledge and accept differences of sexual orientation, recognize that soldiers get involved in sexual relations, that the sexual and reproductive health of everyone involved, military and civilian, must be cared for? Could they welcome constructive conversations about it, and make caring policies?

Can we imagine a peacekeeping operation that includes diminishing the adverse effects of militarized masculinity in the local society, and lending support to those women (feminists and others) and men (such as conscientious objectors) who are trying to demilitarize local society and transform patriarchal gender power relations? Ultimately, what would it take to make a force like SFOR into an army in which part of *soldiers' very professionalism* included an expertise in understanding the part played by gender relations in war and postwar reconstruction?

In 1993 Cynthia Enloe invited us to think about the gender relations of the UN 'blue beret' soldiery. She wondered whether bearing arms for an international peacekeeping military might 'call forth different notions of masculinity' than soldiering for a state (Enloe 1993:34). In concluding this chapter we have suggested the kind of change in the gender regime of an international peacekeeping force that might be involved if the needs of some organized and concerned women in a host community are to be met. Change in these terms is as yet unthinkable to most military leaders and strategists.

There are signs however, as we saw in the Introduction, of a new gender awareness in the United Nations, which fields most international peacekeeping missions. Its most important expression to date is UN Security Council Resolution 1325 of 31 October 2000 on 'Women, Peace and Security'. It was passed in the very month we carried out our research field work This document expressed concern 'that civilians, particularly women and children, account for the vast majority of those adversely affected by armed conflict', reaffirmed 'the important role of women in the prevention and resolution of conflicts and in peace-building' and called, among other things, for:

- increased representation of women in decision-making at all levels including international institutions and particularly in conflict resolution and peace processes;
- more women to be appointed by the UN Secretary-General as special representatives and envoys of the UN, and an expanded role and contribution of women in UN field-based operations, and especially among military observers, civilian police, human rights and humanitarian personnel;
- gender-specific training guidelines and materials to be made available to member states sending soldiers on peacekeeping missions.

Subsequently there have been moves to establish a Gender Unit in the United Nations Department of Peacekeeping Operations. Training materials are being developed within the Department for use by Member States in training military personnel and civilian police participating in UN peacekeeping operations (Mazurana 2001).

The new UN gender-awareness concerning armed conflict, peace processes and peacekeeping has to date shown itself more in utterances about women and gender difference than about men, masculinity and gender power. It is also expressed more in statements of principle than mechanisms of practice. Women's evaluation of SFOR reported in this chapter and the conclusions we draw from it could help to make operational the new policy within national militaries of 'peacekeeping countries' – which is where the practical changes must be achieved. If military hierarchies and military cultures prove unable to respond to women's experience, or if their adaptations are merely cosmetic, we shall have let slip from our hands a chance to humanize gender and military relations simultaneously.

We would like to warmly thank the women of Anima, Buducnost, DOM, Koraci Nade, Lara, Medica, Vrelo, and Zena Mostara *for spending time with us and entrusting us with their insights.*

Material with no references is drawn from the SFOR websites, <http://www.nato.int/ifor and http://www.nato.int/sfor>

Notes

1. R.W.Connell uses the term 'gender regime' to mean 'the state of play in gender relations in a given institution', Connell 1987, p120.

2. See Chapter 4 in this volume, and United Nations Office of the High Commissioner for Human Rights (UNOHCHR) 'Terms of reference for the Gender Co-ordinating Group'. Internal document 1999, Sarajevo.

3. *SFOR Informer Online*, Sarajevo, issues of 15 March, 26 April, 24 May, 7 June, 5 July and 30 August, 2000, reporting activities of Italian, Dutch, Czech, German and Nordic-Polish battle groups.

4. *SFOR Informer*, Sarajevo 7.06.00.

5. Personal communication.

6. The close association of Western European militaries with organized prostitution is borne out in research sponsored by the European Commission's Daphne Initiative, Euler and Welzer-Lang 2000.

7. Here and subsequently, when citing SFOR e-mail communications, we refer to e-mails we received from Media Operations, SFOR Headquarters, Sarajevo, dated 18 October and 2 November, 2000.

8. Personal communication.

9. United Nations Security Council Resolution 1325 of October 31, 2000, for instance does not make reference to prostitution in relation to UN peace-keepers, but in Paragraph 6 it requests the Secretary-General to provide training guidelines and materials for military and civilian personnel of peacekeeping operations on 'the protection and rights of women', and 'invites Member States to incorporate these elements as well as HIV/AIDS awareness training in their national training programmes for military and civilian police personnel in preparation for deployment', United Nations 2000. Eugenia Piza-Lopez, speaking for the Non-governmental Coalition on Women and International Peace and Security, the pressure group that laid the groundwork for the Resolution, was more, though not fully, explicit when she told the Security Council they should 'ensure that all peacekeeping and peace support operations are mandated to protect women and girls against all sexual violence, abduction, prostitution, trafficking and threats imposed by the military and paramilitary, and *to uphold peacekeeping codes of conduct*' (from 'The role of women in achieving

peace and maintaining international security', a statement read out at the Arria Formula Meeting of the United Nations Security Council on 23 October, 2000, by Eugenia Piza-Lopez of International Alert, <www.international-alert.org>).

10. *SFOR Informer Online*, issue No.82, 1.03.00.

11. A minority might dissent from such a view, however, in the belief that women should never be soldiers. One woman for instance felt soldiering would detract from women's femininity. The valuable feminine values related to their caring and domestic role would be damaged. In other words we encountered in Bosnia something of the difference of opinion that has divided feminists worldwide about the increasing recruitment of women to the military. For some interventions in this long-running debate see Chapkis 1981; Enloe 1988 and De Groot and Peniston-Bird 2000.

Enduring ambivalence: the Dutch armed forces and its women recruits

JOLANDA BOSCH AND DÉSIRÉE VERWEIJ

For a few years now the Dutch Armed Forces (DAF) have recognized that their customary recruits, white males, have become less willing to be recruited. This has motivated a shift of view in the DAF. Today, white women, and both men and women of ethnic minorities, have come to be seen by military recruiters as appropriate personnel for the army, navy and air force. Our research however has shown that the policy to recruit women is not followed through with a wholehearted intention to secure for them a place in the armed forces as full and equal members. The experiences the women themselves recounted to us indicate that the military still has difficulties in changing its structure and practices so as to become an institution that is as much female as male, as much feminine as masculine. The military hierarchy shows little inclination to adapt and change the military itself – its rules, cultures and attitudes – in order to accommodate women, or to use and reward women's strengths. And in the practices of many individual men, despite some awareness of the 'unacceptability' of sexism, women in the DAF still experience objectification, discrimination and marginalization.

There is thus a contradiction between, on the one hand, the dual motivation of the DAF to supplement their normal source of supply of new recruits and to get in line with international standards on gender equity, and on the other hand the intractability of the military as a deeply masculine institution and culture.

This is an interesting moment in time to probe the practices and thinking of the Dutch military with regard to women. During the nineties, like its many European counterparts, the DAF has come to see itself, and is widely seen in Dutch society, not only as war waging but also as a peacekeeping army. To the bearing this may have on recruitment of women we return below.

First we need, as certainly the Dutch military policy makers have needed, to shed light on certain beliefs about women and the military. Women are commonly assumed to be absent from the military, in practice, and in principle, incompatible with its categories. However, the facts are somewhat different. Throughout the globe women have been taking part in armed conflicts. In Europe, women participated in both the First and the Second World War in a variety of capacities, as indirect supporters of 'war efforts', as well as direct participants on the front lines.[1] The relationship between women and arms may have been ambivalent, but women in the army are there to stay. Thus, their position in the military is worthy of study.

Our chapter addresses this long lasting ambivalence of women in arms within the Dutch Armed Forces. We analyze official policies regarding the presence of women in the DAF, as well as women's experiences of daily life in the military.

Women in the Dutch armed forces: numbers and positions

Notwithstanding the greater emphasis in recent years on actively recruiting women, the Dutch Armed Forces (DAF) have officially recognized women as active participants in the military for more than five decades. From April 1944 female soldiers worked in separate, women's supporting corps, known as the 'Marine Vrouwenafdeling' (MARVA) in the Navy, 'Militaire Vrouwenafdeling' (MILVA) in the Army and 'Luchtmacht Vrouwenafdeling' (LUVA) in the Air Force.[2]

Eventually, under the pressure of international treaties and laws women were given access to (almost) all military institutes and training centres in 1978.[3] In 1982 the separate women's corps were abolished and from that moment military women were supposed to have the same rights, possibilities and duties as their male colleagues. With the exception of the Marine Corps and the submarine service, all departments, positions and training facilities are in principle open to women today, and they are formally accorded equal opportunities with men. Personnel management has a positive policy of recruitment, retention and integration of women. In order to attract and keep women, different physical requirements are stipulated for the two sexes.

Despite these efforts, however, it seems difficult to hold women on a long-term basis in the Dutch military. As shown in table 1 the number of military women in the Dutch armed services is still relatively low. In the four services – Navy, Army, Air Force and Military Police – women's percentage ranges between 7.2 and 9.2 per cent. Compared to some other western countries, however, the Netherlands are somewhere in the middle. Germany's military has only 1 per cent of women, Denmark and Norway 5 per cent, Belgium, UK and France approximately the same percentages as the Netherlands, and US, Canada and Australia about 15 per cent.[4] If these figures are desegregated to show personnel on short-term as opposed to long-term contracts (table 2) we find that only about 25 per cent of women have long-term contracts, as opposed to over 60 per cent of men. Women obviously make different choices when it comes to the military career, than men. Finally, women cluster in the lower ranks. Table 3 shows that over 66 per cent of all women, compared with less than 35 per cent of all men, remain in the lowest rank of privates. Only 13 per cent of women reach high officer ranks, compared to almost 20 per cent of men. In the DAF there are no women in the vital top positions, and there are only two female colonels. The predictions also vary as to when will we see the first female general.

Table 1: Numbers of military personnel by services (31-12-2000)

| | Male | | Female | | Total |
	Number	%	Number	%	Number
Navy	11266	90.8	1138	9.2	12404
Army	21418	92.8	1668	7.2	23086
Air Force	10465	92.0	905	8.0	11370
MP	4823	91.3	459	8.7	5282
Total	47972	92.0	4170	8.0	52142

Table 2: Numbers of military personnel on long-term and short-term contract (31-12-2000)

| | Male | | Female | | Total | |
	Number	%	Number	%	Number	%
Long	29644	96.0	1185	4.0	30829	60.0
Short	18328	86.0	2985	14.0	21313	40.0
Total	47972	92.0.	4170	8.0	52142	100.0

Table 3: Numbers of military personnel by rank (31-12-2000)

| | Male | | Female | | Total | |
	Number	%	Number	%	Number	%
Officers	9190	94.0	560	6.0	9750	19.0
NCOs*	20067	96.0	844	4.0	20911	40.0
Corp/Sold	18715	87.0	2766	13.0	21480	41.0
Total	47972	92.0	4170	8.0	52142	100.0

* Including Navy Corporals

In addition to this vertical sex segregation, there are indications of horizontal segregation – women are more typically found in one type of unit than another. For example, though technically open to women, the infantry, cavalry and engineering regiments (pre-eminently combat units) have few women. Women on the other hand predominate in the 'additional services'. Finally, the Marine Corps and the submarine service are still forbidden territory for women. The reasons given for the ban on women in these naval units are lack of appropriate accommodation for women on board ship, the lack of privacy and women's inferior physical capacities.

So, today, while officially Dutch women can be active participants in any armed conflict in which the Dutch national forces engage, it would be incorrect to say that DAF's proclaimed intention to 'integrate' women into the military structures has succeeded. The Dutch media regularly report incidents of sexual harassment in the DAF.[5] In the light of what we learned from interviewing and observing women, these reports might be read as a proof of trouble within. What is actually going on?

Different and unequal: representations of gender
Since gender is such a central issue in this chapter, we should perhaps begin by defining the meaning we ascribe to the term. An opposition between the meanings of sex and gender has been firmly established in sociology since the 1970s.[6] 'Sex difference' now commonly refers to a biological dimorphism in humans with male and female bodies differentiated as a result of their complementary roles in human reproduction. 'Gender difference' has come to signify the difference produced through social and cultural shaping of children and adults with the intention of producing acceptably distinct and complementary men and women, masculinity and femininity. Simone de Beauvoir's aphorism neatly illustrates the latter position: a woman isn't born, she is made.[7] A man likewise.

The concept of gender has been refined and strengthened by Judith Butler and others who have shown how biological 'sex' differences are themselves not untouched by social and cultural forces and understandings, and that, besides, genders themselves are not so much dichotomous as various and plural.[8] Thus, it makes sense to speak of masculinities and femininities, as many authors in this book choose to do.

We shall see at work, in the context of the Dutch Armed Forces, certain key aspects of gender relations. First, we shall see that identities are strongly gendered, including military identities. Gender discourses represent what it is to 'be' a man or 'be' a woman in a given society. By a multitude of more or less subtle codes children learn to acquire a sense of self and to project an identity of boy or girl, man or woman. Part of learning to be a proper man is to try on the identity of a soldier, and part of learning to be a soldier is to affirm the identity of a certain kind of man, a militarized man. Where does this leave the girl and woman? The answer to that question addresses one of the problems faced by the military in re-shaping an army of men, by men and for men, to meet the needs of women, and problems faced by women in adopting an identity normally projected as quintessentially masculine. The problem is of no less importance for those (military) men who wish to see traditional military cultures changed so as to accommodate different kinds of masculinities, and different ways of soldiering.

Second, gender entails dichotomous thinking. The contrasted and complementary genders, masculine and feminine, have so deeply entered human thinking as to become metaphors through which to order the world. Dichotomous gender stereotypes are created and perpetuated (e.g. Morgan 1986). For example, doing, logical, rational, aggressive and independent may be contrasted with their opposites: being, intuitive, emotional, empathetic and dependent. Though any one individual may realistically be endowed, to varying degrees, with any of these qualities, in contemporary Western society they are represented as mutually exclusive, the first set characteristic of, and appropriate for, men, the contrasted set of and for women. What is more, the former are accorded higher value, they are considered more useful and more powerful than the latter. They are seen as the basis of rational thought and public action. It is not difficult to recognize their significance for the military.

Third, gender structures social institutions and organizations. Brouns (1995) terms organizations 'gender-loaded'. Certain assumptions about masculinity and femininity are considered standard, and thus normative (Benschop en Doorewaard, 1999). Gender inequalities are manifest in 'the complex system of organizational measures with regard to the structure and the culture of organizations, social processes with regard to the way in which people associate with each other and identify themselves and others' (Benschop en Doorewaard 1999, p184). Institutions reproduce difference and inequality, perpetuating gender power relations and differentially affecting the lives of men and women within them.

The perpetuation of gender discrimination

In the past, sex-discrimination in military recruitment and war fighting was of course routine, open and absolute. What we find today, from interviewing women in the Dutch military and analyzing military policy documents, is that, despite an official change of policy (women are now valued as recruits) and an international shift in perceptions of women's human rights (including the right to work), discriminatory gender representations persist in the Dutch military. They are muted. Often they surface, and are more visible, in individual behaviours than in institutional practices. But they are indicators of a continuing ambivalence towards women on the part of the military authorities.

History provides many examples of images of overt gender discrimination in the military. In the past the DAF were quite explicit: armed forces were for men. During the seventeenth and eighteenth century women were not recruited into the armed forces. It was men who fought wars, while women stayed at home and took care of the family. Despite this blanket ban on female soldiers and sailors, a handful did manage to slip into the Dutch Armed Forces (Dekker and van den Pol 1981). They entered disguised as men, accompanied men into battle and (in some cases) remained undiscovered. Paradoxically, this was possible precisely because in the seventeenth and eighteenth century the sexes were so rigidly differentiated. Wearing a skirt and having a braid of hair was so universal for European women as to vouch for a female. A person with a short haircut, trousers and a broad hat was a man. Since androgyny was not anticipated, there could be no ambiguity. The very power of convention thus made it relatively easy for a woman disguised as a man to go unquestioned.

Two centuries later gender relations within the DAF had changed. In line with the prevailing social relations of the nineteen-forties and fifties women were acceptable supporters of the national armed forces and the national cause. As already mentioned, their place however was limited to the so-called 'support' staff. They were subject to restrictive conditions of employment in terms of education, career potential and dismissal from the service in case of marriage or pregnancy.

During the 1970s the images of female military personnel were sold to the potential recruits, the country at large and within the military by means of an emphatically feminine representation of the militarized woman. A recruitment poster of a 'Marva', colouring her lips, illustrates the times. The text reads: 'Marva, you make the navy look nicer'. Unsurprisingly many Marvas did not approve of this poster.

'Marva you make the navy look nicer' – from a
recruitment poster from the seventies

When in 1978 women gained access to military training centres and in 1982 the separate women's corps were abolished, military women were supposed to have the same rights, opportunities and responsibilities as their male colleagues. As we shall see, however, while DAF's structures and practices have been marginally modified, their gender relations have by no means transformed. Nor did it mean that the old beliefs and representations of gender difference and asymmetry entirely disappeared. For all the official policy, many have continued to believe that 'the armed forces are only for men' and 'female military personnel belong in a supporting role'. The illustration below suggests too the survival of a belief that 'females are an adornment to the armed forces'.

Woman soldier in camouflage

Women's experience of deployment:
ambivalence and contradiction

The Dutch Armed Forces are a profoundly masculine institution, both historically and today: in authority structure and formal values, in terms of the majority of their personnel, and in their various organizational cultures and subcultures.

The predominance, in terms of numbers of white young males, of the rank and file largely determines the values and norms of the organization as a working environment. Alvesson and Billing (1997, p116) describe male-dominated working environments in terms in which we can easily recognize the army, navy or airforce:

> In all-men work groups gender is active in the creation of their own workplace culture. Beer drinking and talk about women in sexual terms underscore the shared masculinity. Rough joking between men, for example giving each other insulting nicknames, also fulfils this function. 'Real men' can take a hard conversational tone, it is assumed. Sometimes gender displays highlight masculinity through a show of physical strength, toughness and daring – safety rules may be neglected for example.

How do women entrants in the DAF experience such a male-oriented organization? Although much research has been done on women and the military in other countries, until now this knowledge has been lacking in the Netherlands.[9] Some research was done at the beginning of the eighties on women in the DAF, particularly in the Navy.[10] But since the new recruitment policy was introduced, in the mid-nineties, no research has been done either on female experiences of military life or on military experiences of gender diversity. Jolanda Bosch's research, mentioned below, is a start towards obtaining concrete information about gender relationships in the Dutch Armed Forces. The project is exploratory, and is concerned only with the Army and the Air Force. The central question is a comprehensive one: 'What are military women's experiences of deployment?' 'Deployment' means service in the field – elsewhere than in the home country, the Netherlands. So far, sixteen white military women with experience in such out-of-area operations have been interviewed.[11]

A preliminary analysis of the interviews suggests an extraordinary degree of ambivalence. On the one hand, women were delighted with their experience. On the other, they experienced treatment that they found troubling, and which demanded from them a large investment in adaptive strategies.

The women interviewed are generally very enthusiastic about their experience of deployment. They evaluate their work as having been intensive and diverse. They experienced a high level of autonomy and responsibility, and say they learned a lot about themselves and their work, in the course of deployment. Examples they gave of learning experiences included helping to reconstruct a country, giving advice, solving a range of logistic problems, negotiating, co-operating with people of many different nationalities, being far away from home for a long time and coping with loneliness. They also mention examples of learning new skills, such as using cold steel.

Many women stated that there were a number of factors that were important for their well being during employment. Among them, good health, and the possession of good social and communication skills seem to be the most important. They mention skills such as being able to accept other persons, not being egoistic, having a positive attitude, flexibility, empathy, and mental strength. Being together twenty-four hours a day sometimes leads to an increase of the mutual strain. One woman sergeant gave the following example as an indication of the importance of a steady mental state during out-of-area operations:

> My commander was a workaholic. Sometimes he got very tense and started to throw things around. If we asked: 'Is everything all right?' he answered by throwing diskettes at our heads. In these circumstances we would go out for a ride in the car. After four or five hours we came back, and everything was all right. He never reverted to the subject.[12]

While this example shows that interpersonal skills are indeed necessary for creating good working relations, the military women in the main typified the working climate as one of collegiality and comradeship. Most of those interviewed had felt fully accepted by the team members with whom they were directly co-operating. Every interviewee said that she had a 'buddy' on whom to lean, within her immediate environment. Buddies keep an eye on each other. They take care of each other in stressful moments. Most of the women interviewed had had male buddies whom they trusted greatly, and whom they considered good listeners. But almost every one has a 'dip' at some time during the deployment. Their stories illustrate that 'feeling bad' was accepted as part of the challenge.

With regard to the vertical relations between military women and their subordinates the research indicates that the leadership styles of the female leaders varied from participative to directive. The women in the interviews felt they were generally accepted as leaders and their experiences of leadership were positive. Few military women have led other military women during deployment, so information about a female chain of command is lacking. However, female leaders state that, back in the Netherlands, in normal working conditions, they had tended to treat female personnel differently. A few female lieutenants stated that they were stricter with female recruits, as well as more patronizing. They felt that, as women, they might be in a position to be ashamed of women recruits, should they fail to achieve the required standards. As examples later in the chapter will attest, this ambiguity of female-female encounters in the DAF seems to exist in both vertical and horizontal relationships.

So the women interviewed were positive about the deployment, which they characterized as diverse, intensive and instructive. However, their reports of 'a good experience' of deployment cannot be taken as meaning a good experience of gender relations in the military. On the contrary. It appears to have been good in spite of some highly unsatisfactory experiences in terms of gender. We gained the impression that relations between male and female military personnel involve markedly stereotyped representations of masculinity and femininity. The study by Hummelink (1999) confirms the impression from the research by Bosch. And it comes as no surprise. Rosabeth Moss Kanter's (1977) classic research on gender and organizations almost a quarter of a century ago led her to conclude that in units where women are few in relation to men (as they are in the military) they tend to be treated tokenistically – as 'something special'. Such a situation can be provocative for men and uncomfortable for women. In Bosch's research we see both male and female military personnel responding to this 'special' position women in the military have.

Daily life of women soldiers: men's reactions as observed by women

First, consider some reactions of male military personnel to the presence of female military personnel, as women experienced and reported them. They include hostility, a heightened awareness of women/femininity, type-casting and sexualization. A particular medic, the only woman who regularly joined social patrols during a peacekeeping operation, gave a striking example of hostility that she had experienced:

> ... there was a rather fanatic platoon. They were clearly anti-woman. The platoon commander showed that openly and encouraged the members of the platoon to do the same. That bothered us (women) a lot. A lot of provocative and sick remarks were made, but when we passed by, we were ignored completely.

When asked whether she went on patrol with these men, she replied:

Yes, you are walking all day, silently, without saying a word.

A second reaction pattern within an all male group, and within groups in which women form a minority, is a singling out for notice, and being derogatory about, women and the feminine. The following example, in Hummelink (1999, p50) was echoed by women soldiers with whom Bosch spoke:

> When I enter a room there's always somebody making remarks, whereas this doesn't happen when a man comes in.

A woman military surgeon described what happened when she wished to visit an Egyptian battalion:

> I wanted to visit a little Dutch signal unit under Egyptian command. I was in front of the gate but I wasn't allowed access, because I was a woman. 'But I'm the doctor', I argued. His answer remained no. I was a woman and nothing else mattered. In the end the sergeant major had to make a deal with the Egyptian commander, so that I was allowed to enter.

The first and decisive thing that is noticed about a woman is the fact that she is a woman. Moreover, male military personnel with women in their team are also first and foremost remarked on for that fact:

> Oh, you are working in that company with those two female lieutenants?

A third kind of reaction is that military men see women as people who require protecting. So women often get benevolent, but uninvited and unwanted, help. A female sergeant was quoted in Hummelink (1999, p53):

> My commander stressed my womanhood. I didn't want that at all. For example, in meetings he urged the men to remove the porno-pictures in the private rooms because of my presence. But I didn't mind at all: the boys pay for their rooms, so they pay for their privacy. The commander put me on a pedestal that wasn't funny. It gave me the feeling I had to walk on tiptoe. I only wanted to do my job in the normal way.

Similar statements given to Bosch included:

> I was the queen bee.
> I was their mascot.
> I was their mother.

The research also produced examples of women working in this male-dominated environment being considered as objects for hetero-sexual fun, thrills and excitement. This sexualization of women was not always expressed openly. But it surfaced in 'blue' jokes and obscenities, or sexually explicit posters and screensavers. A female lieutenant for instance said:

> A platoon was standing to attention after doing sports. Two mili-tary women passed by. The sergeant in front of the platoon shouted: 'Eyes right'. As a result all eyes of the platoon were glued to the two women, who felt embarrassed.

Women's reactions and strategies

The 'special' position female military personnel are accorded as a minority in the organization also affects the way they themselves behave. Many women feel it is hard to be yourself in surroundings where you are conspicuous and attract attention. It makes them wish to keep a low profile. They have a number of well-worked-out strate-gies. One is to be at pains to demonstrate the right, or rather, the desired attitude, especially in relation to physically testing activity. The 'right' attitude implies perseverance, no whimpering. Thus military women sometimes force themselves to achieve ultra-high physical standards. A female captain said:

> The physical tests, look at me, I'm just like a fool, I want to attain the male physical standard. Why? It's not my standard. And it's the standard of the youngest category. So I have to contend with young men. Last year I made up my mind, I wouldn't do it again and in the end ... I'll do it again. I'm expected to do my very best.

A second reaction is cultural over-compensation. Women may adopt a super-macho personal style, in behaviour and language. One lieutenant explained that she resisted this tendency and managed to remain herself, unlike many women in her platoon. She said:

I sometimes get the impression that some women think that they should have an extra big mouth.

Another lieutenant was asked about the reaction of the rest of the platoon to the only female chauffeur. She said:

I think that in the eyes of her colleagues this female chauffeur did not fit in the category 'female'. She did not behave that way. I think she more or less played a role in order to belong; she was one of the guys. I think that is the best way to describe it.

When asked how she knew that this chauffeur was playing a role, the lieutenant answered:

Because, to my mind, it was obvious that she put the male values and norms into practice in an extreme way. I always thought this cannot be normal.

A third reaction visible in Bosch's research shows women minimizing negative, sexist remarks and adopting an attitude of indifference. A sergeant recounts how, when during military training she was confronted for the first time with an objectionable remark about her breasts:

I left. But I lay crying on my bed in secret.

This had been a few years previously. Now, she said, she was no longer touched by such remarks. She had reacted by learning to make equally unpleasant remarks herself. This attitude of indifference, or sometimes, as here, forced indifference, seems to be quite common among women. Rather than reacting to unpleasant remarks:

I act normal as if I am not touched.

A female corporal told how an older male colleague had harassed her for a considerable period. He would always choose to take a shower when she took one. While they were working together he would make sexually suggestive remarks. The corporal's response, in interview, shows clearly her ambivalence. Superficially unaffected, she is in fact deeply troubled by such treatment:

On principle these remarks don't affect me, but I get extremely angry about them.

It is remarkable, in the circumstances, that, out of compassion, she has not disclosed this colleague's behaviour to his superiors.

… A fifty year old man, with five more years to go – does he really have to be put on trial?

The interviews illustrate that the 'minimizing' approach also holds for sexual harassment. Sexual harassment was mentioned by the military women in more than fifty per cent of the interviews. Either the woman had experienced sexual harassment herself, or she knew of other women deployed in the same period who had experienced harassment.[13] It is noteworthy that while the women interviewed make it clear that sexual harassment is undesirable, they do not stress its unacceptability.

A further response women sometimes favour in dealing with 'special treatment' is humour. A sergeant said for instance:

The battalion commander thought that I was in Bosnia to make coffee for him. So the first time I saw him, I entered the room and he threw his mug to me and shouted: 'catch, you know what you have to do with this'. My direct commander, a major, said I should hurry to make coffee. I clammed up. In this kind of situation I get very angry. Ultimately, I put the mug back. After a while the lieutenant colonel came back and wondered where the coffee was. I said to him, very politely, that I lack the right 'caring-attitude'. He never again shouted to me in that way.

Finally, one other recourse is for a woman to dissociate herself from other women. A female lieutenant states for instance:

I'm not the kind of person who wants to have more women in my direct environment. On the whole it is better for me when there are no other women. My relation with the average woman in the organization is not good.

The dire implications of this for women's mutual support and solidarity needs no comment. It is interesting to note that in Bosch's research 75 per cent of the interviewees prefer not to be addressed on the basis of their femininity. They regularly stress the fact that they just want to do their job and that they are not dissimilar to their male colleagues – just 'ordinary military personnel'.

We have seen here that women have been recruited by the military to join the men at all levels and in most functions of the modern armed forces – but it is women, not the Army or the Air Force and their male incumbents, that have been expected to adapt. Unsurprisingly, therefore, the experience has been a very mixed one for women. They show a high degree of ambivalence. What exactly is it that the military policy-makers have in mind, then, in recruiting women?

Ambivalence in military decision-making

Given the male-dominated history and masculinist culture with which female military personnel are confronted when they join the armed forces, it might ideally be expected that the DAF's policy of recruiting women would be accompanied by a policy of transforming the gender structure, gender relationships and gender representations current in the institution. However, while gender mainstreaming is becoming an expertise in the Netherlands, its results still seem to be far from the policy makers in the DAF.[14] Furthermore, neither the affirmation of women and feminine identities nor gender transformation of institutions has ever been on the agenda of DAF. In this section we examine two particular documents that reveal something of the thinking of the military policy makers. From them we can see that their aims have been, rather, (1) the emancipation of women and (2) their integration into the military, and we see something of how these things are interpreted.

The documents we have examined in detail are the 'Policy letter on emancipation' by the Ministry of Defence (1997) and the 'Emancipation Targets' (formulated by the Ministry of Defence under the authority of the Ministry of Social Affairs and Employment) of the Ministry of Social Affairs and Employment (1999). From them we can see: first, that the Ministry of Defence's policy lacks any appreciation of the positive value of gender-diversity for the execution of the tasks for which the DAF are responsible. Emancipation policy is merely a tool of personnel managers and it is, besides, formulated ambiguously. The 'Policy letter' begins by stating that the 'emancipation process', and the 'integration of women', has been disappointing in preceding years – but that the DAF has been continually held responsible for this by the Inspector General of the Military and by politicians.[15] This poses a problem that calls for a solution. However, later in the letter we find an increase in female recruitment represented as the solution to a different problem: that of the Armed Forces as an institution, suffering from a shortage of personnel. Women are needed to fill empty seats in the organization. Finally the letter rather lamely suggests that an increased influx of women will eventually of itself 'in a gradual and natural way have a positive effect on integration' (Ministry of Defence 1997, p12).

Second, gender as a concept is neither mentioned nor addressed in either document. In the Policy letter (1997) there is a reference to a paragraph from the national emancipation policy. It quotes ' ... the decrease of unequal power relations between men and women based on images about masculinity and femininity that exist in society, by which the male values and qualities are seen as the standards'. But the letter does not elaborate on what this might mean for the DAF. For instance, while it mentions measures regarding 'image forming', 'mutual accep-tance' and 'treatment' of women, these mentions are superficial. 'Image forming' for instance refers only to representing soldiering in a way that will attract women to join the forces, to appointing female recruit-ment officials, and to improving information about the functions of the forces. Representations of masculinity and femininity current in the DAF, visible in illustrations in DAF magazines and instructional films, and in posters and calendars in offices, in everyday language and jokes, are not up for discussion.

The measures with regard to 'mutual acceptance' and 'treatment' also lack depth. Some attention is paid to education for tolerance and diversity and there is a mention of the value of 'the confidential adviser'. But the really sensitive gender issues that so badly need addressing in DAF – sexualized aspects of masculine culture, vulnera-bility/aggression, intimacy/distance – these things are passed over entirely in the policy letter and the DAF emancipation policy. This is despite the fact that in preceding years several steps have been taken by various services of the armed forces towards addressing such problems. Thus a series of videos has been made and circulated on sexual harass-ment, homosexuality, discrimination and bullying. And an official framework has been set up for implementing policy on sexual harass-ment. Practical progress however has been slow. For instance, research into undesirable behaviour, including harassment, was planned, but has been deferred.

Third, there is no analysis in the Policy letter of the way in which the structure and culture of the DAF preserve male power and author-ity in the organization. Women military personnel, not the institution, are represented as the problem. Thirteen of nineteen measures listed are in fact 'solutions' to 'problems' concerning the physical demands of work in relation to women's capabilities, the combination of 'work and care' supposedly of particular concern to women (not men), and the poor level of entry and progression of female military personnel. The physical demands of tasks are not themselves questioned. The adequacy of 'work and care' policy in the DAF and the attitude of officials responsible for personnel management are not put under scrutiny.

Yet there was already experience available to the DAF that could have changed perceptions of 'the problem'. Research on 'women and ergonomics' had been started by the DAF in 1998 (Miedema et al 1999). For a long time, stories had been circulating about 'small women' who were incapable of erecting 'bow-tents' or lifting injured 'tall male colleagues' onto stretchers. The design of equipment had not till then been interrogated. The question was inevitably raised however in four pilot-projects on ergonomics (Miedema et al 1999). They showed that modest adjustments to equipment can result in benefit not only to women but also to many men. With this insight, the title of the project was changed from 'women and ergonomics' to 'human beings and ergonomics'. In a similar way it should be possible to examine the genuineness of the imperative of the physical demands of some tasks. That physical demands are no more than relative may be inferred from the fact that since 2000 the Dutch airforce engages pilots with a slight eye-dysfunction. For decades perfect eyesight had been an unquestioned and unchangeable physical requirement for the job of pilot.

With regard to part-time work the Ministry of Defence has formulated targets that only focus on women and are thus seen as part of emancipation policy. They seek an increase in the number of women working part-time – on the assumption that it is only women, not men, who are interested in part-timing.[16] Prior questions would have been relevant: is this true? What are the real reasons there are so few part-timers of either sex at present? What are the attitudes of personnel managers on part-timing? Research by Hummelink (1999) and Storm-Bleijenberg (2001) shows, for instance, that personnel managers may have too rigid an attitude, rejecting initiatives by personnel (men and women) to develop their own careers. Many military personnel who try to switch different services have encountered bureaucratic obstacles. Could this also be a factor frustrating individuals in the DAF who might want to shift to part-timing or change the direction of their careers?

Finally it is striking that the Policy letter does not take into account the many differences that exist among and between women. Measures to increase the progression of women in the Armed Forces are directed exclusively towards the upper echelons. Little attention is paid to the prospects of female NCOs and lower ranks. There is also a striking absence of attention to the position and needs of black women and lesbians.

New personnel for a new model military?

We conclude from our research that the Dutch Armed Forces' goal of recruiting and integrating women into the military is being impeded by a lack of any real understanding of gender. The DAF demonstrate a lack of understanding of how gender relations work, how they perpetuate power imbalances and are maintained through particular discriminatory cultures and the representations of women and men they generate. Their policies thus do not address the root causes of the problem they perceive themselves (and women) as having. This is evident in the weak designation of the policy on women (the fact that it is termed emancipation policy, and not gender policy) and in the emphasis on 'integration' of women as substitute for (and no doubt protection against) transformative change in the organization.

The ambivalence of the Ministry of Defence and the armed forces is clear. They introduce change only in re-action to recruitment problems, and to political and social pressure from outside the military – when the image of the organization as such is under fire. Gender discrimination thus continues, despite the policies. We have seen how, whatever the formal position, certain long-lived beliefs are still perpetuated – that 'the army is for men', 'women are a problem', 'women are not fully effective', they 'do not give full value in the armed forces', are 'the natural support-troops', a mere 'adornment'. The only force shaking these old beliefs is a new dawning of the thought that 'women might be a possible solution to (our) problems'.

Women themselves, as we have seen, are not less ambivalent. They are disinclined to challenge the discrimination they encounter, to question the military's practices or its cultures. No doubt they perceive that their survival depends on adapting their own behaviour and remaining inconspicuous. But the low profile women have kept has not led to them being perceived and accepted as 'ordinary military personnel'. Women continue to be treated tokenistically, as 'something special'. Covertly and overtly, sexism and gender discrimination persist, unchallenged, both institutionally and in individuals.

Neither DAF policies, nor research undertaken or sponsored by DAF, have yet focussed on what a modern army might gain by introducing gender diversity to its personnel and its cultures. This might be considered surprising given other changes that are occurring in conceptions of the Dutch military. As Joachim and Zarkov (2001, p31) point out:

> During the last ten years, the Dutch Armed Forces have seen dramatic change, of two kinds. First, instead of an army of conscripts, it has become a professional army. Second, like its counterparts in other European countries, it is no longer supposed to be defending the 'free world' from a communist/Russian threat, but to be a peacekeeping army. Taken together, these two changes are seen as requiring a mobile and highly trained professional army, ready to go and perform peacekeeping operations wherever the government sends it. In spite of this, in other ways the military has hardly changed at all.

There is evidence that having women present and playing a full role can be beneficial to an army involved in peacekeeping operations. Miller and Moskos (1995) have shown that during operation 'Restore Hope' in Somalia, women and black men in the military were more likely to adopt humanitarian strategies, less likely to adopt warlike attitudes. Because of their cultural backgrounds, they were more likely to act as monitors of misbehaviour than were soldiers in units that were all male, or of a single ethnicity. There have also been suggestions that gender-diversity can increase co-operation with NGOs and local population. If military men are used to co-operating with women in their own units, it may be easier for them to co-operate with NGOs and local population (Winslow 2000; see discussion in Cockburn and Hubic, Chapter 7 of this volume).

By contrast, in 1994 the Dutch government resisted the deployment of female UN monitors in former Yugoslavia, with the argument that Moslems in Bosnia would not accept a female negotiator. The Dutch had to revise this notion when Scandinavia and the United Kingdom successfully deployed females as UN monitors. Interestingly, one of the women interviewed in Bosch's research also reported a personal experience that strongly counteracted any suggestion of female professional incapacity. A UN monitor reported never having experienced any disadvantage in the field from the fact of being a woman:

During negotiations I observed that I was easier to approach for the Moslems than my male colleagues. Obviously a woman was more accessible for them.

The Dutch military are slow to learn however. As one of the respondents, a captain, observed, there had been a difference between the way the Dutch staff treated their own army-interpreters and the way they treated the local interpreters, who were mainly women. The latter were treated, she said, 'as doormats'.

In a recent discussion at the Personnel Directorate of the Dutch Army, a member of the personnel management team stated his belief that women might pose a problem during the Kosovo peacekeeping mission.[17] It would be risky to put them on guard duties due to 'the fact' that the local population would be unimpressed by female soldiers.

Meantime, thinking in the Netherlands is swiftly being overtaken by new thinking internationally. As Dyan Mazurana reports in Chapter 3 of this volume, the United Nations has recently taken serious steps to introduce concepts of gender and an awareness of the significance of women both in war and in the processes of peace-making and peace-keeping. Despite its cautious steps towards recruiting women, installing 'emancipation' measures and 'integrating' women – the Dutch Ministry of Defence and the Dutch Armed Forces are not yet in line with this new thinking. There is clearly an urgent need to bring into a single focus the new requirements of the military and the continuing expectations of women for their human rights and fair treatment in employment.

With a view to a future when this will be achieved, we would like to offer some recommendations for the army, and indicate new issues for further research on gender relations in DAF. For it seems obvious that such research is a necessary precondition for effective gender-policies generating a positive climate for the transformation of gender relations and appreciation of gender difference and diversity.

It is advisable for the DAF to discuss practices and images of masculinity and femininity existing in their ranks, not to conceal them. In that respect it is important to highlight the differences among women and men, and to discuss openly the fact that men feel uncomfortable with the arrival of women. Discussing these issues openly will lead to more gender awareness, which is important for both men and women of all ranks. It is also relevant to pay attention to gender issues such as vulnerability versus aggression, intimacy versus distance, macho behaviour and sexuality. When these subjects are not discussed openly they continue to play a latent but persistent role in daily practices.

With regard to research, we find it especially relevant to conduct research on different images about female military personnel within the DAF. What is the effect of these images, not only on the individuals, but also on the military culture and structure? How persistent are they? How is the forming of the images influenced by traditional gender roles in the Netherlands? Furthermore, given the male-oriented culture of the DAF, the education of both male and female military personnel is clearly based on a male perspective. What is this perspective, and what are the ideas of the cadre and supervisors about femininity and masculinity? Are the personnel aware of the enormous impact these perspectives have on their attitude, and vice-versa?

We hope that such research would prevent the army from making 'a man of you', no matter whether you are male or female.

Empirical data to which this chapter refers are collected in the research conducted by Jolanda Bosch, in the period Spring/Summer 1998, in the Netherlands.

Notes

1. Elisa Kant (1996), lists five roles of women in armed conflicts. Women are victims of sexual violence in war. They are important actors in helping their families to survive. They sometimes actively support the troops. They are at times active participants or aggressors in war. And finally they are sometimes among the political or military decision-makers carrying their countries into war.
2. 'Supporting jobs' were those in administration, signal units, medical corps, service corps, transport units, fighter control and air traffic control (Staf, 1994).
3. European Community law in 1976 followed an earlier 1953 United Nations declaration concerning the political rights of women. The latter was signed by the Netherlands in 1968 and approved by Dutch Parliament in 1971. No exception was made for military functions, including combat function.
4. National reports of the different countries were presented by each delegation at the conference of the Committee on women in the NATO-forces, Brussels, May 2000.

5. Most recent are articles dating from spring 2001, referring to incidents within a 'school battalion'. One Officer and ten NCOs were charged with fornication with female soldiers.

6. A. Oakley, *Sex and Gender*, 1972.

7. S. de Beauvoir, 1976, p323.

8. Cf. J.Butler, 1990 and 1993.

9. See, among others, Cock 1994 and Enloe 1983.

10. In 1979 the Navy started an experiment with women on the supply ship Hr.Ms. Zuiderkruis. The central question in this experiment was: how can the working and living together of men and women on board a ship be organized in the best way? This is the only research within the DAF on co-operation in mixed teams, 'Met vrouwen naar Zee. Rapport over ruim een jaar varen met mannen en vrouwen aan boord van Hr.Ms. Zuiderkruis', Ministry of Defence, SWO Directie Personeel Koninklijke Marine,1982. In further text: Met vrouwen naar Zee.

11. Ten of them have been deployed in Bosnia (Army) and six in Villa Franca in Italy (Air Force). They rank from corporal to lieutenant colonel; the number of years in service varies from one year to twenty-two and their ages range from twenty to forty-seven. Ten respondents are on long-term contracts and six on short-term contracts; two respondents had children during their deployment. Five respondents live together with a partner who also has a job in the military. Five respondents were deployed twice. The respondents have diverse jobs, for example, sergeants, managerial position at company level, UN-monitor, surgeon, interpreter, medical assistant, forklift truck driver, and mechanic.

12. Unless indicated otherwise, this and other excerpts in the pages that follow are all from the interview material collected by Bosch.

13. There was frequent mention too of excessive drinking by military personnel during deployment, both in relation to harassment and as a separate issue.

14. Mossink and Nederland, 1993; Ministry of Social Affairs and Employment, 2001.

15. For example, the report of 1999 of the Inspector General of the Ministry of Defence states: 'Sexual harassment and lack of respect occur more often within the military than is assumed'.

16. Only 0.9 per cent of the military personnel is working part-time: 210 male military part-time workers (0.4 per cent of the total male personnel) and 271 female military part-time workers (6.5 per cent of the total female personnel).

17. At the monthly management meeting (September 2000) of the Personnel

Directorate of The Dutch Army the chairperson of the network of women in the Defence organization was invited to elucidate the standpoints of the network about the emancipation policy.

PART 3:
SOLDIERING AND THE NATION: MASCULINE RELATIONS

The unheroic men of a moral nation: masculinity and nation in modern Dutch history

STEFAN DUDINK

War and the military have undoubtedly been major forces in the making of modern Western masculinity. And in its turn the nexus of war-military-masculinity has contributed substantially to constructions of the nation, nationalism and national identity as we find them in the West from the late eighteenth century onwards. The part of a militarized masculinity in shaping modern nations and nationalisms has often been taken for granted in studies of the nation.

Thus, in his 1882 lecture 'Qu'est-ce qu'une nation?' ('What is a Nation?'), that has continued to inspire scholars of the nation up until the present day, French historian and philosopher Ernest Renan told his audience: 'A heroic past, great men, glory ... this is the social capital upon which one bases a national idea' (Renan 1996, p52). And almost a century later anthropologist Benedict Anderson in his highly influential *Imagined Communities* wrote: 'the nation is always conceived as a deep, horizontal comradeship. Ultimately it is this fraternity that makes it possible, over the past two centuries, for so many millions of people, not so much to kill, as willingly to die for such limited imaginings' (Anderson 1991, p7). Both Renan and Anderson propose to think of the nation as resting on foundations that are thoroughly social ('social capital') or cultural ('imaginings'). And they also seem to be aware of the importance of a military masculinity in establishing these foundational fictions – but both fail to explicitly reflect on this.

Feminist scholarship on nation and nationalism has explored the extent to which the foundational fictions of the nation are produced by gendered stories. As the work of scholars like Cynthia Enloe, Nira Yuval-Davis and Anne McClintock shows, the rhetoric of gender is crucial to accumulating the 'social capital' and to conceiving the 'imaginings' that construct nations and nationalism (Enloe 1989; McClintock 1995; Yuval-Davis 1997). Providing nationalist projects with – among other things – a powerful and emotional language and an ability to 'naturalize' historical and socio-cultural categories, gender is central to nationalism and to the establishment and maintenance of nations and nation-states.

'Nationalism', writes Cynthia Enloe, 'typically has sprung from masculinized memory, masculinized humiliation and masculinized hope' (Enloe 1989, p44). We do well to note that Enloe describes the sources from which nationalism springs as masculin*ized*. They are not 'naturally' or 'necessarily' masculine, but are rendered masculine in a process of articulation that connects national memory, humiliation and hope to masculinity, and goes on to present this ensemble as natural and necessary. In order to maintain the powerful appearance of naturalness and necessity the elements that constitute a masculinized nationalism have to be connected again and again. The stories that weave together masculinity with national memory, humiliation and hope have to be repeated endlessly if they are to produce the seemingly seamless web of nationalism.

In this chapter I hope to tell the story of masculinity and nationalism in a way that brings to light the workings of the processes that connect them. To do so I will explore the contingent nature of their relation that Enloe refers to when she uses the word 'masculinized'. Perhaps going against the grain of her argument, I will try and give as much space to contingency as I can in my analysis of the way masculinity and nationalism are wedded. Where Enloe seems to assume that nationalism generally is constructed through masculinity ('nationalism *typically* has sprung'), I will focus on an instance where nationalism and classical military masculinity do not articulate together easily. And where she speaks of 'masculinized' without exploring what sort of masculinity it is that we are dealing with, I will discuss various masculinities that do not all represent the sort of masculinity one would expect to fuel nationalism.

In what follows I will present aspects of modern military and polit-ical history of the Netherlands that suggest that a successful combination of classical military masculinity and nationalism was not always an easy thing to achieve in the course of Dutch history. More specifically, a masculinity of a military kind was not privileged in repre-senting the virtues and values that were supposed to be at the heart of the Dutch nation since time immemorial. Focusing mainly on repre-sentations of the nation, I want to show that a masculinity of a military kind had to compete with other constructions of masculinity in repre-senting the assumed essence of Dutch national identity. And although the state of my research and that of others does not allow for any defin-itive conclusions as to whether the Netherlands are an exception in the history of masculinity and the nation, I want at least to suggest that looking for (national) differences in the processes in which masculinity and the nation were articulated is a line of inquiry that is worth explor-ing – for the Netherlands and possibly for other nations as well.

South African scholar Thembisa Waetjen recently remarked: 'Masculinity may have for gender theory the same metaphoric value it has for nationalism – an overstated cohesion of interests, forces, and ideologies' (Waetjen 2001, p123). By concentrating on the various ways different masculinities and nationalisms have been linked and by taking into account the failure of certain sorts of masculinity to always artic-ulate well with specific kinds of nationalism, we might contribute to the deconstruction of the story of masculinity and nationalism as a seamlessly connected tandem. Since this story is already the subject of such compulsive re-telling in modern politics and society, we do well to carefully choose our own narratives and words in order not to partake of this compulsion.

Softies and machoes – a brief genealogy

In May 2000 one of the Netherland's national newspapers interviewed military scholar Rob de Wijk, who because of his regular appearance on television during the Kosovo war had become a well known public intellectual. In the course of the interview de Wijk complained of the low esteem in which soldiers and the military are generally held in the Netherlands. Public opinion, according to de Wijk, is too suspicious of the danger the military might pose to civil liberties. In fact, de Wijk claimed, the prudent family men that make up the Dutch military are very much like everybody else in the country and far from a threat. Perhaps somewhat surprisingly, the interviewer went on to ask if de Wijk thought that Dutch soldiers are 'softies'. De Wijk replied

Oh yes! The number of machos in the (Dutch) military is much smaller than in that of the US. And the British aren't so pleasant either. Our army is rather gentle. That is why the Dutch are extraordinarily efficient in peacekeeping operations. A Dutchman will not be armed when he does an inspection of identity papers. An American will put his machinegun against your head. Americans don't like to participate in peacekeeping operations. To them that is a pathetic job. I really worry about the Americans – who happen to be stationed in the most dangerous area of Kosovo. I am sure they will get into trouble and find themselves caught up in fights with the UCK (Wal 2000, p15).

Remarkable as it may seem, this quotation is only one of the many found in public utterances on Dutch national identity that defines this identity in terms of being problematic or unusual in relation to traditional military values and behaviour. Throughout the twentieth and a large part of the nineteenth century remarks like these form a substantial part of the discourse on Dutch national identity. Time and again we find scholars, politicians and journalists who write and speak about Dutch national identity locating it in – among other things – a 'different' relation to military values, heroism and war. This difference is constructed through a comparison to other nations and their relation to the military and war. And very often the Dutch attitude to these matters is presented in a manner that betrays pride. For the country's lack of regular military credentials is presented as a virtue rather than a weakness. It is presumed to actually make the country highly qualified to excel in other areas – for instance those of peacekeeping and international relations.

Those who are familiar with the history of Dutch foreign politics will hear how Rob de Wijk's remark about Dutch soldiers and their extraordinary efficiency in peacekeeping operations echoes older assumptions of a more general nature about the Dutch role in international politics. The idea that a small country like the Netherlands is innocent of the power politics that govern the foreign policies of great powers has over the last 150 years helped to shape notions of the Dutch role in world politics (Boogman 1991; Voorhoeve 1979, p49; Wels 1982, p21). The text that historians often refer to here is a 1913 pamphlet published by the Leiden professor of international law Cornelis van Vollenhoven. In what was intended as an address to the Dutch nation, van Vollenhoven argued that the Netherlands should become a leading force in the development of international law and in the creation of an international police force that would enforce it (Vollenhoven 1913).

Writing on the eve of the 1915 international peace conference in The Hague, van Vollenhoven tried to convince his compatriots that no other country was more suited to executing this elevated task in international relations than the Netherlands. As opposed to the 'monomaniacs of power' like Germany or other great states whose politics had been grounded on nothing but egoism, a small country like the Netherlands could lead the way to an international community that would voluntarily abide by the rules of general interest (Vollenhoven 1913, p11). It was partly because of the country's self-interest – that was served better by peace than by war – that the Netherlands were destined to this task, but also because of its great past, a legacy that was to be revived in the present. The Dutch, van Vollenhoven claimed, were 'a small people but a great nation' and in order to provide the historical evidence that supported this claim, he pointed to humanist philosophers and to artists – Spinoza, Grotius, Rembrandt – rather than military heroes (Vollenhoven 1913, pp13, 95).

Those who are familiar with Dutch colonial history may hear yet other, but nonetheless related, echoes in de Wijk's estimation of Dutch excellence in peacekeeping. In the late nineteenth and early twentieth century the Netherlands prided itself on the specific way it managed its colonies, and in this discourse too, the virtues of a small nation were contrasted with the hunger for power and the proclivity for violence of great powers. In 1914 Professor Johan van Eerde, Director of the Anthropology Section of the Colonial Institute in Amsterdam wrote:

> When history calls upon small nations to engage with energy and intelligence in the demanding work of empire, a little country such as Holland provides better guarantees than larger nations to implement the appropriate policies. Bigger European countries have a proclivity to use brute force in colonial administration – a blunt violence that is grounded in their self-assurance as a society that can wield superior political and military might. Large countries tend to ignore the gradual adjustment process and evolutionary development that indigenous people must go through in order to achieve a higher level of civilization (Eerde 1914, p54, quoted in Gouda 1995, p39).

Here it is not the development and enforcement of international law that 'a small people but a great nation' excels at. It is the efficient management of a colonial empire, that at the same time lives up to the mother country's duty to civilize the natives, that is presented as a specific quality of the Dutch. This conviction that Dutch colonial rule was characterized by a degree of sophistication and gentleness that would benefit all significantly shaped ideas about Dutch self-identity as a colonial power.

The works of van Vollenhoven and van Eerde have become sources for historical analysis; they are generally no longer considered to be adequate representations of Dutch national identity. That should not lead us to believe however that – elements of – their overall estimation of the nature of Dutch national identity do not return in historical works that are still read and quoted. One of them is historian Johan Huizinga's 1934 classic essay on Dutch national identity. Huizinga was the Netherland's most respected historian of the interbellum years and he still counts as one of the great Dutch historians. With the resurgence of matters of national identity in Dutch historiography and public debate over the last fifteen years, his essay has become a much quoted classic in this field.

What made Dutch national culture and identity what it was, Huizinga wrote, was the fact that it is '"burgerlijk" in every sense one would want to attach to that word' (Huizinga 1934, p13). 'Burgerlijk' is a word that is hard to translate into English, for like the German 'bürgerlich' it refers to both the 'bourgeois' and the 'citizen' (Velde and Aerts 1998). It denotes a socio-economic stratum, the habitus associated with it, and a certain civic political disposition. It was with this amalgam of qualities evoked by the term 'burgerlijk' that Huizinga characterized Dutch national character. The main contrast he used to elucidate the meaning of the 'burgerlijk' nature of Dutch national character was heroism. The Dutch, according to Huizinga, were not and had, at least since the seventeenth century, never been a heroic nation (Huizinga 1934, p11).

Huizinga did not explicitly say anything about the masculinity of this decidedly unheroic nation. But implicit references to masculinity can be spotted where Huizinga favourably compared the Dutch lack of heroic qualities with the 'false heroism' of ultra-nationalism, fascism and communism – ideologies that have centred around ostentatious and rigid notions of masculinity (Huizinga 1934, pp12-13; Mosse 1996).

Today, the words of van Vollenhoven, van Eerde and Huizinga are easily dismissed. It is all too easy to read them as evidence of hypocrisy, a misplaced self-congratulatory sense of moral mission, or a nationalism that hides behind a façade of an ostentatious condemnation of the nationalism of others. In this chapter, however, I am not interested primarily in the relation to empirical fact of these pronouncements on Dutch national identity.

I do not want to engage in debunking, partly because such a pose sometimes obscures what I find most interesting about constructions of Dutch national identity, i.e. their difficult relation to stereotypically militarized notions of masculinity. Political historians that have wanted to distance themselves from van Vollenhoven's ideas have sometimes done so by waxing ironical about his vision of the Netherlands as a peacekeeper – and especially about van Vollenhoven's calling the Netherlands a Joan of Arc among nations (Boogman 1991, p31; Fasseur 1998, p474). In doing that, they not only try to establish themselves as sound – and manly – thinkers, but also foreclose explorations into the construction of Dutch national identity that might unearth some unexpected variations in formations of gender. And it is precisely these variations that I am interested in.

So rather than dismissing them, I will read these texts as threads of a dense web of intertextuality in which Dutch national identity is continuously invented (Hobsbawm and Ranger 1983). In what follows I will try to show that notions of Dutch national identity as discussed above rest on an idea of national self that gradually arose in the course of the nineteenth century. Constructed in reaction to the country's adventures in the political turmoil of the late eighteenth and early nineteenth century, this sense of self was created and expressed through, among other means, representations of the country's past. As I hope to show by reference to these representations, the Netherlands confront us with something of a fault line within a European tradition of imagining the nation through the military, war and classical heroic masculinity.

War, nation and masculinity

The European political and military upheavals of the years around 1800 caused great changes in the interrelated fields of nation, war, the military and masculinity. The 1789 French revolution and other democratic revolutions of this period produced a concept of the nation that was deeply political. The nation became the sole and supreme source of political authority, replacing authority that was derived from God or historical precedent. As sovereign political power, the nation would rule itself through direct or indirect political participation. And although this new, sovereign nation was presented as inclusive, not everybody was to be granted full rights of citizenship. Women were to be represented through their husbands or fathers: the sovereignty of the nation rested on the right of self-determination of its male members.

Europe not only witnessed the invention of a new idea of the nation, it also saw the advent of a new kind of war. The wars of the French revolution and the Napoleonic wars were *national* wars. Wars of and for 'the people' replaced the old dynastic wars. These new wars, waged in the name of 'the people' – a concept often fraught with democratic connotations – were to be fought by national armies. The army of conscripts, that in principle could include all able men of the country, replaced the standing armies and armies of mercenaries of the ancien régime. And since revolutionary ideology declared the performance of military duties one of the conditions for acquiring full citizenship in the nation, (democratic) politics and the military became strongly connected (Best 1982). After the democratic experiment of the revolution had faltered, the legacy of national wars and national armies remained – stripped, of course, of its radical democratic aspects. Under Napoleon the ideas and practices of national wars and armies were further developed and exported to countries under French rule, and during the Napoleonic wars the French example was followed by France's adversaries, Prussia most notably (Frevert 1997). National wars and national armies had become a European reality.

The rise of national wars and armies rested upon and produced a democratization of formerly exclusive constructions of military masculinity. Aristocratic and chivalric notions of man as an honourable warrior were called upon, as were republican concepts of the citizen as an arms-bearing man willing to fight for the liberty of his political community (Mosse 1996). They were declared relevant – and accessible – to all men. Heroic death, too, was no longer the 'privilege' of the elite officer class. As part of attempts to legitimize mass mobilization, heroic death, and its 'rewards', were extended to the common soldier who sacrificed his life for the nation (Hagemann 1996, 1997). What resulted was a configuration of nation, the military and masculinity that to a certain extent is still hegemonic in the Western World. In this configuration the male soldier hero is one of the main symbols of the nation, the special relation of men and masculinity to the nation has been institutionalized in the military, and narratives of soldiering in service of the nation have a prominent part in shaping male subjectivity.

The main elements of this, admittedly somewhat sketchy, history of the nation, masculinity and the military have been taken from the history of France and Prussia in the revolutionary and Napoleonic era. It can, however, with some justification be read as a European history (as is clearly the case in the work of George Mosse 1990, 1996). As the dynamics of revolution, counter-revolution and restoration spread from France to the rest of Europe, the new meanings of, and links forged between, nation, the military, war and masculinity established themselves all over the continent. But the legacy of revolution, counter-revolution and restoration also always interacted with local meanings and circumstances. How does Dutch history of the period fit into this general scheme?

Unlike most other European states, the Dutch state of the ancien régime was not a monarchy but a republic, a federation of provinces that was the product of the sixteenth-century Dutch revolt against the Spanish king. The Dutch republic was a highly decentralized state that prided itself on its political and civic liberties, but nevertheless harboured monarchical tendencies at the heart of its constitutional system. In the Dutch republic the princes of the House of Orange occupied the post of 'Stadholder'. Officially the Stadholder was the servant of provincial estates and the Estates General, the provincial and national representative bodies that appointed him Stadholder and gave him his powers. In practice, however, these powers were of such a nature that they allowed the Stadholder to become the most powerful person in the republic. As a result, much of the political history of the Republic was a history of continuous struggle over political power and privileges between Stadholder and provincial estates and Estates General (Israel 1998; Jacob and Mijnhardt 1992).

In the later years of that history we see the emergence of two configurations of nation, military and masculinity that would further be developed in this specifically Dutch path through the age of democratic and nationalist revolutions. The first rises with the democratic *patriot movement* of the 1780s, in which we find constructions of politics and masculinity that are very much in line with developments elsewhere. The patriot movement wanted to regain prosperity and international prestige for the Netherlands, and it considered the restoration of liberty as the main means to achieve this. The central character in patriot discourse about the restoration of liberty, and in a sense the most important embodiment of patriot notions of citizenship, was the citizen-soldier.

Harking back to traditional republican concepts of virtue and citizenship (Pocock 1975), the patriots called for Dutch citizens to arm themselves, form local militias and thus prepare themselves to defend liberty – invariably presented in female allegorical form – against her attackers from within and outside. The citizen-soldier not only represented patriot notions of citizenship, he also embodied Dutch national character. His love of liberty and willingness to fight for freedom were time and again presented as the outstanding features of the Dutch. This quality was given a past that reached back to Roman times when the tribe of the Batavians – who were considered as the ancestors of the Dutch nation – had successfully revolted against their Roman oppressors (Grijzenhout 1989; Woud 1990).

This way of providing national character with historical origins was also a way to establish the fact that Dutch love of liberty was an outspoken masculine disposition. In a speech in 1784 for the manly members of the patriot militia in the city of Zwolle, patriot leader Joan Derk van der Cappellen tot den Pol told his audience that their forefathers had been able to maintain their liberty because they had armed themselves and had, thus, remained men. Their masculinity was the precondition for establishing and maintaining a free society. To try and have liberty in an 'effeminate nation' was a pure chimera (Capellen tot den Pol 1981, p152). This was not just a representation of the nation as masculine. Van der Cappellen's speech also established a continuity between a great past and a great future through an endangered, but in the end unbroken, spirit of masculine virtue. Masculinity was the link between the past, present and future of the nation.

Another, very different configuration of masculinity and nation emerges after the final overthrow of the Dutch ancien régime – with the help of French troops – in 1795. Thereafter the Dutch democratic regime gradually became, first, a French Satellite State and then part of Napoleon's empire. Resistance to the French occupation was minimal and no national army of volunteers was established to liberate the Netherlands. From Napoleon's final defeat in 1815 onwards the country was at the mercy of the great European powers. After Napoleon's fall, the Congress of Vienna (1815) decided to unite the Netherlands and Belgium into one kingdom in order to have a middle-sized state as a buffer at France's Northern border. The House of Orange was to supply this newly created monarchy with its kings.

The transition to a new state and to a monarchy was made in a climate where leading politicians and citizens wanted to leave behind the dramatic political events of the past. Especially the patriot movement and revolt were forced into the background of official national memory (Schutte 1987). As a result, representations of the Dutch national past and identity no longer foregrounded the manly citizen soldier – emblem of the period of radical democratic politics and civil war. He was to be replaced by the industrious and homely citizen that was much better suited to the political climate of the restoration era (Aerts 1999, p46; Stuurman 1992, p49). Dutch poetry of this period, predominantly written by men and addressing other men, spoke ceaselessly about the bliss of domestic life. Poets presented an aptitude for domesticity as a national trait that went back to the seventeenth century (Krol 1997).

The citizen-soldier, however, returned once more when in 1830 the Belgians revolted against the union with the Netherlands. In the Netherlands this revolt that became a war gave rise to a spirit of fierce, martial nationalism. In 1830 and 1831 citizens took up arms once more, especially the students of the student militias. The mythological Batavians were once again called upon to inspire military fervour in Dutch men. 'Your liberty is at stake; forward Batavians! / Imagine the ancestors looking at you', a choir sang in the auditorium of an Amsterdam philosophical society in February 1831 (Kinker 1831, p1). The Batavians returned, but not as the ancestors of radical democratic citizens. They had become the loyal subjects of the House of Orange who fought for King and Country. The military enthusiasm of the 1830s notwithstanding, the Netherlands did not win the war. The mood of martial ardour soon faded away, as did the cult of worship around the heroes of the Belgian war (Vries 1988). The Belgians gained independence and the Netherlands had to begin the long and painful process of adapting to the status of a minor European nation.

A moral and colonial nation

The Dutch nation sought to accomplish this adaptation through a process of compensation, where compensation for political and military weakness in Europe was sought – and found – in two things. On the one hand there was the assumed moral superiority of the Dutch nation (Kossmann 1984, p111). On the other there were the immense colonial possessions of the country that increasingly became a source of national pride and the ground for claiming a higher rank for the Netherlands among European nations than it could be granted on the basis of its power within Europe (Wels 1982, p100).

Depicted as the weak and vulnerable victim of the corrupt and selfish politics of the great European powers, the Netherlands was made to appear as the epitome of morality. From the 1830s onwards notions of Dutch national identity started to centre around the idea that the Netherlands, despite, or perhaps because of, its weakness was the home of justice and morality (Kossmann 1984, p112). Such ideas could successfully build on a Christian notion of the Dutch nation as consisting of virtuous and pious citizens whose primary allegiance lay with the nation. In the late eighteenth century the construction of a modern idea of the nation in the Netherlands had relied heavily on this religious idea of the nation as a moral community (Rooden 1999). Political events of the first decades of the nineteenth century gave it a new impetus and caused it to spread into new directions.

The notion of a moral nation manifested itself in various spheres. In the course of the nineteenth century it started to shape ideas about the Dutch role in international politics, culminating in van Vollenhoven's appeal to the nation of 1913. It also left its imprint on notions of Dutch identity in national political life. Especially after 1848, when the shock-waves of revolutionary upheaval that went through Europe had left the Netherlands relatively untouched, Dutch politics was increasingly represented as an oasis of stability and moderation in a world perverted by revolution. As the Dutch State gradually became a constitutional, liberal monarchy in the course of the nineteenth century, the assumed moderate nature of Dutch political life was turned into a source of national pride. This idea of Dutch politics was part of a political typology that rested on a juxtaposition of revolution and gradual reform. Of course France and its revolution figured prominently in this scheme. The revolution, and French politics and national character more generally, were represented as the opposite of all political virtues that could be found in the Netherlands. The chief local virtue was that of timely and prudent adaptation to changing circumstances – a quality that was thought to be totally lacking in French politics (Stuurmann 1993).

Naturally, such a view of Dutch politics that emerged around the mid nineteenth century could not easily accommodate the years of intense political conflict and civil war the country had gone through around 1800. Dutch historiography of the nineteenth century tended to diminish this period as an anomaly that was not in line with the true nature of Dutch political life. The true course of Dutch politics was that of moderation, consensus and reform; the revolutionary years were an unfortunate incident in an otherwise admirable continuity of political stability (Stuurmann 1992, pp21-53). This way of moulding the Dutch past into a history that suited a self-image of high morality in politics and elsewhere deeply affected symbolical representations of the Dutch past – and also the constructions of masculinity that we find in them.

Monuments to honour the 'great men of the past' were one of the major nineteenth-century nation-building technologies. All over Europe figures cast in bronze or iron helped to create the heroic past that was the sine qua non of the modern nation-state. France had its 'statuomanie' and Germany its 'Denkmalswut'. In the Netherlands, too, the nineteenth century was the age of the statue, but in comparison with other European countries relatively few statues were created (Beeman et al 1994, p23).

More telling, perhaps, than the number of statues are the conventions employed to immortalize the military heroes of the Dutch past. It is a striking feature of nineteenth-century Dutch statues that they depict even military figures of history predominantly in poses of introspection and contemplation. So the seventeenth-century naval hero De Ruyter was shown in the same way as were the painter Rembrandt or the poet Vondel. It seemed as if the men involved in the invention of a national past preferred the contemplative to the classically heroic. They decided to represent the distinctive qualities of the nation through what we might call a masculinity of moderation and contemplation.

The political past was imagined in the same way. Between 1845 and 1848 two statues of William of Orange, leader of the sixteenth-century revolt against Spain, were erected in The Hague. One, paid for by the king and placed in front of his palace, did indeed show 'the father of the fatherland' as a man-at-arms, riding a horse and holding a truncheon in his right hand. The other, the result of a citizen's initiative and the favourite of the public and professional critics, was very different. It depicted a statesman, standing, pensive and with a sword that was less visible than in an earlier design of the statue (Wal 1983).

The turn to the colonies as a source of national pride seems perhaps not very surprising. It was only in the course of the nineteenth century, however, that Dutch national identity and nationalism began to thoroughly depend on the status of the country as a major colonial power. In the early 1830s when the loss of Belgium caused a deep crisis in national self-esteem and identity, the country did not immediately look to its colonial possessions to boost its morale. One might have expected it to do so, for in 1830 the Netherlands had finally suppressed a five year long revolt in Java and had thus re-established Dutch control over the major island of the archipelago. The war had been long and costly, though, and Java itself was still far from the highly lucrative heart of the Dutch colony it was to become later (Doel 1996, pp39-40).

The colonies were nationalized only gradually. The climax of this process undoubtedly was the intense nationalism that was inspired by the war that established Dutch rule over the outer regions of the archipelago at the turn of the nineteenth century. As European nations engaged in intense competition for colonial possessions during the last decade of the nineteenth century, the Netherlands produced its own variant of imperialism by subordinating the unruly outer regions of its empire to Dutch rule. The aggressive nationalism that accompanied this colonial war at home had not been seen in the Netherlands since the Belgian war of the 1830s. It even led to a remarkable rise of the number of men that were willing to join the Dutch colonial army. Earlier in the century the Dutch colonial army always had great trouble recruiting enough soldiers and had to rely on soldiers of dubious background and quality and on soldiers recruited among the colonized. The mood of militant nationalism of the 1890s changed the status of soldiering and gave it an appeal it had lacked previously (Bossenbroek 1992, pp237-239).

This nationalist enthusiasm for a colonial war appears to contradict the picture painted so far of notions of Dutch national identity as they emerged in the nineteenth century. And partly it does. The late nineteenth century colonial war presents us with a moment in Dutch history when the European model of militarized masculinity in tandem with the victorious nation seems perfectly to apply to the Netherlands. However, in the national imagination, even this war was in some ways represented as befitting a moral nation. As Frances Gouda notes, 'The expansionism of the Dutch colonial state in the late nineteenth century was often depicted as a series of delicate political manoeuvres and subtle cultural transactions between wily, sensitive, and above all, knowledgeable, colonial administrators, on one hand, and indigenous sultans, regional chiefs, and local potentates, on the other' (Gouda 1995, p43).

The violence of the war in the colony's outer regions was often presented as a continuation of this political attitude by other means – means that would maintain the spirit of these politics. The general in charge of the operations, J.B. van Heutsz, had, together with orientalist C. Snouck Hurgronje, devised a military strategy that apparently rejected all out military violence. They proposed a strategy of 'functional violence' that was subordinate to the political goals of the war. Surgically precise rather than bluntly indiscriminate, their strategy was presented as being more effective than more traditional and ruthless military operations in gaining control over the colony's outposts (Bossenbroek 1996, pp37-38). When, however, after a period of success, it became clear that the war was fought with much more brutal violence than the public was led to believe, van Heutsz's fame quickly diminished. Public opinion at home turned against him and against his war (Bossenbroek 1996, pp43-47). So when in 1926 the massive and lavishly decorated Colonial Institute in Amsterdam opened its doors, this monument to Dutch empire bore no references to the general or to the war that had completed Dutch rule over the Indonesian archipelago. The extremely rich symbolical ornamentation of the building focused on the uplifting of the colonized rather than on the violence that had subordinated them. In the words of historian Martin van Bossenbroek the building spoke of 'Colonial pride, protestant ethics (and) catholic symbolism' (Bossenbroek 1996, p286). Heroic masculinity was not to be enshrined by the ultimate monument to Dutch empire.

The difficulties of incorporating colonial violence into a sense of national self with strong moral overtones do not stop here. The bloody war over Indonesian independence that the Netherlands fought between 1946 and 1948 was perceived as a mission of mercy, 'a kind of Peace Corps mission, accompanied, alas, by a few police actions' as one historian rightly describes the atmosphere at the time (Pollmann 2000, p95). When from the late sixties onwards the atrocities committed by Dutch soldiers during that war became known to the wider public, these revelations at first met with an 'agitated and shrill' popular response (Gouda 1995, p31). And although the truth of these revelations has by now been acknowledged, this has not fundamentally changed perceptions of the Dutch nation as somehow less militarised and more pacifist than others (Pollmann 2000, p106).

'Softies' and the nation

As Joan Scott writes, politics construct gender at the same time that gender constructs politics (Scott 1986). This holds true for the politics of nationalism and national identity too. I hope to have shown, however, that the ways in which gender helps to produce nationalism and notions of national identity – and vice versa – are manifold and sometimes unexpected. Masculinity definitely played its part in Dutch nationalism and it was invoked to articulate what Dutch national identity was. But an ostentatiously militarized and heroic form of masculinity was not always at the forefront of constructions of 'Dutchness'. It alternated with a form of masculinity more suited to a self image of high morality, of moderation and contemplation, and of a special moral mission connected to its lack of power and specific historical development.

Lest this observation be taken to mean the Dutch nation was blessed with a genuinely and consistently 'nicer' hegemonic masculinity than other nations, two further observations are necessary however. First, a 'soft' masculinity seems just as likely to produce exclusions, subordinations and inequalities as a militarized masculinity does. This 'moderated' and 'unheroic' masculinity that departs from the classic militarized masculine model has by no means always or necessarily been to the advantage of women. In the Netherlands the presence of a 'soft' masculinity – of both a military and a non-military kind – may well have been one of the building blocks of a powerful ideology of family that has both culturally and institutionally hampered women's emancipation. 'Soft' masculinity can besides also function as an appropriation of femininity for men that renders 'real' women obsolete. Second, the fantasies of moral righteousness at the heart of a Dutch national sense of self have, as I have shown, in any case often been contradicted by historical fact.

Still, it is important to distinguish different masculinities and the various ways they help construct nations and nationalisms, rather than concluding that in the end they all amount to the same thing. The use of the word masculinities in the plural is part of the attempt to take difference seriously in gender studies. A reason to insist on the difference between various masculinities is that this is a good way to make clear that there is no such thing as unqualified masculinity – the fantasy of a singular, self-evident, natural masculinity that is at the heart of the modern discourse of gender. It is precisely this fantasy of a singular, natural masculinity that is vital to the construction of modern nationalism, and that has in its turn been empowered by nationalism. It is the persistence of this unholy alliance of nationalism and masculinity – singular, self-evident – that calls for a stress on the plurality of masculinities as part of an attempt to destabilize this alliance. That is not to say that 'soft' masculinity deserves attention because it is better than classically militarized masculinity – in many ways Dutch, soft masculinity is not. It might, however, be a more promising candidate than militarised masculinity for a politics of gender that seeks to appropriate central categories of political discourse in order to put them to a new, 'better' use.

This article is part of a research project on masculinity and nation in the Netherlands, 1780-1848 that is funded by the Netherlands Organization for Scientific Research. An earlier version of it appeared as 'Imagining a Nation Without Heroes? The Trouble With Masculinity in Nineteenth Century Dutch Political and Military History', Potsdamer Studien zur Frauen- und Geschlechterforschung 4, 2000, pp111-124. *I should like to thank Cynthia Cockburn and Dubravka Zarkov for their help and encouragement in thoroughly rewriting this earlier piece.*

A *gentle*men's agreement: Srebrenica in the context of Dutch war history

MARC DE LEEUW

Justinus: *These are the keys to the stronghold and I take the liberty of making the protest that I am handing them over to you much against my will. There is, as you know, no fear that would force me to surrender, as I would find death less heart-rending. This is no treachery but fate that condemns to dust glorious and excellent kingdoms.*

Spinola: *Justinus, I accept the keys and I recognize your courage, because the courage of the conquered is the glory of the conqueror. And in the name of Philip IV, may he reign through the ages with more victories than ever before and prosper as always, I occupy the city.*

Calderón de la Barca, The Siege of Breda, 1625.[1]

What happens the moment following this dialogue from Calderón de la Barca's *El Sitio de Bredá* (The Siege of Breda) can be seen in Diego de Velazquez's painting *The Surrender of Breda* (see illustration below). The conquered general and Dutch stadtholder (governor), Justinus van Nassau, deferentially surrenders the key of the Dutch city to Ambrosio Spinola, a general from Genoa in the service of the Spanish King Philip IV. Shortly after the capture of Breda in 1625 – this would be the last triumph before the definitive fall of the Spanish empire – the King commissioned his court poet, Calderón de la Barca, to prepare a play (from which the dialogue above is quoted) to celebrate the glorious victory.

A number of years later, the King's court painter, Velazquez, was awarded the honour of painting the subject of the conquest of Breda to hang in the 'Hall of Realms' in the new summer palace, *Buen Retiro* (where twelve paintings were eventually to be hung in memory of the Spanish military glory achieved under Philip IV).[2] The interweaving of *armas y letras* – the arts of war, theatre and painting – was unique for the Spanish Golden Age, during which the cruelty of Conquest, the piety of Catholicism, the grandeur of art and the baroque theatricality of the court went hand-in-hand.[3]

The painting *The Surrender of Breda* hangs in the Prado in Madrid and is as essential to the cultural identity of Spain as Rembrandt's *Night Watch* is to the Netherlands: it is an icon of national art and a symbol of the Golden Age. Velazquez's painting was finished in 1635 and two years later Breda was recaptured by Dutch troops. In the case of Velazquez, the order in which fact and fiction, historical event and painted imagining are interwoven becomes clear: a battle is won, the King wants to immortalize this event as a national glory, he gives the court painter the assignment to let his imagination loose on the topic and the result, *The Surrender of Breda*, is first hung in his private chambers and later in the National Museum. As did the play, the painting served as a fictitious representation of actual history: the surrender/occupation by Spanish troops of the city of Breda in 1625. What remains of Spanish glory, after the liberation of Breda, is a theatrical play long since forgotten and a painting, *The Surrender of Breda*, that in the interval has become world-famous. So famous that ironically, since 1931, a copy of *The Surrender of Breda* even embellishes the entrance to the City Hall of the vanquished Breda!

In the canon of art history, Velazquez's painting is known as an exemplary visualization of a return to humanity after war. Instead of glorying in having won the battle, Velazquez pictures men ceremoniously bowing to each other. Thus, the painting reveals nothing of the suffering, the occupation of the city, the murders, but instead represents the surrender of the city as 'making peace'. In doing so, it defines surrender as the re-establishment of mutual respect, humanity, dignity and generosity. Fraternizing with former enemies turns war into peace.

This chapter focuses on how, by examining the way honour, pride and the figure of the *gentle*man warrior are portrayed, we can unearth from beneath a story of 'peacemaking' and humanity, one of masculinity, male bonding and reaffirmation of patriarchal supremacy. *For, from the point of view of maintaining the patriarchal gender order, the restitution of the masculine honour of the vanquished is as important as the celebration of the masculine triumph of the victor.*

I also wish to explore to which extent the *past*, brought alive in

Velazquez's visualization of war, humanity and masculinity, is still *present* today. To that end, I will compare the seventeenth-century painting, *The Surrender of Breda*, with a photograph taken in 1995 during the occupation of Srebrenica by the Bosnian-Serb forces.

In the photograph we see Colonel Karremans, the commander of the Dutch battalion (Dutchbat) of the United Nations Protection Force responsible for the security of Muslim inhabitants and refugees in the designated 'safe haven' of Srebrenica, with General Mladic, commander of the Bosnian Serb forces. It is the moment when Karremans cedes control of the town to Mladic. What would ensue, we now know, is the massacre by Mladic's men of several thousand unarmed Muslim males. The photograph was published in different Dutch newspapers shortly after the fall of Srebrenica, on the 13 and 14 July 1995. Due to the fact that it quickly gained a highly symbolic value in the eyes of the Dutch, this photo was often reprinted and used as an illustration for articles on the topic.

Thus, the artistic visualization of the 'linked pair' Nassau/Spinola will be compared and contrasted with the photographic registration of the 'linked pair' Mladic/Karremans to detect an echo of the first in the second, and see what it tells us about war, peacemaking and masculinity.

I will argue that what we see in both painting and photograph are masculine stories (and stories of masculinities).[4] These are moments of fraternization, restoration of mutual respect between warriors in the transition from war to peace. The warrior also legitimizes his desire to re-appropriate patriarchal supremacy within the community by means of this restoration. Additionally, this staging of a 'fair agreement' by the 'gentleman warriors', usually seen as shrewd diplomacy, can be read as a hollow ritual deteriorating into a *farce* of civil behaviour at the very moment that the victor is certain of his complete domination over the victim.

My comparison of the painting with the photograph will show that the element of farce or charade, the hollowness of the ritual, is neutralized by the medium in which the representation appears. The painting is primarily seen as a product of artistic talent, imagination and aesthetics and not as a statement on war and masculinity. The press photo appears as a neutral registration, a snapshot of an historical event, and not as an interpretation and staging of the event by the photographer or the press editor. I will argue that *both* images evoke particular interpretations of reality, even though they appear in different media and are perceived differently by the public. The painting and the photograph *both* tell us a story about gender and war, about generosity, pride, glory, respect, self-esteem and defeat, loss of national honour and surrender. They show us how particular notions of masculinity and peacemaking are based in gestures of humanity and respect, even in possible friendship. As such, both images are part of our Dutch collective identity because they set up a discourse on the 'peacemaking' abilities of 'gentlemen warriors', on their masculinity and on their staging of humanity within the arena of war.

In order to explore this staging of peace and war through masculinity and male bonding, I plan first to analyze the representation of war, peacemaking and masculinity in Velazquez's painting. Then I will analyze the press photo of the pair Mladic/Karremans and their dialogues and, finally, I will compare the two. I will do this by reflecting on the ontological and social background of male bonding rituals and by employing semiotic analyses of the gestures and the 'mutual glances' that make visible the gentleman warriors' encounters. Of necessity, I will also touch upon the similarities and differences between art and press photography and I will compare the significance of the background scenery used in both images.

Diego de Velazquez, *The Surrender of Breda* (1635), Prado Catalogue, Jose Antonio de Urbin (ed) 1993, London, Scala Publications. In Spain euphemistically referred to as 'Las Lanzas'.

Lieutenant Colonel Karremans (centre) raises his glass with General
Mladic (left) after the fall of Srebrenica (Photograph AP).

A representation of the ideal
surrender: warriors, glory and gallantry

Although the official title of *The Surrender of Breda* points to war and
the imminent occupation of the city, it is immediately clear that the
painter chooses to portray not the war but the making of peace. While
Justinus van Nassau's *gesture* is the handing over of the key to the city
and thus symbolizes the imminent occupation, Velazquez manages to
imbue this gesture with a totally different affect.[5] The two generals
bow to each other. Spinola lays his hand on Justinus' right shoulder. It
looks as if a knowing glance is exchanged: respect, dignity, maybe even
friendship can be read from their demeanours. The special Velazquez
catalogue, available right beside the painting, speaks of 'the generosity
of the victor toward the vanquished';[6] the magnanimity of Spinola, and
thus of Spain, toward the conquered enemy is the official message.
(Never mind that Spinola came from Genoa and was a hired general.)

In the general catalogue of the Prado, one can find a more precise
rendering of Velazquez's sources. It informs us that although the court
painter was not in Breda during the war, he was able to consult the

sketches made by Jacques Callot, who was present. Velazquez had met general Spinola on his trip to Italy in 1629, when they travelled on the same ship. It also states that for the background to Breda in his painting Velazquez used the landscape paintings of Peter Snayers. The catalogue thus implies that Velazquez was *almost* at the site, that his imaginings found their origins in trustworthy witnesses who had experienced historical reality at first hand, rendering the painting an almost faithful representation. The ensuing paragraph explains that the positioning of the principal characters in the painting consciously echoes a painting by Bernard Salomon whose motif was the Bible story of Jacob of Esau (Genesis 1.33). Further, the Prado catalogue links the painting to the play: ' the theme ... became an exemplary representation, which was much imitated later on. The *anecdote* (my italics) seems to have been inspired by a comedy by Calderón de la Barca entitled *The Siege of Breda*'. In short: this text accompanying the painting in the exhibition in the Prado in July 1998 refers to five sources from which Velazquez derived information for his impression/depiction of the surrender: one personal meeting between Velazquez and Spinola, two eyewitnesses, Callot and Snayers, and the images they registered of the events, two literary references, the biblical motif and Calderón's final dialogue (quoted above).

There is a contradiction here between the text/title and the pictorial image. While the foregrounded motif refers to a biblical story of forgiveness, reconciliation and new-found fraternity, the title '*The Surrender of Breda*' refers to war, occupation and violence. Velazquez' painting, however, covers the war tableau with a tableau of peace. Instead of a brutal occupation he shows dignity and appeasement. It is not the painting itself but the chosen title that locates the image: it is not called 'The chamberlain gives the key back to his king', but 'The Surrender of Breda'.[7]

Whether the surrender takes place violently, with dignity or jovially is not revealed to us. The title is factual. The painting appears to say: 'the surrender referred to in the title took place in a dignified fashion'. The representation of the historical event finds its central focus in a gesture: the giving of the key. The *movement of giving* implies that Spinola does not 'conquer', he 'receives' from the giver. The 'key gesture' is framed by affective gestures: hand on shoulder, people bowing to each other. These gestures stand for mutual respect, reconciliation and dignity within the official European code of behaviour.

This behavioural code qualifies the *knight* or *gentle*man warrior – who unites in his person military violence, humanism and the beguiling of court ladies. But is this the only way to read the portrayal? Is this sudden transformation from war to fraternity rather a further humiliation of the enemy? Is the boundary between humility and humiliation, expressed in the bowing, a very fine line indeed? Is the attribution of valour to a vanquished general a too easy, too masculine, rhetorical *trick* meant to enhance the victor's own glory?

The sentence in the play '*I recognize that you are courageous for the courage of the conquered is the glory of the conqueror*' is like a maxim, summing up the military moral principles of knighthood. Seen in conjunction with this dialogue, Velazquez's painting becomes a comic strip or a Hollywood film complete with happy ending; everyone is satisfied. The one is courageous and undergoes his fate with dignity; the other achieves glory and is allowed to rule. In this way a rhetorical *barter* takes place between generals; this is a *gentle*man's agreement, a *tête-à-tête* of comrades, of pals.

As enemy generals, their positions are opposed. But by attributing to them complementary and parallel characteristics (courage – glory) suddenly a human equality is assumed. A rhetorical figure gives rise to a seemingly fluid transition from a war tableau to one of peace. Given that courage denotes glory and glory courage, the generals dissolve into one and the same person recognizing and acknowledging each other's manly-cum-military pride.[8]

In the light of this it is possible to interpret Velazquez painting as meaning: the enemy is reclaimed as a friend to restore his masculine honour and to avoid his revenge. In *The Surrender of Breda* thus one can see the portrayal of dignity as a portrayal of 'war by other means'. The defeated general and stadtholder, Justinus van Nassau, in being forced to play this diplomatic game, is doubly humiliated. And his humiliation is portrayed as an ideal of Humanism.

The existential quality of the ordinary soldier is complemented at the level of the generals by their equality within the patriarchal social order they serve. Again we see an identification with the (enemy) Other: the man with identical military power, social status and historical responsibility. In addition to the rhetorical barter – courage for glory – there is thus a social exchange with the Other. The generals recognize and acknowledge each other as peacemaking *gentlemen*.

The strength of this emotional, existential and fraternal connection determines also the internal dynamics of every *Männerbund* (male bonding; see Theweleit 1987). In the 'masculine tête-à-tête' loss of face automatically means loss of masculinity. The 'dignified surrender' saves face. The reinstatement of mutual respect *can* lead to a friendly tête-à-tête, one that *can* be acted out by the actors as a pseudo role-play. This role play becomes ritual and has another important goal: the right of the men (vanquished as well as victor) to take up their patriarchal positions once more within the symbolic social order of the community they left behind to do battle. In order to be able to demand their rightful position in this social order after the violence, they must avoid irretrievable loss of their masculinity, their potency on the battlefield. Only he who, after a defeat, can return to the community with head held high and with some residual prestige can successfully demand his former patriarchal position back. Therefore, the ritual of peace, in which the men mutually confirm and restore (rather than further undermining) each other's manliness, is crucial for the preservation (rather than the assailing) of the patriarchal order after the war.

A war which has really been lost is one in which both soldiers and generals count solely as a negative memory – as a moral scar – within the community.[9] See the examples of World War Two for Germany, Vietnam for the USA, and Afghanistan for the USSR. After these wars, the men who returned had definitively lost their status, honour and dominance within the social order. The nation did not honour them; they were not heroes; they symbolized only the national guilt and the futility of the battle fought. No matter how courageous they had proved themselves to be, they nevertheless became synonymous with defeat and disgrace. The loss of face meant a corrosion of the national identity as well.[10] Soldiers who lose without honour are emasculated and lose both their status and their identity.

The reality of Srebrenica's surrender

Can this kind of interpretation now be used to find the key to the image of *The Surrender of Srebrenica*? The press photograph (p166) that I perceive as a counterpart of Velazquez's painting shows the meeting – the tête-à-tête – between the Dutch lieutenant colonel, Ton Karremans, and the general of the Bosnian-Serb forces, Ratko Mladic, during the retreat of Dutchbat and the deportation of the refugees. The photograph shows Karremans drinking, while he stares intently at Mladic. All others present watch Karremans expectantly and seem to be asking themselves: 'Is he drinking with us or not? Yes he is'. The masculine tête-à-tête portrays, just as in Breda, the giving up and surrender of a stronghold. In this version the key has become a champagne glass, the painter (who was not present at the surrender of Breda) is a photographer (who most definitely was there in Srebrenica). The exhibition in Buen Retiro (opened ten years after the surrender) is replaced by a front-page news item (appearing two days after the event).

Four men stand in a half-circle, facing the photographer. Their clothing reveals, to a lay person, hardly any difference in rank. Each holds a glass. Karremans and Mladic exchange a glance while Karremans drinks and Mladic watches him. The photographer appears to be an absent presence – no one looks into the lens. This endows the image with a feeling of authenticity, of this being a 'snapshot'. Untitled, without an accompanying text, this could perhaps be a snapshot of the festivities at a military birthday party! One of the captions applied to this photograph was: 'Lieutenant Colonel Karremans (centre) raised his glass with General Mladic (left) after the fall of Srebrenica. (Photograph AP)'.[11] The news source, Associated Press, neutralizes the Bosnian-Serb photographer, who actually served in Mladic's army, following the troops, and took this photograph on Mladic's order.

In the photo, just as in the painting, the winner records the victory. But, while most of the museum visitors would look on the painting as a fictitious, aesthetic interpretation/representation, most of the newspaper readers would look on the press photograph as a neutral registration of an actual event. The painting is elevated to art because creativity coincides with craftsmanship and evokes reality through the materialization of Velazquez's imagination. The photograph evokes reality through the registration and materialization of the photographer's subjective choice of a particular moment, person, gesture, lighting and composition.

In his excellent book *War Photography. Realism in the British Press* John Taylor (1991) shows how ideas of a 'natural world' underpin photographic realism, and its assumption that photography opens a window through which we can see 'the real thing' happening, making us witnesses of 'living history'. Instead of accepting the 'silent authority' of this assumed 'account of the real' in photographic realism, Taylor suggests we should ask: 'What is photography's *position* in the power relationships of this time?'. This means that we need to remain cautious of the apparent reliance on 'the reportable war' (p8) and 'see photographs in *places* and put to particular *uses*'(p16). Furthermore, Taylor cites Sekula as stressing that the consequence of photographic realism is that our 'awareness of history as an *interpretation* of the past succumbs to a faith in history as *representation*. The viewer is confronted, not by *historical writing*, but by the appearance of *history itself*' (p15). Thus, photographic realism 'hides the procedures of the groups who use it by offering in the first place an immediate *experience*' (p15).

In every image, painting or photograph, representation and interpretation shift in relation to each other. But, because photography implies realism and authenticity, the photograph can be employed as a *witness to the truth of the event*. Each and every image offers us a surface upon which we can project our interpretation/reading of what (we think) we are seeing. The photographer is also the witness to an event for which the photograph is evidence: the photograph proves the fact of the photographer as witness. In the case at hand, there is a photograph of the get-together of Mladic and Karremans but there is no photograph of the executions, of the mass murder. Karremans and Mladic are, in their turn, witnesses to the moment at which a photograph was taken of them, their tête-à-tête is materialized by the photograph and thus made part of a reality outside the moment when, and the location where, the encounter took place. The presence of the photographer or a camera team makes the scene part of a discourse on 'making visible'; the photograph announces, just like the catalogue of the Velazquez painting did, 'this happened in this way'. Karremans and Mladic are witnesses to how they themselves were made visible witnesses to their own tête-à-tête. For Mladic this visibility functions to enforce his legitimacy, for Karremans it underscores his impotence, his humiliation and his future role as the personification of the failure of Dutchbat and the UN.

In spite of the fact that the victor, Mladic, would be the most important figure in the eyes of the photographer, he has consciously made the central figure in the photo the defeated, drinking, UN representative, Karremans – who is of course the most important figure for the Dutch public. Unlike the Surrender of Breda, there are no generals to be seen on a hill against the background of a burning battlefield; there are no gatherings of exhausted officers and men; there is no bowing and no subservience. Instead, there are interpreters present, and the media. The humane, peacemaking gesture consists in this case of four men raising a glass together. The newsworthiness of this image is derived from the unexpected way in which the 'general at war' and the military 'protector' of the refugees are portrayed during the surrender of Srebrenica. Serbian propaganda and the Western media subsequently made this image into a symbolic representation of what became known as *The Fall of Srebrenica*.

Thus, having a drink together makes the meeting between enemies into a serene tableau of peace, a masculine tête-à-tête during which generals reach a 'fair agreement' as *gentle*men. While the photographer is shooting this film, the execution and ethnic cleansing of thousands of

Moslem men is being set in motion outside the location and outside the frame of the photograph.[12] In this way an unpleasant reciprocity is set up between an aesthetic, ethical and ethnic 'cleansing'. The minutely planned genocide is hidden behind a portrayal of courtesy: wine for generals and – as we get to learn from other sources – bread, water and candies (!) for the refugees, distributed by Serb soldiers.

While Karremans calls Mladic a 'great strategist', the preparations for the executions are well underway. The extent to which the Bosnian-Serb army leaders wished to use the UN leaders to legitimize their actions became apparent only after the deportation and genocide of the refugees, when Major Franken of Dutchbat and the representative of the refugees, Nesib Mandñiç, were forced to sign a document in which both officially declared that the evacuation of the refugees had proceeded correctly. At the same time, the Bosnian-Serb forces camouflaged themselves with material confiscated from the UN Blue Helmets in order to mislead inhabitants who had fled from the enclave and in order to create the impression that they were safe and could come out of hiding (Honig & Both 1996, p53).

Thus, for the cameras, Mladic and Karremans behaved according to the military tradition in which generals shake hands as a continuation of politics and/or war by other means. They conformed to the behavioural code that dictates that a masculine tête-à-tête restores the mutual respect of the generals and a 'fair agreement' concerning the retreat and help for victims leads to peace. But *The Surrender of Srebrenica*, more clearly than *The Surrender of Breda*, shows us that the official military tradition is nothing more than a masquerade covering up massacres, absent from both the photograph and the painting.

But the 'as if' of the masquerade – the men playing/staging the ideal of military/male honour – covers *both* the behaviour of the victorious Mladic and that of the vanquished Karremans. Both simultaneously have a secret agenda: Mladic orders massacres, Karremans orders assistance and the withdrawal of his troops. Both men drink while behind the scenes – outside the painting/picture – Bosnian-Serb forces separate the men from the women with the support of Dutchbat. Thus, Karremans, as a defeated general, becomes a victim of the military masquerade, which he himself, as a representative of this specific military tradition, keeps reaffirming. One could also further argue that Karremans becomes simultaneously an accomplice and a victim. But Karremans was able to ensure that both he and his troops returned home, while it is probable that more than 7000 Moslem men were killed. Consequently, we have to conclude that this photo is nothing more than a mise-en-scène of war as politics, and politics as war by other means.

At first sight, one could argue that Karremans and the UN peace-keeping forces, in their attempt to protect victims of war, symbolise exactly the opposite of such a politics as well as male domination and oppression. My argument is, however, that the manners of peace-keeping are still embedded within a militarized tradition of male honour and pride. As I show above, masculine honour and pride remain every bit as important in the case of the male peacekeeper as in the case of the victorious warrior. As long as we cannot funda-mentally change these codes of male honour and pride, our peacekeeping operations will continually perpetuate the problems they purport to resolve.

Farce, masquerade and massacres

In this section I will turn from the pictorial images to the spoken word, and compare the rhetorical exchange (dealing with glory and bravery) between Justinus and Spinola from the final scene of the play *El Sitio de Bredá* (*The Siege of Breda*) with a tape recorded dialogue between Mladic and Karremans during the fall of Srebrenica. I will ask: how does this staging of the masculine tête-à-tête and the exchange of masculine honour, humiliation and fraternisation influ-ence the 'fair agreement' and what does this mean for the fate of the Moslems?[13]

The following dialogue consists of excerpts from the so-called 'Mladic-tapes', which the British documentarian Leslie Woodhead found and used for his film *A Cry from the Graves* (BBC/NPS 1996).

Mladic: Do I understand correctly that you ordered your men to kill my soldiers and that you ordered the NATO air force to carry out attacks on my troops?

Karremans: I repeat, those things are not mine to decide. This is ordered by higher authorities, based on information received by the UN in New York from the base.

Mladic: Don't make me partner to your fantasies, lieutenant colonel. Answer my questions. Did you or did you not order your troops to fire on my army?

Karremans: I issued an order for self-defence.

Mladic: Against whom were your troops to defend themselves if no one was being attacked?

Karremans: I was attacked by mortar fire and tanks.

At this point Mladic changes the subject, but later returns to the same point:

Mladic: Lieutenant colonel, in conformance with the agreement of April-May 1993, it was your job to disarm the Moslems in Srebrenica. But you provided them with arms instead; you helped them smuggle in weapons and you allowed them to prepare themselves to fight the Serbs. Furthermore, you also gave your troops the order today to open fire on my soldiers.

In this way Mladic answers his own question, attributing the blame to Karremans. They then move on to the subject of what is to happen to the refugees in the enclave. Karremans emphasizes the function of the UN as provider of help. Mladic suddenly asks:

Mladic: A cigarette?
Interpreter: Do you smoke?
Karremans: Usually I do, yes. But the last while I've smoked so much...
Mladic: Here, have one; it certainly won't be your last.
Karremans: The military assignment of Dutchbat is over.
Mladic: End of that story then.
Karremans: I've been asked to provide as much aid as possible to the refugees.
Mladic: Ha. Good. Anything else? ...
Karremans: Something personal. I want to thank the Serb military leaders for treating the soldiers well.
Mladic: You don't have to thank me for that.

After this sequence – a seemingly friendly gesture extended by Mladic to Karremans (they smoke together) – Mladic establishes that they have reached 'the end of the story'; Karremans thanks him and turns again to the question of humanitarian help and the civilian population. Mladic is provoked by this:

Mladic: Yeah, yeah. You helped the Moslems and the Croats. And you all isolated us, especially that Van den Broek of yours. He is one of those who has destroyed our dream and our collective nation, both for us and for the Moslems. My dear man, we were a content country. All the sectors of the population were content. And we had a good life together, both in Srebrenica and here.

Until the Moslems started to do what Van den Broek, Zimmerman and other Western Mafiosi told them to. When I was standing in front of the City Hall in Srebrenica, I could see that machine-gun fire was coming from your observation post. I brought this along to show you. Your troops shot at me personally.

Karremans: I know nothing about that, but if it's true, I apologize. As a man and as a military man. Usually we don't shoot at generals.

Mladic: I usually never shoot either. How old are you? Where were you born?

Karremans: In 1948. I'm 47.

Mladic: You're six years younger than I am. Is this your first war?

Karremans: No.

(...)

Mladic: And so you've come to Srebrenica. This is the first war of my career. And this is my country.

Karremans: I realize that.

Mladic: It is not your country. There is not one single reason why you should shoot at me from your tank.

Karremans: Once again, my apologies.

Mladic: Because you are taking shots at me in my own country. I'm not going to go shooting at people in the Netherlands. Where do we go from here?

So, from the moment of the offer of 'a cigarette?', matters of general human interest, military affairs and masculine discourse become interwoven in the Mladic-Karremans dialogue. We hear Karremans, who up to this moment kept strictly to the military UN discourse, beginning to reveal personal information. At the end of a plea for safe conduct for the citizens and for his own battalion, Karremans unexpectedly says something that was particularly shocking when revealed in the Dutch media – and that, like the photographic image of Mladic and Karremans clinking their glasses, reinforces the impression of Karremans as a coward:

Karremans: But I've never been there (Sarajevo), so I don't know how it works. I'm only the piano player, as I've repeatedly said. Don't shoot the pianist.

Mladic: You are a bad pianist.

175

With this 'don't shoot the pianist' Karremans is describing his own position in terms of an image from a Hollywood western: while wild cowboys are demolishing the saloon, the pianist plays cheerfully on, out of the line of fire. His responsibility is just to provide the musical accompaniment to the fight. A paragon of virtue, he makes absolutely sure he doesn't get involved. Here Karremans offends against the traditional military code of courage and glory: he is afraid. When he again starts to speak of the fate of the civilian population, Mladic interrupts him:

Mladic: Are you married and do you have children?
Karremans: I have two children.
Mladic: How old are they?
Interpreter: How long has it been since you saw them?
Karremans: Half a year.
Mladic: And are you keen to see them again?
Karremans: Of course.
Mladic: My soldiers felt the same way, the soldiers you killed today in Srebrenica.

A bit later Mladic dictates to Karremans what he is to tell General Nikolai, supreme commander of the UN peace forces:

Mladic: UNPROFOR is, in spite of the air attacks of NATO and the acts of war of your troops against my soldiers, as yet, not a target. Your soldiers and officers have but one life, just as you do. I am sure you do not want to lose your life. Therefore, I demand complete cooperation. Moslem citizens are not our targets. I wish to help you. Even though you do not deserve it. Neither as a man nor as an officer. But I am doing this for the young men, the children of UNPROFOR, because I do not want them being sent back to their mothers in coffins. I also wish to help the Moslem citizens, because they are not guilty of what is happening here. That is why I want to ask the following of you: Are you capable and willing to come here with the representatives of the citizens? I wish to conclude agreements with them; you can all succeed in this or you can all stay here or you can all die here. I do not want you to die. Should the Moslem army of Srebrenica wish to speak, then you must also bring along their representative ...

Now, how can the 'linked pair' Karremans/Mladic be compared to Nassau/Spinola? In the above excerpt we see that Mladic places himself at the heart of the classical military tradition of humanity, respect and honour. He states his readiness to spare the lives of both his enemies: NATO and the Moslems. And, in the same move, he denies them status as equals by addressing them both as *civilians*: 'children of UNPRO-FOR' and 'Moslem citizens'. By doing this he enhances his own military and masculine honour: it is beneath him to fight those who are not his equals – who are not military, not men, nor adults. He seems to agree with Spinola that the 'courage of the defeated is the glory of the winner'. But as his soldiers begin to slaughter Moslem refugees, these statements only show that the wine-drinking performance Mladic stages for his official photographer is a farce.

The farce that characterizes the meeting of Mladic and Karremans is there too, already, in Velazquez's composition. Justinus van Nassau had neither the freedom *not* to come, nor the freedom to escape. The *honourable failure* and the *dignified transfer* had as their most impor-tant goal – after a siege lasting some months and an imminent occupation – the symbolic and triumphant confirmation of the surren-der. Van Nassau had to capitulate alive or die; the only way out of the dilemma was a reconciliation with what Calderón de la Barca calls his *fate*. Van Nassau's freedom amounts to no more than a choice between life and death. Represented as 'fate', Van Nassau can accept his giving up, his surrender to the enemy, as God's will. Thus he becomes a 'brother' in the Christian ethic and can reconcile himself to failure with his head held high.

Karremans too saw his fate determined by a higher power – the United Nations – and could likewise see himself as free of blame. He was only the 'pianist', with no lines to speak. The Mladic tapes do in fact show that Karremans used the little latitude he was given to try to help the civilian population. But he was caught between a rock and hard place – a passive UN and a general who had already fashioned his own plan. An apparent negotiation for an unopposed withdrawal of the civilian population turned out to be just as *fake* as the gestures of reconciliation – 'A cigarette?'. The *gentlemen* have agreed that they themselves don't shoot – and prefer not to be shot at.

So, the exchange between courage and glory degenerates into the handing over of the Moslems and a humiliating withdrawal by Dutchbat. The '*gentle*man's agreement' keeps up the appearance of diplomatic negotiations that are alternately fierce and friendly and that sometimes seem like a discussion of military men among themselves.

Mladic is offended that UN troops dared to shoot at him and now asks for cooperation in the evacuation of the civilian population. It is in this moment of pretence that it becomes clear, within the context of the masculine tête-à-tête, that the ethical ideal (reconciliation of enemies and aid for victims) is a *farce*. Humanistic gestures, staged as *farce*, reveal that the masquerade of generals is the bitter reality of refugees. In his talk with Karremans, Mladic *appears* to be concerned with the fate of the civilian population, but his soldiers have already been commanded to separate the men from the women and children and to cart them off for execution.[14]

As Zarkov shows in Chapter 11 in this volume, the impotence and humiliation of Karremans and the Dutchbat (and the UN) symbolised also the humiliation of the Dutch as a nation: we proved ourselves unable to uphold the moral order, which for the Netherlands meant protecting the refugees. The men who were sent out not to fight but (contemporary heroes) to protect refugees, came home as cowards: they were not 'man enough' for the task. They might even have been accomplices, through negligence, to the crime of ethnic cleansing. By staging a drama of their own legitimacy, the Serb leaders made criminals of Dutchbat and the UN. Both the taking of Srebrenica and the ethnic cleansing that followed were organized as propaganda events, as much as incidents of war:

> As a propaganda stunt, bread was being distributed by the Bosnian Serbs everywhere and was eagerly accepted by the hungry masses. But a request by the BSA (Bosnian-Serb Army) to stage such a scene within the compound and film it was denied. Mladic, filmed by his own camera crew, reassured the Moslems: 'All of you who wish to go will be transported, large and small, young and old. Don't be afraid, just take it easy. Let the women and children go first. Thirty buses will come and take you in the direction of Kladanj. No one will harm you' (J.W. Honig and N. Both 1996, p35).

Here the farce of the tête-à-tête and masquerade of safety come together. The trick worked: the refugees flocked to the waiting buses while Serb soldiers pushed back Dutchbat soldiers, separated men from women and children and took over the camp. And the executions began.

This is how, on a smaller scale, Srebrenica became a Vietnam for the Netherlands' national identity. It was a 'dirty' war in which we fouled ourselves. Belief in contemporary Dutch innocence, in the decency of 'our boys', was destroyed. We needed them to be heroes, and not just ordinary guys who joined the army because they thought it was a tough thing to do, because they felt the army to be justified and necessary, or because they simply wanted to earn money.[15] 'Srebrenica' thus undermined what was an extremely positive Dutch self-image, fed by a conscious orchestration of 'religious tolerance' in the seventeenth-century, and the myth of the 'massive resistance' of the Dutch populace against the occupier in the Second World War. In the Netherlands it is still possible to call the colonial war in Indonesia a 'police action', and the war in Kosovo was called (like in almost all NATO countries) a 'humanitarian intervention'. With such euphemisms we deny our own oppressive, aggressive and violent actions. It is against the background of such a national self-image that our own peacekeepers are idealized as pseudo-modern knights.

Within this particular historical-military discourse, Karremans might try to justify his own behaviour regarding *The Surrender of Srebrenica* – the behaviour that *echoes* the standard set by, among others, Velazquez' painting. As a Lieutenant Colonel, serving under United Nations orders, given their failure to respond to his calls for support, he can accuse the United Nations.[16] But, as an individual with a responsibility for his own deeds in history, Karremans can be deemed 'guilty by reason of negligence'.

Conclusion: honour, pride and identity

In this paper I reflected on the relationships of gender and military by looking at the codes of masculinity, male bonding, fraternization and patriarchal supremacy using the visualization of a 'get-together' between victors and vanquished. I argued that we need to understand the relationship between the ways of making visible the code of masculinity (gestures, glances, bowing) and the traditional military code of honour and generosity in order to gain insight into the *politics* of patriarchal fraternization. The aesthetic representation of an ideal surrender and the photographic representation of a real surrender are both shown as being simultaneously theatrical, functional and strategic. The notions of making peace serve multiple functions: the affirmation of total control, the avoidance of the enemy's revenge and the mutual affirmation of maleness through an exchange of gallantry and glory.

But, when the staging of the rituals and codes of the *gentle*man warrior becomes a play in itself then the fictions of masculinity show its real face: *farce* and *masquerade*. For the victor this farce and masquerade is just another phase in the staging of *his* war game: both farce and masquerade demonstrate how easily he can set a trap for another warrior. His pride and honour are not reaffirmed by his violence but by his cleverness. War has become a man's game without rules: a game within a game, a ritual within a ritual and a farce within a farce. In short, the theatricality of the *gentle*men's encounters can, at any moment, fall into the farce of its own masquerade.

The concepts of heroism vs humiliation are of central importance to understanding the similarity between the 'praxis of war' and the 'praxis of peacemaking'. Both are founded on the praxis of fraternization. Whereas fraternization in the Christian tradition points to the fundamental brotherhood (!) of all men under the guidance of God, it can also be used as a strategy to reproduce the social structures of male domination and, in this strategy, keeping one's male dignity appears to be the absolute necessity. Thus, images of the 'gentlemen warriors making peace' demonstrate not only how masculinities and militarization govern the war arena but also how they govern our peacekeeping practices. Because the identity of the peacekeeper is still embedded in masculine and militarized notions of self-esteem, respect and humanity, the rules of 'making peace' are still the rules of the man's game of mutual confirmation or destruction of maleness. This game is a game of honour and pride, played by individuals, nations and states.

I would like to thank Dubravka Zarkov, Harry Kunneman, Annemie Halsema, Martien Schreurs, Peter de Leeuw, Amade M'charek, Sonja van Wichelen, Markha Valenta, the ASCA-workshop and Mieke Bal for their inspiring comments on this text.

Notes

1. *El Sitio de Bredá* was written as a theatre play, a comedy. In it, the Spanish playwright Calderón de la Barca stages the siege of Breda by the Spanish troops and their final victory on 2 June 1625. The manuscript was probably commissioned by Conde-Duque de Olivares, the 'most intimate servant' of the King and was written between 15 June and 5 November 1625, and was thereafter performed for the members of the court. It first appeared in print in 1632.

2. Vosters calls this hall a 'type of Spanish pantheon of heroes or a propaganda poster', 1993, p206.

3. Compare with Curtius 1948, p550.
4. I use here the concept of masculinity/ies as developed by Connell 1995.
5. Whitaker states 'that Velazquez depicted the capitulation in his great painting *The Surrender of Breda* as Calderón had depicted it on stage, for the delivery of the keys is found in no other account. In addition, Spinola's compassionate gesture to Justin in Velazquez' painting corresponds to the magnanimous words Spinola addresses to him in an effort to raise his spirits in the moment of defeat', 1978, p529. See also S. Vosters 1993, and the *Bibliographisches Handbuch der Calderón-Forschung*, 1979, p453.
6. See F. C. Serraller 1998, p20.
7. The chamberlain in the Spain of Philip IV was a very important figure: he held the keys of all the chambers of the courtrooms and this symbolic task was accompanied by great influence on the king. As the chamberlain actually could be in a position to give back keys to his king, this would make the painting for the public in those days *a true story*.
8. With his mise-en-scène Velazquez' painting refers back to a long Hellenistic, Christian and Islamic tradition in which reconciliation, forgiveness and fraternising with the enemy are the central themes. This fraternization is paradoxical. While it is, on the one hand, the very basis of patriarchal order, on the other hand, it seems to contradict the point of departure for every war, namely, that the Other – even if he is my brother – could be my enemy. In his *Der Begriff des Politischen* (The Concept of the Political) the controversial German legal philosopher of law, Carl Schmitt 1927, p14, describes the political enemy as 'the Other, the Stranger; in essence it is enough that in a very intense way that person is existentially Other and Strange, so that in an extreme situation, conflict with him is possible'. Only when a person is abstracted to the Other – the Stranger – can a conflict with him *as* an enemy be justified. For Schmitt, the essence of every political deed is the distinction between friends and enemies, in which friends are chosen in relation to one's enemy. One can see in Schmitt the often cited dictum of Carl von Clausewitz – War is the continuation of politics by other means – re-interpreted to read: *Politics is continuation of war by other means.*
9. For an examination of the de- or remasculinization of the nation state in relation to war see G. L. Mosse 1990.
10. For the most recent fine analysis of the specific relationship between gender, nation and war from the feminist perspective, see Melman's collection *Borderlines. Genders and Identities in War and Peace, 1870-1930*, 1998. The chapters focus on the changing definitions, perspectives and attitudes towards masculinity, femininity and national identity evoked by the experiences of the First World War, Colonialism and the subsequent

reshaping of the European Empires and/or nation states. See specially Ilana R. Bet-El's chapter *Men and Soldiers: British Conscripts, Concepts of Masculinity, and the Great War*, pp73-95.

11. Dutch daily *NRC Handelsblad*, 29.05.96. Of course there were many other captions, like: 'Lieutenant Colonel Karremans was forced earlier this week to take a drink with the Serb leader Mladic after the Serbs had conquered the enclave of Srebrenica with the capture of Portocari', *Brabants Nieuwsblad*, 14.07.95. Here Karremans (and with him the Dutch nation) immediately becomes another victim of Mladic, as the caption clearly states that Karremans 'was forced' to drink with Mladic.

12. J. W. Honig & N. Both 1996, reconstructed the chronology of the events leading up to the fall of Srebrenica and the subsequent genocide. They especially focused on the diplomatic and military errors made in the decision-making process of the UN-forces in comparison to the strategy of siege of the Bosnian-Serb forces.

13. The Mladic-tapes, made by a camera team of the Bosnian-Serb forces to document their offensive in the region of Srebrenica, served as propaganda. After the transmission of Wood's documentary on Dutch television, the transcripts of the dialogues were made available on the Internet by the Dutch broadcasting organization NPS. I had access to Dutch translation of the dialogues, and these are here translated back to English (original language of the dialogue). The quality of English in the original is poorer.

14. In this act of separation, masculine conflict is once again elevated – this time in a humanistic gesture – through masculine friendship and the restoration of the masculine community's social order: men as soldiers, women-and-children as 'real' refugees.

15. There is no denying that we, Dutch, actually love 'ordinary guys' – witness our everyday expression 'act normal and then you're crazy enough'.

16. Karremans claims to have asked five times in vain for air support from UN headquarters – after five refusals Karremans had no choice but to surrender Srebrenica.

Srebrenica trauma: masculinity, military and national self-image in Dutch daily newspapers

DUBRAVKA ZARKOV

When I first read the word *trauma* in the title of a newspaper article about Srebrenica – 'Srebrenica-trauma is difficult to process' (*Het Parool*, 30.10.95, p7) – I thought that the piece would be about the war traumas of people who had survived Srebrenica and lived without knowledge about their missing family members. But, I couldn't have been more wrong. The word *trauma* had nothing to do with the tens of thousands of Bosnian Moslem refugees who were expelled from the so-called UN Safe Haven, or those who perished in the process. As the excerpt below attests, the *trauma* referred exclusively to the feelings of Dutch soldiers who served in Srebrenica, and to national sentiments regarding the matter:

> The liquidation of refugees took place hardly 200 meters from the Dutch Compound in Potocari. Thus, literally, before the eyes of Dutch soldiers who saw the events but did not, or could not, do anything to prevent them. This passivity and powerlessness gets to the very root of the Srebrenica-trauma that now weighs on the Dutch armed forces [...] The confrontation with their own powerlessness has left deep wounds [...] The Netherlands, that in the past gladly appointed itself as conscience of the world, suddenly saw itself depicted as a laughing stock [...]

Several years after reading that article, I decided to go back to Dutch newspapers and examine their writings about Srebrenica, for my presentation at the expert seminar on Gender Relations after War that

Cynthia Cockburn and I organized in October 2000. I was soon to learn that the texts that appeared in the Dutch press seldom offered clear-cut reports on actual events surrounding the take over of Srebrenica by the Bosnian Serb forces in July 1995. Rather, the stories were much more about the Netherlands: Dutch history, Dutch norms and values, Dutch traditions and feelings were consistently invoked and examined against the backdrop of the war in the little town in eastern Bosnia. In many ways, Srebrenica provided a mirror through which the Dutch press engaged in a dialogue with its own national image. It is this self-image, and the role of militarized masculinities in it, that I wish to examine here.

For the sake of clarity, I wish to emphasize that I am not analyzing actual events surrounding the fall of Srebrenica, although I will refer to them. I am not dealing with the questions of who did what and why and how, or whose responsibility it was that thousands of Moslem refugees found death and despair, instead of safety. I analyze only a small segment of Dutch press and their representation of the events, and even then, only in as much as these allow me to investigate how militarized masculinities find their place in Dutch national self-images.

My analysis is focused on one of the key discourses through which the fall of Srebrenica was represented in the Dutch press: the *Srebrenica trauma*.[1] I argue, first, that the discourse of the *Srebrenica trauma*, as constructed by the media, rested on an assumption of two interrelated militarized masculinities: a classical, heroic one, and an ethical, moderate one. Secondly, that it is the failure of both that has turned the fall of Srebrenica into a specifically Dutch *national* trauma. Finally, that the discourse on *trauma* has a specific function: it offers possibilities for remedy and recovery.

My analysis, in many ways, is both a follow up and a challenge to some of the arguments presented in the two previous chapters. I agree with Dudink that the contemporary Dutch national self-image is constructed through categories of moral superiority, with moderated, 'soft' masculinity as its chief guardian and bearer. However, unlike Dudink, I argue that classical, heroic masculinity, in the case of Srebrenica became the very condition against which the moderate, moral masculinity was measured. I agree with de Leeuw that the contemporary politics of peacekeeping is produced through the same gendered imagery that produces war-waging. But this same imagery, and the relations of power that underpin it, functions by separating (Karremans) a 'man' from (Karremans) a 'general' and makes one morally responsible, while pardoning the other. As Bosch and Verweij confirm in this volume, there are no women generals in the Dutch army as yet. So, in this case, literally, the *man* was the *general*. Symbolically, separation further sustains the narrative of war, instead of challenging it.

A note on methodology

Conducting an analysis of the press – be it a text, a caricature or a photograph – often evokes questions of methods. How do we researchers select our material (from a load of texts on a subject)? Are the selected texts really representative enough of the press writings on the specific subject? Do we leave out the pieces that contradict our arguments? How do we know what effects these texts have on the readers? Do we forget that beyond the words and images in the press there are real events, real people?

The answers to these questions depend very much on the particular methodological assumptions within which we situate our analysis of media representations. We can assume a direct link that connects an event, a text about it in the press, and an opinion of a reader. But if we do that, we also assume that the media are simple transmitters of the facts. Much mainstream and feminist research on the media has already discarded such an approach, asserting that the media engage in a practice of representation, with an arguable relation to 'facts'.[2]

Taylor (1993, p36) argues that representations are not 'innocent, transparent or true; they do not simply "reflect" reality. They help constitute it'. This is also the starting point of my analysis of media representations. I assume that the link between an event, a text about it in the press, and the way readers understand it, is never direct or transparent. It is produced by different practices, discourses and relations of power. Notions of femininity and masculinity, norms of heterosexuality, definitions of national, religious or ethnic identities are among some of the most significant producers of the words we read and images we see. Furthermore, we all – readers and journalists, politicians and soldiers – share the social worlds in which these different practices and discourses co-exist and compete.

The media discourse on the *Srebrenica trauma* is produced in just such a complex social world of practices and power relations within one nation-state and the competing meanings of its war history, its national and international politics and its self-image. The media are taking part in the struggle to control these meanings (van Zoonen 1991, p43). This is maybe easier to recognize in a situation of tightly controlled or censored media, as for example, in the former Yugoslavia, during its disintegration.[3] It would be naïve however to think that absence of censorship implies an absence of struggle to control the meanings.

The fall of Srebrenica: facts

Srebrenica was declared a UN Safe Haven in 1993. On 6 July 1995 the Bosnian Serb forces started their offensive on the town. At the time of its fall, the large number of Moslem refugees from other parts of eastern Bosnia were gathered in Srebrenica, expecting the protection of the UN peacekeepers – a Dutch battalion ('Dutchbat') with about 400 personnel. But the protection failed. Despite repeated requests for air support by the Dutch Colonel Karremans, UN officials in charge decided not to engage militarily.

On 11 July, Bosnian Serb forces finally took over the town. They immediately started evacuating the refugees. The evacuation lasted only a couple of days and was overseen, and even aided, by the Dutchbat. In the process, several thousand Moslem men disappeared; presumed or confirmed killed, with soldiers of the Dutchbat suspecting or knowing what was going on, if not directly witnessing the killing. Some of the murders were actually already occurring during the evacuation, in a house just across from the UN compound guarded by Dutch soldiers where the refugees were staying. A number of the refugees were escorted by Serb soldiers from the UN compound straight to this house, and Dutch soldiers could actually hear the shots and the screams of the victims.[4] Furthermore, 55 Dutch soldiers who were kept hostage by the Bosnian Serb forces in a nearby village have confirmed, upon their release, that as they travelled back to the UN compound, they saw dead bodies scattered about the roads. They also reported seeing a lorry full of bodies and a bulldozer digging a grave (Bakker Report 2000, p195).

On 21 July 1995 the Dutchbat was finally allowed by the Bosnian Serb forces to leave the enclave. They went to Zagreb, Croatia, and, after a great deal of partying, and receiving a hero's welcome by the Dutch Prime Minister and the Crown Prince, who were visiting troops in Zagreb at the time, they were transported back to the Netherlands.

During the fall of Srebrenica, and after it was taken over, the Dutch commander, Colonel Karremans, and Bosnian Serb commander, General Mladic, had several encounters. They negotiated the release of the Dutch soldiers who were taken hostage, the free exit of the Dutchbat from the enclave, and the free passage of the refugees to other regions. These encounters were tape-recorded, filmed and photographed. Some of that material was used in the subsequent numerous reports and investigations about the events surrounding the take over of Srebrenica. A lot of it was published in the Dutch national press, or used in documentary production for television. The media use of the material had considerable consequences. About a year after the fall of Srebrenica, in May 1996, one TV documentary, one photo and a few texts in the national daily *NRC Handelsblad* featuring Colonel Karremans prompted a number of Parliamentary questions.[5]

The fall of Srebrenica: inquiries

The inquiry into the Dutchbat's and Dutch government's role in the fall of Srebrenica began almost immediately. Many different institutions – from political to academic – have been involved in these inquiries in the years since the fall of Srebrenica, but the media as well as some individual MPs remain unhappy with the lack of openness and the depth of the investigations.

The latest line of inquiries started in May 2000. Conducted by the so-called Bakker Committee, it was established by the Dutch Parliament, and named after its chairman, an MP, Mr A.D. Bakker. The task of the Committee was to examine decision-making processes regarding Dutch peacekeeping operations in general, and Srebrenica in particular. It was in no way supposed to find out what actually happened in Srebrenica, or who was responsible for it. In September 2000 the Bakker Committee offered its findings to the public, in the form of a 500 page *Report of the Temporary Committee for Decision-making on Peacekeeping* (henceforth: the Bakker Report).

According to the Bakker Report, Dutch participation in peacekeeping operations has been too often driven by internal political motives and power struggles between different ministries and ministers, instead of a consistent and informed international policy (Bakker Report 2000, pp479-498). Communication between different ministries, and especially between those for Foreign Affairs and Defence, has often been insufficient and competitive. The Parliament often had too little relevant information for decision-making, or was put under pressure by the Cabinet, or by the media.

All of these failures in communication and decision-making were relevant for the circumstances surrounding the fall of Srebrenica. The Bakker Report concluded that the first information about the murders of refugees reached the senior politicians in the Netherlands only on 18 July 1995, thus after the executions were already over (p488). But the information about the executions had been sent to The Hague three days earlier (see p195). As responsibility was not the issue for the

Bakker Committee, it only quoted the UN Secretary General's report to the effect that the Netherlands can be blamed only inasmuch as it was a part of the international community. Beyond that, it bore no specific responsibilities for which it could be blamed (p488).

Nevertheless, it was clear from the Bakker Report that many questions are yet to be answered. Among them: Have Dutch soldiers and responsible military and political leaders actually committed offences that are punishable under either Dutch national or international law? From the Bakker Report it is clear that the Dutch political authorities were aware of the seriousness of this question, and have actually done everything to prevent 'eventually punishable facts' ever reaching the public.[6]

Some of the facts from the ground however – punishable or not – did reach the press. Armed with photos, transcripts of tape-recorded and filmed conversations and testimonies of witnesses, the press conducted its own investigation into the guilt and responsibility of the Dutchbat and Dutch political leadership, from the very first day the news broke about the fall of Srebrenica. And, as they started publishing their stories, the expression *Srebrenica trauma* came up over and over again.

The excerpt at the beginning of this chapter gives an indication of what this expression the *Srebrenica trauma* refers to: the overwhelming feeling of powerlessness of the Dutch soldiers and Dutch military stationed in Srebrenica, and the sense of humiliation of the Dutch nation, in the eyes of the world. By writing the words in italics I wish to stress that they are not just an expression, but a discourse, in which masculinity, military and nation are linked in a very specific way.

Masculine failures, national traumas

The word *trauma* was used in many texts in its literal meaning – as emotional suffering or a disorder, characterised by emotional pain.[7] Many of the texts asserted that the soldiers who served in Srebrenica had to 'endure more shocking things than other peacekeepers'[8] and had experienced 'profoundly fundamental events'.[9] Military commanders were sometimes accused of being either too dismissive of the soldiers' pain and their need for counselling, or too busy to give attention to their own men.

The attitude of the public was also questioned. Negative publicity was described as 'the sword of Damocles that hangs above [soldiers'] heads every time [when Srebrenica is mentioned]',[10] and was said to have 'deepened soldiers' wounds'.[11]

I do not wish to deny or belittle the fact that many Dutch soldiers did suffer *post-traumatic stress disorder* after their experience during the fall of Srebrenica. However, I wish to stress the following. First, one could question whether Dutch soldiers serving in Srebrenica had more reason for suffering trauma than soldiers witnessing atrocities in any other war zone, and why there were no media stories about trauma in the case of the latter. Second, the word *trauma* acquired a different meaning once it became the *Srebrenica trauma*: it was not any longer a psychological disorder of individual soldiers, but a deep national senti-ment. Finally, within the discourse on the *Srebrenica trauma*, the events before, during and after the fall of Srebrenica, and the experi-ences of the Moslem refugees have almost completely disappeared, both as *actual events*, and as a *media story*. Within this particular discourse, the fall of Srebrenica was deemed significant only when transformed into an element of Dutch national sentiment – crucial as it may be. I will come back to that later. For now, I wish to examine these two particular feelings – powerlessness and humiliation – that have been singled out in the discourse on the *Srebrenica trauma* as the core cause of both soldiers' and national traumas. I argue that these feelings are indicative of the place occupied by militarized masculinity in the Dutch national self-image.

From philosophy and psychoanalysis to anthropology and law, feminist women and men studying masculinity have all pointed out that *power* is one of the core constitutive elements of notions of masculinity in the West.[12] At the level of social and cultural organiza-tion, power translates into the hierarchical advantage of the masculine and subordination of the feminine. At an everyday level, that power translates into male domination over women. But masculinity as power has much deeper ontological consequences, which are not necessarily related to femininity. Maleness and manhood are defined by power. A man cannot be 'the Man', unless he embodies power.

When it comes to wars and conflicts, the issue of power gains extra significance. Classical works by Theweleit (1987, 1993) and Connell (1985) have already shown that in wars, virility, aggression and violence are easily translated into, and celebrated as, militarized masculine power. Other authors have shown that men in war and armed conflict are ultimately seen as representatives of their respective (warring) communities, and as such, their masculinity is the very symbol of what they fight for, be it the nation, the race, or colonial mastery. It is this symbolic function of masculinity within the nation that often prohibits the exposure of powerlessness in men belonging to the dominant, or in Connell's (1995) words, hegemonic masculinity. Sharpe (1991) has shown, for example, that in the British press in the nineteenth century, bodies of colonial European men were never represented as mutilated, while the bodies of European women and native women and men were. Bourke (1996) has analyzed social discomfort with the mutilated male bodies of soldiers after the First World War. In my own analysis of the national press during the disintegration of Yugoslavia I concluded that the main Croatian daily and weekly newspapers never exposed Croat men as victims of sexual violence, while Moslem men were depicted as castrated (Zarkov 2001). In each of these cases, men who belong to the dominant social group are represented as powerful, because they symbolically embody the power of their respective group. Because masculinity is constitutive of other social identities – in the above cases, those of colonizers, white European men, and a particular ethnic group – public exposure of their powerlessness is a direct threat to the identity of the social group to which the specific men belong.

In that respect, the discourse on *trauma* may be thought to be one of the few acceptable discourses in which the powerlessness of one's own (military) men could be made *public* and tolerated by the nation. I will argue later that this discourse is also appropriate for yet other reasons: it carries in itself a possibility for dreaming as well as a possibility of healing.

A piece that is especially poignant in making the link between the power of military men and the honour of the nation is an article about the Minister of Defence, Mr Voorehoeve. So often criticized in other texts about Srebrenica, he received gentle treatment in an article describing his own trauma following the fall of Srebrenica: 'Voorhoeve's Trauma'.[13] Written on the occasion of the Minister's visit to Bosnia in 1998, the text begins by comparing the man that the Minister was just after the fall of the town in 1995, and the man at the moment of writing. In many ways, the language of the piece betrays the underpinning assumption of contemplative and moderate masculinity that Dudink writes about (Chapter 9, this volume). Voorhoeve is depicted as someone who neither seeks glory, nor falls into despair over mistakes. He simply does his duty, with contemplation and moderation. The way the Minister talks about Srebrenica is an example:

> Of course this follows me still. This experience will always stay with me. It keeps dominating my thoughts. Still. It was one of the most horrific war crimes of recent years and it happened while I was a Minister. Each interview begins with it. This is how things are. I understand that.

He is a man who accepts his lot, dark side included, and carries on doing his best. That his bad lot was undeserved, we learn already in the very first sentence: 'Why, of all the people, did this have to happen to him, a minister who was everywhere praised for his integrity?' the journalist asks. And then he goes on to portray this man of integrity, with a long list of all the good things the Minister had done in recent years. The readers are informed that Voorhoeve refused to resign after the fall of Srebrenica because he 'did not want to give a false impression that the Netherlands is accepting blame for a big Serbian war crime'. Instead, he stayed and, refusing to 'give in to self-pity', worked hard for the army and for the Netherlands. 'Pained' by the state of the Dutch army after Srebrenica, he put all his effort in transforming it. Success followed:

> Three years after the occupation of the Moslem enclave of Srebrenica by Serbs, that saddled the Netherlands and especially its military with a trauma, the number of Dutch peacekeeping missions increased [...] The Dutch blue helmets that he met on his first visit to Bosnia in 1994, in Srebrenica, for that matter, were a part of a powerless, badly led UN mission without a mandate. In 1998 the Dutch are taking part, within the SFOR, in armed actions against Serb and Croat war crime suspects. They strictly control the warring parties' observance of the Dayton peace accord. They also oversee the return of refugees.

By comparing what the Dutch army lacked during the fall of Srebrenica, and what it eventually regained – power and control – this text offers us a clear insight into the assumed links between masculinity, military and national self-image. The Dutch do not have to be ashamed of themselves any longer: their men carry and use their arms again! The nation, embodied in its military men, is again, visibly, manly.

Of course, one could assume that women are similarly bearing arms, and exercising power and control. After all, as Bosch and Verweij show in this volume, women also served in the Dutch military within UN forces, and were stationed in Bosnia. However, not a single text on the *Srebrenica trauma* explicitly referred to women soldiers. The overwhelming majority of the public figures mentioned in these texts – from counsellors to military and political officials – were men.

The absence of female soldiers from this discourse on war and nation is not surprising. Other authors have already shown that national self-representations found it difficult to cope with the combination of femininity and soldiering. In her investigation of the British press during the Gulf war, Forde (1995) concluded that one of the dominant strategies of the press was simply to ignore the presence of women soldiers among the allied forces fighting in the Gulf. If and when women under arms were included in the national imagery, their femininity was constantly stressed at the expense of their military expertise. They were mothers, sex objects, or vulnerable girls in need of male soldiers' protection. A small number of texts represented an image of emancipated Western women, skilled and capable of any duty, including soldiering, but that image was not coupled with similar images of male soldiers, but rather with the images of victimised Arab women. Finally, the image of a woman soldier as female Rambo was also present, but in such cases soldiering was obviously constructed as incompatible with femininity. My own research shows that the Serbian and Croatian main daily and weekly newspapers engaged in a substantial negotiation of feminine versus military skills, stressing the perfectly fitting uniforms on curved bodies, or flowing locks of hair, every time a woman's military expertise was mentioned (Zarkov 1999).

I speculate that the absence of women from the discourse on the *Srebrenica trauma* can be further explained by the fact that this discourse is about *failed* militarized masculinity. In other words, women's military presence is tolerated within the national self-imagery only when men as soldiers are the prototype of the heroic, or at least, unbeaten military. This speculation also makes sense in the context of *gendered narratives of war*, where tales of glory and defeat ascribe very different, and often very definite roles to men and women.[14] When stories about the *Srebrenica trauma* appeared in the Dutch press, they did not fall into a vacuum. They fell onto the fertile soil of these narratives, in which, as Dudink points out, Dutch military heroism and moral superiority have both been ascribed to *men*. The performance of the Dutchbat in Srebrenica was measured against the background of these narratives. And against the background of these narratives, the traumatised nation dreamed another – heroic – version of the Srebrenica story.

Battlefield hero and a champion of the weak
In his text 'The Lost Fatherland', published in *NRC Handelsblad* on 13 July 1996, during the first commemoration of the fall of Srebrenica, the Dutch media historian Henri Beunders asks:

Why did we believe so much in Castro's revolution? Was it because it says clearly on the coin, around the head of Che Guevara: 'Patria o muerte', the fatherland or death. Why have we reserved heroism for them, and not accorded it ourselves? Maybe then the 400 Dutchbatters would have fought to the death, for the fatherland of humanity [....]

What would have happened if Karremans and his 400 Dutchbatters had fought to the death on behalf of the Moslems? Would the Netherlands have won everlasting fame, instead of being mocked and vilified? We do not know that. 'History does not unveil its alternatives', according to Voorhoeve. Maybe the world's reactions ought to have been even more scornful. Maybe Dutchbat ought to have been ridiculed as the dummies of the century, for being unprofessional and for not following the rules. The Government ought to have stepped down, and Voorhoeve ought to have become a professor in a province.

We do not know. What W.F. Hermans said remains true: 'A hero is someone who is not punished for not being careful'. Now we certainly know one thing: the non-hero who is careful will certainly be punished. But with Voorhoeve one has to conclude that the guilt does not lie with the Dutchbatters. For how can anybody become a hero with the home front still preoccupied by freedom from commitments, by luxuries, illusions and a belief in one's own inviolability?

It is this unfulfilled yearning for heroes who would die for the 'fatherland of humanity' that ravaged Dutch national self-images. Suddenly, the nation that, through the last two centuries, had imagined itself as a principal, if reserved, champion of humanity all over the world, found itself yearning for a just warrior who would sacrifice himself defending the weak rather than accept defeat. The careful one, the moderate one, the one who follows the rules, is suddenly faced with the alternative never chosen, always left to the others – heroic death, eternal glory, all in the name of the fatherland.

A reader of this analysis should have no illusion: the 'fatherland of humanity' that Beunders mentions is not, as one might assume, the world. Rather, it is the Netherlands. Dudink (Chaper 9) points out convincingly that Dutch national identity has been constructed as ethically superior. It is the Dutch, in Dutch national self-imagination, who can teach the rest of the world the moral principles of humanity. Thus, when the author laments the fatherland of humanity, he is actually lamenting the Netherlands, its ethical spirit, its moral tradition and the military men who would carry them all. These he sees as being irrevocably lost with Srebrenica. In doing so, he is not questioning the national self-image of ethical superiority, he is re-affirming it. And he longs for a Hero who would have saved it. The Hero who would not only have fought a war, but also championed the cause of the wronged and powerless, a Hero who would have embodied the best of both classical, heroic military masculinity, and moral masculinity.

Instead of such a Hero, there was Dutchbat, helping the Bosnian Serb forces to separate men, who were to be killed, from their families, who would be expelled. The difference between the fantasy of a Hero and the reality of the defeated battalion that might even be guilty of war crimes was so appalling as to shatter the very core of Dutch national self-understanding. Another historian, Van der Dunk, writes about that explicitly:

> The precarious retreat of Dutchbat-soldiers from Srebrenica is not only a stain on the escutcheon of the Dutch armed forces, but also means a moral failure of the ethical principle that the Netherlands has carried high on its banners, for decades, willingly [...].[15]

As the principles of morality fail, one could assume that the whole national history, especially history of wars, would be seen in a different light. And that happens, albeit in a different way, in both articles. Both historians mention previous wars and their place in the Dutch national self-image. Henri Beunders wonders what had happened in Dutch society 'since the previous national trauma, in 1945?' Have all the values and norms become worthless? Are the Netherlands entering a new era, an era of disillusionment, an era in which it becomes clear that Dutch

> feeling of national moral superiority was based on nothing else but the luck of our smallness. Who is big, commits big crimes, who is small, small.

If so, he asks, how should one deal with past wars and the military? Will colonial wars continue to be seen as having the 'quality of an operetta, and will the military continue to be seen as a "ridiculous institution?" '[16]

While Beunders laments the absence of the classical battle Hero, van der Dunk points to the absence of moral men. He does not take Srebrenica as a marker of a new, immoral era. To the contrary. He shows that the whole history of Dutch wars was immoral. He questions not only Dutch attitudes during World War Two and the colonial wars in the 1940s and 1960s but also the war with the Belgians in 1830 and with the Spanish in the sixteenth century. He lists examples of Dutch trade dealings that express an attitude of 'if you cannot beat the Devil, at least you should rip him off', and shows that the Dutch government's readiness to negotiate with the 'wrong side' in wars has a long history. But most of all, he compares the Netherlands with Germany, to the Germans' advantage! This is something quite extraordinary in the Netherlands, where the big neighbour on the east still carries the can for all the evils of World War Two. Expressions such as 'wir haben es nicht gewust' (we did not know) and 'Kollektivschuld' (collective guilt) are used in German language, but they refer to the Dutch performance in Srebrenica. The dilemma facing the Dutchbatters was called the 'moral dilemma of Auschwitz: knowledge obliges us to intervene, but when intervention demands too much from us, we would rather not know'.

These two texts are significant because they indicate the existence of different, co-existing militarized masculinities in the Dutch national self-image, as well as the possible relationships between them. The first text, and its yearning for a classical hero who will make ethical choices worth dying for, shows us that, in the case of Srebrenica, the classical heroic militarized masculinity, far from being pushed aside or replaced, has become the very condition of Dutch moral masculinity. Heroism has been all along a suppressed and hidden value by which the moderated military masculinity was measured. We could say that Srebrenica became a Dutch national trauma precisely because it exposed the fallacy of the masculinity of moderation through the debacle of its suppressed, heroic image. Furthermore, I suggest that, in this particular context, being a 'softy' is no longer a compliment, nor does it carry the potential for an acceptable alternative military masculinity. It only creates yearning for the 'hard' military masculinity, men who would fight to the bitter end, for the good of the world. This is clear not only in the text on the 'Lost Fatherland', but also from many other pieces. One way or another, newspaper texts expressed dismay and contempt before the fact that Dutch soldiers abandoned the enclave 'without striking a single blow'.[17]

While the 'Lost Fatherland' article brings the classical battlefield hero and the man of morality together, the 'Moral Bankruptcy' article challenges the very idea that either of the two ever existed in the Dutch history of war. The author argues that the choices often made were not for ethics, and certainly not military glory, but for trade and money. Thus he argues that the Dutch history of wars was shaped by neither moral nor heroic masculinity, but rather by corporate interests. In the final section of this chapter, I will argue that the corporate interest lives on and, coupled with a discourse of professionalism and expertise, is creating a new type of military masculinity. This may be the masculinity that will heal the *Srebrenica trauma*.

Traumas and rightful places

I want to go back to my statements at the beginning of the chapter: that experiences of the Moslem refugees were excluded from the discourse on the *Srebrenica trauma*, and that events surrounding the fall of Srebrenica acquired meanings only within the larger framework of national trauma.[18]

This is not the first time in recent Dutch history that the events of a war have been processed collectively as national trauma. Something similar happened in the way the persecution of Jews during World War Two acquired meanings in Dutch society.

Ido de Haan (1997) concluded, in his powerful analysis of the meanings of the persecution of Jews in the Netherlands, that Dutch Jews who survived the war lost, eventually, any influence over the way this persecution would be commemorated. With it, they lost any control over meanings that were ascribed to both the commemoration, and the persecution itself.[19] De Haan showed how these meanings changed over time. The experience of the persecution was, after being ignored immediately after World War Two, eventually acknowledged as a source of deep personal trauma in the Jewish survivors. State funds were provided for their counselling, and the persecution became a public issue, allbeit within this medicalized framework. But, in the course of time, the Jewish war trauma became a metaphor which included not only the experiences of Jewish survivors, but also of other social groups who competed for the status of, and recognition as, war victims. Eventually, the trauma of persecution came to refer more to the reaction to the persecution of the non-persecuted Dutch, and to the war suffering of Dutch society as a whole, than to the Jewish survivors. Currently, de Haan argues, the persecution of Jews is less and less perceived as a crime committed against Jews, and more as a stain on the escutcheon of the Dutch who allowed it, or even took part in it.

The discourse on *Srebrenica trauma* traversed a somewhat different route in the press. It was also named a 'stain on the escutcheon of the Dutch armed forces' and the symbol of 'moral bankruptcy of ethical principles that the Netherlands carried high on its banners'.[20] In the process, actual events, and the experiences of the people who were most affected by them – Moslem refugees sheltering in the enclave – were obscured and transformed. In this the two 'national traumas' are similar. De Haan notes that the experiences of the Jews who survived the war were not only (first) appropriated and (then) disregarded, but also defined exclusively in discursive terms. The 'meaning of Auschwitz', de Haan argues, has completely obscured the hard, mortal reality of Auschwitz (de Haan 1997, p156).

However, unlike the trauma of the persecution of Jews, the *Srebrenica trauma* seems to have been short lived. Judging by the press coverage, the Netherlands is slowly but surely shaking off its traumatic experience of the failed peacekeeping mission. As the years pass, the meaning of the discourse of *Srebrenica trauma* is changing. While in the beginning it was a lament over failed heroic and moral masculinity, and the consequent humiliation of the nation, in recent years it has become a signifier of political opinions. The focus is no longer on the *trauma* itself but on those politicians and journalists who *talk* about it. And these people are accused of dragging the Netherlands through the mud of the past, and by doing so, denying the country its rightful place in the international community.

One of few texts on the *Srebrenica trauma* that actually posed the question of the responsibility of the government and expressed a need for re-thinking Dutch involvement in peacekeeping missions in general appeared in August 1998. Like the others, it drew a direct link between the military and moral failure and the humiliation of the nation, but unlike most of the others analyzed above, it was unforgiving and cynical:

> 'I am joining the army, to do nice things in peace missions', said a girl recently after getting her school-leaving exam results. She is tired of the sorrow and injustice in the world and will not stay and watch from the sidelines any longer. She is impressed with nice TV clips picturing military vehicles protecting children in the war zones.
>
> What the army advertisers do not let her see are the night patrols, the sieges with kalashnikovs and the maimed bodies. The illusion of the land of the guidebooks – the Netherlands – of the Florence Nightingale in an angry world, must not be disturbed.

Three years after Srebrenica we still haven't learned our lesson. Instead of being anxious about new adventures, we are glad to sign up again, and to recruit new young people. After all, we have something to repair. Our shattered reputation has to be restored.[21]

This text still links Srebrenica to the Netherlands. But only a month later, that link, while acknowledged, is loosened. In another text on possible criminal charges against peacekeeping missions, the frame of reference is shifted from national to international, from political to legal. In the text are listed various crimes committed by other peace-keepers in other UN missions (Belgian and Canadian in Somalia), and by the USA in other countries. The author agrees that,

the state of affairs regarding Srebrenica can only be lamented. On the basis of the information that has come out to date [...] it seems that the Netherlands is not taking upon itself full responsibility. This serves not only the Dutch Armed Forces and the Netherlands badly, but the whole system of UN peace missions. From that point of view, 'Srebrenica' is not only 'our' trauma, but that of all UN member states.[22]

Again, I do not wish to deny the fact that responsibility for the massacres of Moslem refugees in Srebrenica should be accounted for, and shared among the military and political leaders of the UN, as well as individual member states who had military in the field. Nor do I deny that many texts were critical of the role of the Netherlands in Srebrenica. My point is that the discourse of the *Srebrenica trauma* had a very specific meaning in the Dutch press in the years following the fall of the town – a meaning of militarily and morally failed masculinity, and of a consequently humiliated nation. The *Srebrenica trauma* was claimed as the Dutch *national* trauma. Disclaiming it, albeit partially, as a *national* trauma is indicative of a new discourse, a new meaning of Srebrenica in Dutch national self-image. This new discourse appears to be about *national recovery*. So, what interests me is: what direction is this recovery now taking and what is the place in it of militarized masculinity?

In August 1999 a short note appeared in the *Trouw*, about a Dutch delegation participating in the gathering of the World Council of Churches. The delegation withdrew from the WCC's statement condemning the NATO bombing of Yugoslavia. The WCC suggested that its refusal to condemn the bombing was caused by the 'bitter memories of the fall of Srebrenica'.[23]

Here we have an indication of both the new meaning of the *Srebrenica trauma* and of the direction in which national recovery is to be sought, and eventually, found. The new meaning is apparent: the *Srebrenica trauma* has ceased to be a feeling of national humiliation and has become an impediment to Dutch functioning within the international arena. The direction is also clear – it is towards international politics. While in the *Trouw* report the 'international' was only in the context of a non-governmental organization, in the texts that follow it is a a matter of global power politics.

In June 2000, one month after the Bakker Committee was appointed, professor emeritus Leon Wecke, an expert from the Peace Studies Department of the University of Nijmegen, wrote a piece in *Trouw* where he defined the new meaning of the *Srebrenica trauma*. The author quotes secret advice given by the Dutch Foreign Affairs Ministry to the Dutch Ambassador in the UN, regarding participation in the Eritrea mission of the UN:

> Dutch troops in that part of Africa will enhance the Dutch position as a member of the UN Security Council and, at the same time, definitely draw the line under the 'Srebrenica-trauma' that has been standing in the way of Dutch participation in peace-missions.

The author goes on to ask:

> But is there a trauma? What is it, who has it and what are its consequences? The so-called 'Srebrenica-trauma' seems describable as an efficient resistance against sending out Dutch soldiers within the framework of (UN) peace operations [...] The view that the Dutch people suffer from a 'Srebrenica-trauma' is incorrect. Considering its policy to send Dutch peacekeepers abroad, nor does the Government seem to suffer from such a thing. Missions of three thousand men in peace troops in Kosovo, Bosnia and Cyprus do not speak of a 'Srebrenica-trauma' on the part of government.
>
> There was a resistance to peace operations from Dutch people, as well as the government, long before 'Srebrenica'. This resistance was not provoked by 'Srebrenica', where the Netherlands had only one victim to mourn. The many thousands of victims on

the Moslem side were recognized only later, and obviously were not considered to be a consequence of Dutch actions. The 'Srebrenica-trauma' exists only in imagination of diplomats, politicians and journalists. Luckily, imagination is not yet in power, in the Netherlands.[24]

It seems that, as the relevance of the *Srebrenica trauma* increases for Dutch *international* politics, its relevance for the *national* self-image decreases. The *Srebrenica trauma* in the piece above does not invoke masculine failures any longer. It has nothing to do with Dutch national humiliation. It is about the Dutch position in international institutions and power brokering and a few individuals who are not aware of, or stand in the way of, Dutch national interests. Thus, from a signifier of national-cum-masculine humiliation, the *Srebrenica trauma* becomes a signifier of politically incorrect behaviour sabotaging Dutch international influence.

In October 2000, one month after the Bakker Committee issued its report, another article pursued this same angle on the *Srebrenica trauma*. The journalist expressed frustration with the 'fundamental insecurity' of certain politicians over Dutch participation in UN missions, and with the MPs of the Christian Democratic Party (CDA) for endlessly debating the issue of sending Dutch troops to Eritrea:

> In calling for yet more certainty and yet another guarantee for the security of Dutch soldiers, the Parliament is not really raising questions about [future] operations in Eritrea, but about the previous war in Bosnia [...] What do we [send our troops to Eritrea] for? Not for the sake of our national ego but to prevent new massacres. We had better stay at home if our concern is contingent on our armed forces being protected from every risk.[25]

The circle of meanings of the *Srebrenica trauma* is closed: from a powerlessness and humiliation before the massacre that was not prevented, and thus affected national ego, to the claim of ego-less prevention of new massacres. At first sight, the moral argument is back. However, I believe this is neither of the two we have been previously observing; not the moderate, contemplative morality, nor the morality of classical military heroes. Rather, it is a corporate morality, in which professionalism and expert knowledge grant one the moral right to tackle a job. In this case, the expertise is in matters of war and peace. The experts are military men.

This chapter is not about disputing Dutch military expertise. It is about how meanings of a specific media discourse change through time. The discourse was produced because one peacekeeping mission failed. I have argued that it was not produced because seven thousand men were killed, but because four hundred men could not save them from the other four hundred who set about murdering them. The *Srebrenica trauma* discourse was produced because even the Netherlands – this least heroic of all countries – would still rather have its top military men die as heroes than live as ordinary men.

Five years on, and the discourse has changed. It did not change because the first failure had been resolved. It changed because other wars were ending and other peacekeeping missions beginning. And the Netherlands wants to be an important player in world politics. That's all.

I would like to thank Marga Altena, Cynthia Cockburn, Pauline van Gelder and Halleh Ghorashi for their suggestions, criticism and encouragement during my work on this text.

Notes

1. The newspaper articles analyzed here are all found in a database of a local library in Wageningen, The Netherlands, that keeps data on texts published in five national dailies: *Trouw, De Volkskrant, NRC Handelsblad, Het Parol* and *Algemeen Dagblad*. I searched for articles that had *Sbrebrenica trauma* either in the title or in the text. I also looked for titles where words such as 'moral' ('ethics'), 'shame', 'disgrace', 'debacle' and 'homeland' (plus 'motherland' or 'fatherland') were linked to the word 'Sbrebrenica'. There were about 30 such texts published from 11 July 1995 (the day of the fall of Sbrebrenica) to 1 October 2000 (a pragmatic choice, linked to the deadlines). Only a small section of the newspaper articles analyzed is presented here.

   Of course, there were many more texts that reported the events surrounding Sbrebrenica without using any of the words listed above. This particular database has over 1000 texts mentioning Sbrebrenica in the given period.

2. See among others van Dijk 1988; van Zoonen 1991, 1992; Meijer 1993, and Taylor 1991.

3. See Colovic 1994.

4. This is a statement by a Dutch soldier, from the documentary, *Crazy*, by a Dutch woman filmmaker, Heddy Honigmann.

5. The Bakker Raport (2000, p8) explicitly mentions the texts published in

NRC Handelsblad, on 29 May 1996 (cover page and pages 6 and 7), and the TV documentary produced by Dutch *IKON* and British *Channel 4* shown on the Dutch TV programme *Nederland 1*, on May 30 1996, at 8.30pm. Both the texts and the documentary argued that the Serb forces and the UN made a deal, a 'herenakkoord' (gentlemen's agreement), as analyzed by de Leeuw in Chapter 10 in this volume. The photo in question is also the one de Leeuw analyses.

6. The Bakker Report mentions among other things: driving over the refugees with vehicles, assisting Serb forces to separate men from women, withholding medical help from wounded local population, pp210-11.

7. The Oxford Dictionary defines trauma as follows: '1 any physical wound or injury. 2 physical shock following this (…). 3 Psychol. emotional shock following a stressful event, sometimes leading to long-term neurosis (…)', 1995.

8. 'Dutchbatters uit Srebrenica hebben meer last van trauma's' (Dutchbatters from Sebrenica suffer more trauma), *Trouw*, 24.08.98, p3.

9. 'Srebrenica blijft trauma Dutchbat' (Srebrenica remains trauma of the Dutchbat), *Het Parol*, 05.06.96, p1.

10. 'Srebrenica blijft trauma Defensie' ('Srebrenica' remains trauma of the Ministry of Defence), *NRC Handelsblad*, 14.07.99, p3.

11. 'Veel trauma's bij Dutchbatters', (Many Dutchbatters suffer traumas), *Het Parool*, 22.08.98, p1.

12. In masculinity studies see Chapman & Rutherford 1988; Brittan 1989; Easthope 1992; Craig 1992; Seidler 1994, 1997 and Murphy 1994.

13. 'Het Trauma van Voorhoeve' (Voorhoeve's Trauma), *de Volkskrant*, 22.04.98, p13.

14. See especially Huston 1982.

15. 'Srebrenica toont moreel failliet' (Srebrenica points to moral bankruptcy), *NRC Handelsblad*, 22.08.98.

16. 'Het Verloren Vaderland' (Lost Fatherland), *NRC Handelsblaad*, 13.07.96.

17. Original: 'zonder slag of stoot'; emphasis added. 'Indrukwekkende satire op Dutchbat-debacle' (Impressive satire about Dutchbat-debacle), *Trouw*, 17.05.96, column: Theather.

18. I have already showed that individual traumas of the soldiers were part and parcel of the national trauma.

19. I am grateful to Stefan Dudink for referring me to this text and the arguments on trauma in relation to the persecution of Jews in the Netherlands during World War Two.

20. From the already quoted piece 'Srebrenica toont moreel failliet', *NRC Handelsblad*.

21. 'Trauma Srebrenica', *de Volkskrant*, 15.08.98, p19.
22. 'Trauma Srebrenca is zaak van alle leden van de VN' (Srebrenica trauma is a matter of all UN member states), *De Volkskrant*, 01.09.98, p9.
23. 'Nederland laat zich leiden door Srebrenica-trauma' (The Netherlands let itself be led by Srebrenica-trauma), *Trouw*, 28.08.99, p16.
24. 'Het trauma-Srebrenica is louter verbeelding' (Srebrenica-trauma is purely an imagination) *Trouw*, 14.06.00, p16.
25. 'Srebrenica-trauma brengt CDA'ers op dwaalspoor' (Srebrenica-trauma brings members of the CDA to a dead end), *Trouw*, 11.10.00 p3.

References

Aerts, R. (1999) 'Een staat in verbouwing. Van republiek naar constitutioneel koninkrijk 1780-1848', in R. Aerts at al (eds) *Land van kleine gebaren: Een politieke geschiedenis van Nederland 1780-1990*, Nijmegen: SUN, pp11-95.

Alvesson, M. and Billing, Y.D. (1997) *Understanding Gender and Organizations*, London: Sage.

Anderson, B. (1991) *Imagined Communities: Reflections on the Origins and Spread of Nationalism*, London/New York: Verso.

Anderson, M.B. (1996) *Do No Harm: Supporting Local Capacities for Peace through Aid*, Cambridge, Mass: The Collaborative for Development Action Inc.

Bakker Report (2000) *Rapport van de Tijdelijke commissie besluitvorming uitzendingen* (Report of the Temporary Committee for Decision Making on Peacekeeping), Twede Kamer, vergaderjaar 1999-2000, 26 454, nrs. 7-8.

Bank, J.T.M. (1990) *Roemrijk vaderland. Cultureel nationalisme in Nederland in de negentiende eeuw*, Gravenhage: SDU.

de la Barca, C. (1969) El Sitio de Bredá, *Obras Completas*, Vol. II, Madrid.

de Beauvoir, S. (1976) *De tweede sekse. Feiten, mythen en geleefde werkelijkheid*, J. Hardenberg (trans), Utrecht: Bijleveld.

Beeman, M., Burkom, F. and Grijzenhout, F. van (1994) *Beeldengids Nederland*, Rotterdam: Uitgeverij.

Beilstein, J. (1995) 'The role of women in United Nations peacekeeping', *Women 2000*, 1 (December): n.p.

Benschop, Y. and Doorewaard, H. (1999) 'Verhuld genderonderscheid in organisaties' in Glastra, F. (ed) *Organisaties en diversiteit. Naar een contextuele benadering van intercultureel management*, Utrecht: Lemma, pp181-197.

Best, G. (1982) *War and Society in Revolutionary Europe 1770-1870*, London: Fontana.

Bet-El, I. R. (1998) 'Men and Soldiers: British Conscripts, Concepts of

Masculinity, and the Great War', in Melman, B. (ed) *Borderlines. Genders and Identities in War and Peace 1870-1930*, London: Routledge, pp73-94.

Boogman, J.C. (1991) 'Achtergronden, tendenties en tradities van het buitenlands beleid van Nederland', in N.C.F. van Sas (ed), *De kracht van Nederland. internationale positie en buitenlands beleid in historisch perspectief*, Haarlem: Becht, pp16-35.

Bosch, J. (in preparation) 'Experiences of military women in out of area operations'.

Bossenbroek, M. (1992) *Volk voor Indië. De werving van Europese militairen voor de Nederlandse koloniale dienst 1814-1809*, Amsterdam: Van Soeren & Co.

Bossenbroek, M. (1996) *Holland op zijn breedst. Indië en Zuid-Afrika in de Nederlandse cultuur omstreeks 1900*, Amsterdam: Bert Bakker.

Bourke, J. (1996) 'Fragmentation, Fetishization and Men's Bodies in Britain, 1890-1939', in *Women, A Cultural Review*, 7(3): 240-250.

Bozinovic, N. (1994) 'Key points in the history of the women's movement in former Yugoslavia', in Centre for Women's Studies, *What Can We Do For Ourselves*, Report of the East European Feminist Conference, Belgrade 1994, pp13-18.

Brahimi Report (20000): *Report of the Panel on United Nations Peace Operations*. Report on-line [cited 6 November 2000]. Available at <www.un.org/peace/reports/peace_operations>

Breines, I., Connell, R. and Eide, I. (eds) (2000) *Male Roles and Masculinities: A Culture of Peace Perspective*, Paris: UNESCO.

Briscoe, D. (2000) 'Pentagon to send soldiers to Nigeria', *Yahoo News/Associated Press*, Article on-line [posted and cited 10 October 2000]. Available at <www.dailynews.yahoo.com/h/ap/20001010/pl/us_nigeria_1>

Brittan, A. (1989) *Masculinity and Power*, Oxford: Basil Blackwell.

Brouns, M. (1995) 'Kernconcepten en debatten', in Brouns, M., Verloo, M. & Grünell, M. (eds), *Vrouwenstudies in de jaren negentig.Een kennismaking vanuit verschillende disciplines*, Bussum: Coutinho, pp29-51.

Bryer, D. and Cairns, E. (1997) 'For Better? For Worse? Humanitarian Aid in Conflict', *Development in Practice*, 7(4): 363-74, Oxford: Oxfam GB.

Butler, J. (1993) *Bodies that Matter. On the Discursive Limits of 'Sex'*, New York: Routledge.

Butler, J. (1990) *Gender Trouble. Feminism and the Subversion of Identity*, New York: Routledge.

Capellen tot den Pol, J. D. v. d. (1981) *Aan het volk van Nederland* (W.F. Wertheim & A.H. Wertheim-Gijse Weenink, eds), Weesp: Eureka.

Chandler, D. (1999) *Bosnia: Faking Democracy after Dayton*, London: Pluto Press.

Chapkis, W. (1981) *Loaded Questions: Women in the Military*, Amsterdam: Transnational Institute.

Chapman, R. & Rutherford, J. (1988) *Male Order: Unwrapping Masculinity*, London: Lawrence & Wishart.

Chinkin, C. and Paradine, K. (2001) 'Vision and reality: democracy and citizenship of women in the Dayton Peace Accords', *Yale Journal of International Law*, 26(1): 103-178.

Clifton, D. and Williams, S. (1999) '*Gender assessment of Oxfam's emergency response to the Kosovo refugee crisis in Albania and Macedonia*', Internal report to Oxfam GB, June.

Cockburn, C. (1998) *The Space Between Us: Negotiating Gender and National Identities in Conflict*, London: Zed Books.

Cockburn, C. (2001) with Rada Stakic-Domuz and Meliha Hubic *Women Organizing for Change: A Study of Women's Local Integrative Women's Organizations and the Pursuit of Democracy in Bosnia-Herzegovina*, Second Look, no.5, Zenica Bosnia-Herzegovina: Medica Women's Association Infoteka, and Budapest: Soros Foundation Open Society Institute. Also published in Bosnian language as Zivjeti Dolvojeno.

Cohen, R. and Rai, S. (2000) 'Global social movements: towards a cosmopolitan politics' in Robin and Rai (eds) *Global Social Movements*, London and New Brunswick NJ: The Athlone Press, pp1-17.

Colovic, I. (1994) *Bordel ratnika (Brothel of the Warriors)*, Beograd: Slovograf/XX Century Book (No.78).

Connell, R. (1985) 'Masculinity, Violence, War', in Patton, P. & Poole, R. (eds) *WAR/Masculinity*, Sydney: Interventions.

Connell, R.W. (1987) *Gender and Power*, Cambridge: Polity Press.

Connell R.W. (1995) *Masculinities*, Cambridge: Polity Press.

Connell, R.W. (2000) *The Men and the Boys*, Cambridge: Polity Press.

Craig, S. (1992) *Men, Masculinity and the Media*, London: Sage.

Curtius, E.R., (1948) *Europäische Literatur und lateinisches Mittelalter*, Bern: Francke.

Dao, J. (2000) 'Army orders peacekeepers to sessions on rights', *The New York Times On-line*, Article on-line [posted and cited 2 December 2000]. Available at <www.nytimes.com/2000/12/02/world/02ARMY>

Dekker, R. and Pol van de L. (1981) *Daar was laatst een meisje loos. Nederlandse vrouwen als matrozen en soldaten een historisch onderzoek*, Baarn: Ambo.

DFAIT/DFID (2000) *Gender and peace support operations*, Canadian Department of Foreign Affairs and International Trade and United Kingdom Department for International Development.

van Dijk, T.A. (1988) *News as Discourse*, New Jersey & London: Lawrence Erlbanm Associates.

Dobash, R.P., Dobash, E.R., & Wilson, M. (1992) 'The myth of sexual symmetry in marital violence', *Social Problems*, vol. 39, pp71-91.

Doel, H. W. v. d. (1996) *Het Rijk van Insulinde. Opkomst en ondergang van een Nederlandse kolonie*, Amsterdam: Prometheus.

Duffield, M. (2001) *Global Governance and the New Wars: The Merging of Development and Security*, London and New York: Zed Books.

Durch, W. (1993) *The Evolution of UN Peacekeeping: Case Studies and Comparative Analysis*, New York: St Martin's Press.

Easthope, A. (1992) *'What a Man's Gotta Do' – The Masculine Myth in Popular Culture*, London and New York: Routledge

Eerde, J. C. v. (1914) *Koloniale Volkenkunde. Eerste Stuk: Omgang met Inlanders*, Amsterdam: Koloniaal Instituut.

Eisenstein, Z. (1979) *Capitalist Patriarchy and the Case for Socialist Feminism*, New York: Monthly Review Press.

Enloe, C. (1988) *Does Khaki Become You? The Militarization of Women's Lives*, London: Pandora Press/Harper Collins.

Enloe, C. (1989) *Bananas, Beaches & Bases: Making Feminist Sense of International Politics*, London/Sydney/Wellington: Pandora.

Enloe, C. (1993) *The Morning After: Sexual Politics at the End of the Cold War*, Berkeley, Los Angeles, London: University of California Press.

Enloe, C. (2000) *Maneuvers: The International Politics of Militarizing Women's Lives*, Berkeley and London: University of California Press.

Euler, C.A. and Welzer-Lang, D. (2000) 'Developing best professional practice for reducing sexual abuse, domestic violence and trafficking in militarised areas of peacetime Europe', Report on Project No.98/043.WC, Leeds Metropolitan University, March.

Fasseur, C. (1998) *Wilhelmina. De jonge koningin*, s.l.: Balans.

Fetherston, A.B. (1998) 'Voices from warzones: Implications for training UN peacekeepers', in *A future for Peacekeeping?*, Moxon-Browne, Edward (ed), London: Macmillan Press, pp158-175.

Fine, R. and Rai, S. (eds) (1997) *Civil Society: Democratic Perspective*, London and Portland: Frank Cass.

Forde, C. (1995) '"Women warriors": Representation of Women Soldiers in British Daily Newspaper Photographs of the Gulf War' (January to March 1991), in Maynard, M. & J. Purvis (eds), *(Hetero)sexual Politics*, Bristol: Taylor & Francis, pp108-123.

Frevert, U. (1997) '"Das Militär als, Schule der Männlichkeit": Erwartungen, Angebote, Erfahrungen im 19. Jahrhundert', in U. Frevert (ed), *Militär und Gesellschaft im 19. und 20. Jahrhundert*, Stuttgart: Klett-Cotta, pp145-173.

Gouda, F. (1995) *Dutch Culture Overseas: Colonial Practice in the Netherlands Indies*, Amsterdam: Amsterdam University Press.

Grijzenhout, F. (1989) *Feesten voor het Vaderland. Patriotse en Bataafse feesten 1780-1806*, Zwolle: Waanders.

De Groot, G.J. and Bird-Peniston, C.M. (eds) (2000) *A Soldier and a*

Woman: Sexual Integration in the Military, Harlow: Longman/Pearson Education.

De Haan, I. (1997) 'De betekenis van het vervolgingstrauma', in de Haan, *Na de ondergang. De herinering van de Jodenvervolging in Nederland 1945-1995*, Den Haag: Sdu Uitgevers, pp131-156.

Hagemann, K. (1996) 'Nation, Krieg und Geschlechterordnung. Zum kulturellen und politischen Diskurs in der Zeit der antinapoleonischen Erhebung Preußens', *Geschichte und Gesellschaft* 22(4): 562-591.

Hagemann, K. (1997) 'Of "Manly Valor" and "German Honor": Nation, War and Masculinity in the Age of the Prussian Uprising Against Napoleon', *Central European History* 30(2): 187-220.

Held, David (1987) *Models of Democracy*, Cambridge: Polity Press.

Helland, A., Karame, K., A. Kristensen, and I. Skjelsbaek (1999) *Women and Armed Conflict: A Study for the Norwegian Ministry of Foreign Affairs*, Copenhagen: Norwegian Institute of International Affairs.

Hobsbawm, E.J. and Ranger, T. (eds) (1983) *The Invention of Tradition*, Cambridge: Cambridge University Press.

Honig, J.W. and Both, N. (1996) *Srebrenica. Record of a War Crime*, London: Penguin Books.

Huizinga, J. (1934) *Nederlands geestesmerk*, Leiden: Sijthoff.

Hummelink, K.M. (1999) *Het draaideureffect. Een kwalitatief onderzoek naar de redenen waarom vrouwelijke militaren de Nederlandse krijgsmacht (willen) verlaten. Eindstudie*, Breda: Koninklijke militaire academie.

Huston, N. (1982) 'Tales of War and Tears of Women', in *Women's Studies International Forum* 5(3/4): 271-282.

Independent Bureau for Humanitarian Issues (1998) *The Local NGO Sector within Bosnia-Herzegovina: Problems, Analysis and Recommendations*, October, Sarajevo.

Independent Human Rights Law Group (1999) *Izvjestaj NVO-a o zenskim ljudskim pravima u Bosni i Hercegovini/A National NGO Report on Women's Human Rights in Bosnia and Herzegovina*, Sarajevo.

International Council of Voluntary Agencies (1999) *The ICVA Directory of Humanitarian and Development Agencies in Bosnia and Herzegovina*, April: Sarajevo.

Israel, J. (1998) *The Dutch Republic: Its Rise, Greatness and Fall 1477-1806*, Oxord: Clarendon Press.

Jacob, M.C. and Mijnhardt, W.W. (eds) (1992) *The Dutch Republic in the Eighteenth Century*, Ithaca/London: Cornell University Press.

Jancar, B. (1985) 'The new feminism in Yugoslavia' in Ramet, P. (ed) *Yugoslavia in the 1980s*, Boulder and London: Westview Press, pp201-223.

Joachim, K. and Zarkov, D. (2001) 'Changing the soldier or changing the military? The case of the Dutch armed forces', in *Peace News*, No. 2443, pp31-32.

Jünger, W. (1920) *In Stahlgewittern. Aus dem Tagebuch eines Stosstruppführers*, Hannover: Selbstverlag (Leisnig).

Kandiyoti, D. (1993) 'Identity and its discontents: women and the nation', in Patrick Williams and Laura Chrisman (eds) *Colonial Discourse and Post-Colonial Theory: A Reader*, New York and London: Harvester Wheatsheaf, pp429-443.

Kant, E. (1996) 'Vrouwen en oorlog: mythevorming of bloedige werkelijkheid', in *Kernvraag*, No. 110, pp42-51.

Kanter, R.M. (1977) *Men and women of the corporation*, New York: Basic Books.

Kaufholz, C. (2001) 'Size of UN peacekeeping forces 1947-2000', *Global Policy Forum*, data on-line [cited 1 January 2001]. Available at <www.globalpolicy.org/security/peacekpg>

Keane, J. (1998) *Civil Society: Old Images, New Visions*, Cambridge: Polity Press.

Keeler, B. (2000) 'A time for peace?', *Our Future*, article on-line [cited 7 December 2000]. Available at <www.future.newday.com>

Kinker, J. (1831) *De heldendood van Jan van Speyk*, Amsterdam: G. Portielje.

Kossmann, E. H. (1984) *De lage landen 1780-1940. Anderhalve eeuw Nederland en België*, Amsterdam/Brussel: Elsevier.

Krol, E. (1997) *De smaak der natie. Opvattingen over huiselijkheid in de Noord-Nederlandse poëzie 1800-1840*. Hilversum: Verloren.

Kvinna till Kvinna (2000) *Engendering the Peace Process: A Gender Approach to Dayton – and Beyond*, Stockholm: The Kvinna till Kvinna Foundation.

Laumann, E.O., Gagnon, J.H., Michael, R.T. and Michaels, S. (1994) *The Social Organization of Sexuality: Sexual Practices in the United States*, Chicago: University of Chicago Press.

Leijenaar, A. (2000) 'The dichotomy of gender and gender mainstreaming within the United Nations and its peacekeeping operations', Working paper, New York: United Nations Department of Peacekeeping Operations, 23 May 2000.

Linz, J.L. and Stepan, A. (1996) *Problems of Democratic Transition and Consolidation*, Baltimore and London: John Hopkins University Press.

Mackay, A. (2001) 'Gender and peacekeeping: Training experiences in UNTAET and UNMEE', paper presented at *Challenges of peacekeeping and peace support into the 21st century*, Nova Scotia, Canada, 28 May – 1 June.

Mackintosh, A. (1997) 'Rwanda: Beyond "Ethnic Conflict"', *Development in Practice*, 7(4): 464-474, Oxford: Oxfam GB.

Macrae, J. and A. Zwi with M. Duffield and H. Slim (eds) (1994) *War and Hunger: Rethinking International Responses to Complex Emergencies*, London and New York: Zed Books.

Malcolm, N. (1996) *Bosnia: A Short History*, London: Macmillan (updated edition).

Mayer, T. (1994) 'Heightened Palestinian Nationalism: Military occupation, repression, difference and gender', in T. Mayer (ed) *Women and the Israeli Occupation*, London & New York: Routledge, pp62-87.

Mazurana, D. and McKay, S. (1999) *Women and Peacebuilding*, Montreal: International Centre for Human Rights and Democratic Development.

Mazurana, D. (2001) 'Gender, women and peacekeeping', Discussion paper prepared for the 45th Session of the Commission for the Status of Women, New York, USA, March 6-16, *International Alert*, London.

McClintock, A. (1995) *Imperial Leather: Race, Gender and Sexuality in the Colonial Contest*, New York/London: Routledge.

Melman, B. (ed) (1998) *Borderlines. Genders and Identities in War and Peace. 1870-1930*, London: Routledge.

Mertus, J. (2000) *War's Offensive on Women: The Humanitarian Challenge in Bosnia, Kosovo and Afghanistan*, Bloomfield, Connecticut: Kumarian Press.

Messner, M.A and Sabo, D.F. (1994) *Sex, Violence and Power in Sports: Rethinking Masculinity*, Freedom, CA: Crossing Press.

Meznaric, S. (1994) 'Gender as an ethno-marker: rape, war and identity politics in the former Yugoslavia', in Moghadam, Valentine (ed), *Identity Politics and Women: Cultural Reassertions and Feminisms in International Perspective*, Oxford: Westview Press, pp76-97.

Miedema, M.C. (1999) *Defensie: vrouwen en ergonomie. Analyse en aanpak van fysieke belasting*, TNO-rapport 4080166/R9900347 Hoofddorp: TNO.

Miles, A. (1996) *Integrative Feminisms: Building Global Visions 1960s-1990s*, New York and London: Routledge.

Milic, A. (1993) 'Women and nationalism in former Yugoslavia' in Funk, Nanette and Mueller, Magda (eds), *Gender Politics and Post-Communism*, London: Routledge, pp109-122.

Milic, A. (1994) 'Women, technology and societal failure in Yugoslavia', in Cockburn, C. and Furst Dilic, R. (eds), *Bringing Technology Home: Gender and Technnology in a Changing Europe*, Milton Keynes: Open University Press, pp147-164.

Miller, L.L. and Moskos, Ch. (1995) 'Humanitarians or Warriors?: Race, gender and combat status in Operation Restore Hope', *Armed Forces & Society*, 21(4): 615-637.

Ministerie van Defensie (1997) *Verder kijken dan vandaag. Policy letter on emancipation*, Den Haag: Ministerie van Defensie.

Ministerie van Sociale Zaken en Werkgelegenheid (1999) *Actieplan emancipatietaakstellingen Departementen. 1999-2002*, Den Haag: Sociale Zaken en Werkgelegenheid.

Ministerie van Sociale Zaken en Werkgelegenheid (2001) *Gendermainstreaming. Een strategie voor kwaliteitsverbetering*, Den Haag: Sociale Zaken en Werkgelegenheid.

Mladjenovic, L. and Litricin, V. (1993) 'Belgrade feminists 1992: separation, guilt and identity crisis', *Feminist Review*, No.45, pp113-119.

Molyneux, M. (1996) 'Women's rights and the international context in the post-communist states', in Threlfall, M. (ed) *Mapping the Women's Movement*, London and New York: Verso, pp232-59.

Morgan, G. (1986) *Images of organisations*, London: Sage.

Morokvasic, M. (1986) 'Being a woman in Yugoslavia: past, present and institutional equality', in Godout, Monique (ed) *Women of the Mediterranean*, London: Zed Books, pp120-38.

Morokvasic, M. (1997) 'The logics of exclusion: nationalism, sexism and the Yugoslav war', in Charles, Nickie and Hintjens, Helen (eds) *Gender, Ethnicity and Political Ideologies*, London: Routledge, pp65-90.

Mosse, G.L. (1990) *Fallen Soldiers: Reshaping the Memory of the World Wars*, New York/Oxford: Oxford University Press.

Mosse, G.L. (1996) *The Image of Man: The Creation of Modern Masculinity*, New York/Oxford: Oxford University Press.

Mossink, M. and Nederland, T. (1993) *Beeldvorming in beleid. Een analyse vanvrouwelijkheid en mannelijkheid in beleidsstukkenvan de overheid*, Den Haag: Vuga.

Murphy, P. (1994) *Fictions of Masculinity: Crossing Cultures, Crossing Sexualities*, New York & London: New York University Press.

Olsson, L. (1999) *Gendering UN Peacekeeping: Mainstreaming a Gender Perspective in Multidimensional Peacekeeping Operations*, Uppsala: Repro Ekonomikum/Department of Peace and Conflict Research.

Olsson, L. and Tryggestad, T. (eds) (2001) 'Gender and Peacekeeping', Special Issue of *The Journal of International Peacekeeping*, Vol. 8, No. 2,

Oxfam GB (1998) *The Links: Lessons from the Gender Mapping Project*, Oxford: Oxfam GB.

Oxfam Policy Department (1998) *Nothing Can Stop Me Now: Report on the International Oxfam Workshop on Violence Against Women*, Oxford, UK: Oxfam.

Oxford Dictionary, The Concise (1995) London, New York, Sydney, Toronto: BCA (new edition).

Papic, Z. (1994) 'Women's movement in former Yugoslavia, 1970s and 1980s', in Centre for Women's Studies, *What Can We Do For Ourselves*,

Report of the East European Feminist Conference, Belgrade 1994, pp19-22.

Pateman, C. (1988) *The Sexual Contract*, Cambridge: Polity Press.

Perspective, The (2000) 'Nightmares of Nigeria's "peacekeeping" unfold', *Global Policy Forum*, article on-line [cited and posted 11 September 2000]. Available at <www.globalpolicy.org/security/issues/sierra/00912d>

Phillips, A. (1991) *Engendering Democracy*, Cambridge: Polity Press.

Pickup, F. with Williams, S. and Sweetman, C. (2001) *Ending Violence Against Women: A Challenge for Development and Humanitarian Work*, Oxford: Oxfam GB.

Pocock, J.G.A. (1975) *The Machiavellian Moment: Florentine Political Thought and the Atlantic Tradition*, Princeton/London: Princeton University Press.

Pollmann, T. (2000) 'The Unreal War: The Indonesian Revolution through the Eyes of Dutch Novelists and Reporters', *Indonesia* 69: 93-106.

Prism Research (1998) *Women in the Bosnian and Herzegovinian Economy: Current Status and Future Strategies*, Sarajevo: Prism Research.

Reichenberger, K. & Reichenberger E. (eds) (1979) *Bibliographisches Handbuch der Calderón–Forschung*, Part I, Kassel: Thiele & Schwarz .

Renan, E. (1996) 'What is a Nation?', M. Thom (trans), in G. Eley and R. Grigor Suny (eds), *Becoming National: A Reader*, New York/Oxford: Oxford University Press.

Reno, W. (1998) *Warlord politics and African states*, Boulder: Lynne Rienner.

Rooden, P. v. (1999) 'Godsdienst en nationalisme in de achttiende eeuw: het voorbeeld van de Republiek', in N.C.F. van Sas (ed), V*aderland. Een geschiedenis vanaf de vijftiende eeuw tot 1940*, Amsterdam: Amsterdam University Press, pp201-236.

Sargent, L. (ed) (1981) *The Unhappy Marriage of Marxism and Feminism: A Debate on Class and Patriarchy*, London: Pluto Press.

Schmitt, C. (1927) *Der Begriff des Politischen*, Berlin: Duncker und Humlot.

Schutte, G.J. (1987) 'Van verguizing naar eerherstel. Het beeld van de patriotten in de negentiende en twintigste eeuw', in F. Grijzenhout et al (eds), *Voor vaderland en vrijheid. De revolutie van de patriotten*, Amsterdam: De Bataafsche Leeuw, pp177-192.

Scott, J.W. (1986) 'Gender: A Useful Category of Historical Analysis', *American Historical Review* 91(5): 1053-1075.

Seidler, V.J. (1997) *Man Enough. Embodying Masculinities*, London: Sage.

Seifert, R. (1996) 'The Second Front: the logic of sexual violence in wars', in *Women's Studies International Forum*, 19(1/2): 35-43.

Serraller, F.C. (1998) *Diego Velázquez*, Madrid: Fundación Amigos del Museo del Prado y Alianza Editorial.

Sharpe, J. (1991) 'The Unspeakable Limits of Rape: Colonial violence and counter-insurgency', in *Genders*, 10: 25-47.

Smith, T.W. and Smith, R.J. (1994) 'Changes in firearm ownership among women, 1980-1994', paper presented to the American Society of Criminology, Miami.

Sphere Project (2000) *Humanitarian Charter and Minimum Standards in Disaster Response*, Interagency publication, distributed by Oxfam GB.

Staf, E. (1994) *Vijftig jaar vrouw in de Koninklijke Landmacht*, Den Haag: Vereniging Vrouwelijke Militairen Koninklijke Landmacht.

Storm-Bleijenberg, N.S. (2001) *Loopbaangedrag: een kwestie van variabelen? Eindstudie*, Breda: Koninklijke militaire Academie.

Stuurman, S. (1992) *Wacht op onze daden. Het liberalisme en de vernieuwing van de Nederlandse staat*, Amsterdam: Bert Bakker.

Stuurman, S. (1993) 'La centenaire de la Révolution française: les Pays Bas entre la France et l'Angleterre', in P. den Boer and W. Frijhoff (eds), *Lieux de mémoire et identités nationales*, Amsterdam: Amsterdam University Press, pp93-104.

Taylor, D. (1993) 'Spectacular Bodies: Gender, Terror and Argentina's "Dirty War"', in Cooke, M. and A. Woollacott (eds) *Gendering War Talk*, Princeton, New Jersey: Princeton University Press, pp20-40.

Taylor, J. (1991) *War Photography. Realism in the British Press*, London and New York: Routledge.

Theweleit, K. (1987), *Male Fantasies* (vol. 1), London: Polity Press.

Thompson, Martha (1999) 'Gender in times of war (El Salvador)', in *Gender Works*, Oxford: Oxfam GB.

UNICEF – The United Nations Childrens' Fund (1998) *Bosnia and Herzegovina: Women and Children – Situation Analysis*, Sarajevo.

United Nations (1979) *Convention on the Elimination of All Forms of Discrimination against Women*, New York: United Nations Publications.

United Nations (1989) *Convention on the Rights of the Child*, New York: United Nations Publications.

United Nations (1993) *Declaration and Programme of Action*, World Conference on Human Rights, Vienna and New York: United Nations Publications.

United Nations (1996a) *The Beijing Declaration and Platform for Action*, New York: United Nations Publications.

United Nations (1996b) 'Economic and Social Council Resolution 1996/310: Mainstreaming a Gender Perspective into all Policies and Programmes of the United Nations System', Available on website <www.un.org/womenwatch>

United Nations (1997) *Economic and Social Council Resolution 1996/310: Mainstreaming a Gender Perspective into all Policies and Programmes of the United Nations System*, United Nations Economic and Social Council. Available on website <www.un.org/womenwatch>

United Nations Development Programme (1998) *Human Development Report: Bosnia and Herzegovina*, Report prepared by the Independent Bureau for Humanitarian Issues, Sarajevo.

United Nations (2000) *United Nations Security Council Resolution 1325*, see <www.un.org>

United Nations Department of Peacekeeping Operations (2000) *Mainstreaming a Gender Perspective in Multidimensional Peace Support Operations*, New York: United Nations, Learned Lessons Unit, Department of Peacekeeping Operations, 12 May.

United Nations (2000) *Protocol to Prevent, Suppress and Punish Trafficking in Persons, Especially Women and Children*, from the Convention against Transnational Organized Crime, UN General Assembly 7th Session Vienna 17-28 January 2000, New York: United Nations Publications.

UNMIBiH and OHCHR (2000) *Trafficking in human beings in Bosnia and Herzegovina*, a Summary Report of the Joint Trafficking Project of the UN Mission in Bosnia and Herzegovina and the Office of the High Commissioner for Human Rights, Sarajevo, May.

United Nations (2000a) 'Press release SC/6942: Security Council, unanimously adopting Resolution 1325 (2000), calls for broad participation of women in peace-building, post-conflict reconstruction', *Press release* on-line [cited 7 November 2000]. Available at <www.un.org>

United Nations (2000b) 'Press release SC/6937: Stronger decision-making role for women in peace processes is called for in day-long Security Council debate' *Press release* on-line [cited 14 November 2000]. Available at <www.un.org>

United Nations (2000c) *United Nations Security Council Resolution 1325 (2000)*, resolution on-line [cited 31 October 2000]. Available at <www.un.org>

United Nations (2001a) United Nations Department of Peacekeeping Operations, 'Percentages of male and female staff serving in peacekeeping operations as at 30 April 2000', data on-line [cited 2 February 2001]. Available at <www.un.org/depts/dpko/dpko/pub/pdf/6.pdf>

United Nations (2001b) United Nations General Assembly, 'Press release GA/SPD/198: Under Secretary-General for Peacekeeping addresses fourth committee, highlights departments proposed structure changes', *Press release* on-line [cited 24 January 2001]. Available at <www.un.org>

United States Bureau of the Census (1998) *Statistical Abstract of the*

United States: 1998, 118th edn, Washington DC.

Velde, H.te and Aerts, R. (1998) 'Inleiding', in R. Aerts and H. te Velde (eds) *De stijl van de burger. Over burgerlijke cultuur vavaf de middeleeuwen*, Kampen: Kok, pp9-27.

Vollenhoven, C. v. (1913) *De eendracht van het land*, 's-Gravenhage: Martinus Nijhoff.

Voorhoeve, J.J.C. (1979) *Peace, Profits and Princples: A Study in Dutch Foreign Policy*, 's-Gravenhage: Martinus Nijhoff.

Vosters, S. (1993) 'Het Beleg en de Overgave van Breda', in *Geschiedenis, Litteratuur en Kunst*, Breda: Publikatiereeks Archiefdienst Breda Studies 8, Vol. I.

Vries, S. d. (1988) *De lucht ingevlogen, de hemel ingeprezen. Eerbewijzen voor Van Speyk*, Haarlem: Joh. Enschedé.

Waetjen, T. (2001) 'The Limits of Gender Rhetoric for Nationalism: A Case Study From Southern Africa', *Theory and Society* 30(1): 121-152.

Wal, G. v. d. (2000) 'Onze krijgsmacht is redelijk zachtaardig' Rob de Wijk', *Volkskrant Magazine* 36: 12-16.

Wal, M. v. d. (1983) 'Krijgsman of Staatsman? De oprichtingsgeschiedenis van de twee standbeelden voor Willem de Zwijger in Den Haag', *Nederlands Kunsthistorisch Jaarboek*, 34: 39-70.

Walker, L., Butland, D. and Connell, R.W. (2000), 'Boys on the road: Masculinities, car culture, and road safety education, *Journal of Men's Studies*, 8(2): 153-169.

Walsh, M. (1998) 'Mind the gap: where feminist theory failed to meet development practice – a missed opportunity in Bosnia and Herzegovina', *European Journal of Women's Studies*, 5(3/4): 329-343.

Walsh, M. (1999) *Rising to the Challenge: Gendered Impacts of Conflict and the Role of Women's Organizations in Post-Conflict Bosnia and Herzegovina*, A report to the United States Agency for International Development.

Watson, P. (1996) 'The rise of masculinism in Eastern Europe', in Threlfall, Monica (ed), *Mapping the Women's Movement*, London and New York: Verso, pp216-31.

Wels, C.B. (1982) *Aloofness & Neutrality: Studies on Dutch Foreign Relations and Policy-making Insitutions*, Utrecht: HES Publishers.

Whitaker, B.S. (1978) 'The first performance of Calderón's 'El Sitio de Bredá', *Renaissance Quarterly* 31: 515-531, New York: Renaissance Society of America.

Whittington, S. (2001) 'Gender and peacekeeping: The United Nations Transitional Administration in East Timor (UNTAET)' Presentation at *Confidence Building and Conflict Resolution, Asia Pacific*, 4-7 June 2001.

Williams, S. (1999) *Gender and Human Rights in the Macedonian Refugee*

Camps, Oxford, UK: Policy Department, Oxfam.

Wilson, J. (1973) *Introduction to Social Movements*, New York: Basic Books.

Winslow, D. (2000) 'NGOs and the military', *Militaire Spectator*, 10: 525-534.

Woodhead, L. (1996) *A Cry from the Graves*, TV documentary for BBC/NPS.

Woud, A. v. d. (1990) *De Bataafse hut. Verschuivingen in het beeld van de geschiedenis*, Amsterdam/Antwerpen: Contact.

Yuval-Davis (1997) *Gender & Nation*, London: Sage.

Zarkov, D. (2001) 'The Body of the Other Man: Sexual Violence and the Construction of Masculinity, Sexuality and Ethnicity in Croatian Media', in Moser, C.O.N. and C. Fiona (eds) *Victims, Perpetrators and Actors. Gender, Armed Conflict and Political Violence*, London: Zed Books.

Zarkov, D. (1999) *From 'Media War' to 'Ethnic War': The Female Body and the Production of Ethnicity in Former Yugoslavia (1986-1994)*, Doctoral Thesis, Centre for Women's Studies, University of Nijmegen.

Zimmerman, C. (1994) *Plates in a Basket will Rattle: Domestic Violence in Cambodia*, Project against Domestic Violence, Phnom Penh.

Van Zoonen, L. (1992) 'The Women's Movement and the Media: Constructing a Public Identity', in *European Journal of Communication*, 7: 453-476.

Van Zoonen, L. (1991) 'Feminist Perspectives on the media', in Curran J. and M. Gurevitch (eds) *Media, Mass Communication and Society*, London: Edward Arnold, pp33-54.

Notes on contributors

Jolanda Bosch is an organizational psychologist and lectures at the Royal Netherlands Military Academy. She has published various articles on human resource management, managing diversity, emancipation issues and gender in the Dutch Armed Forces. She chairs the Defensie Vrouwen Netwerk (a network of women in Defence). She is currently conducting research on gender in the Dutch Armed Forces.

Cynthia Cockburn is a feminist researcher and writer based at City University London, where she is a professor in the Department of Sociology. From an earlier focus on gender in labour processes, technology and organizations, her interest has now shifted to gender in the making of war and peace. Her most recent book, *The space between us: negotiating gender and national identities in conflict* (Zed Books 1998), concerns Northern Ireland, Israel/Palestine and Bosnia-Herzegovina. She lives in London, where she is active in the women's anti-militarist network Women in Black.

R.W. Connell is Professor of Education at the University of Sydney, Australia. He has been involved in research and action on issues of social justice and peace, and is author or co-author of 17 books including *The men and the boys* (Cambridge: Polity Press 2000), *Masculinities* (Cambridge: Polity Press 1995), *Schools and Social Justice* (Temple University Press 1993) and *Gender and Power* (Polity Press 1987).

Marc De Leeuw is Research Assistant at the University for Humanist Studies of Utrecht, Netherlands. He is currently working on a study of subjectivity and ethics called *Tracing the self. A hermeneutic reconstruction of subjectivity in the face of posthumanism*. His articles cover the field of contemporary philosophy, cultural studies, urban development, science studies, ethics and gender.

Stefan Dudink is Assistant Professor in Gay Studies at the University of Nijmegen, the Netherlands. He is the author of a book on Dutch social liberalism of the late nineteenth century and of various essays on gay and lesbian politics, queer theory, and the history of masculinity. He is currently working on a study of the meanings of masculinity in Dutch political culture around 1800.

Cynthia Enloe is Professor of Government and Director of Women's Studies at Clark University, USA. Her feminist explorations of gender, militaries and militarization have found expression in (among other books) *Does khaki become you?* (Pandora/Harper Collins 1988); *Bananas, beaches and bases: making feminist sense of international politics* (University of California Press 1993, new edition 2000); and *The morning after: sexual politics at the end of the Cold War* (University of California Press 1993). Her latest book, also published by University of California Press in 2000, is *Manoeuvres: the international politics of militarizing women's lives.*

Meliha Hubic was born in Visegrad, in Bosnia-Herzegovina, in 1972. Her undergraduate studies in metallurgy were interrupted by war. From 1995 she has worked in the *Infoteka* unit of Medica Women's Association, Zenica. Her work includes provision of training for Bosnian non-governmental organizations on gender, leadership and organization; training and advocacy on domestic violence; and conflict resolution work among returning refugees. She participated in research for the book on Bosnian women's NGOs, *To live together or to live alone*, published by Medica in 2001.

Dyan Mazurana is a Research Scholar in Women's Studies at the University of Montana, USA. She has published numerous manu-scripts on gender, armed conflict, international intervention, and post-conflict reconstruction including *Women and peacebuilding* (International Centre for Human Rights and Democratic Development 1999) and contributions in *Investigating women's rights violations in armed conflict* (Amnesty International 2001). She is a leading author on the United Nations Secretary-General's study on Women, Peace and Security, as requested by the Security Council in Resolution 1325.

Madeleine Rees is currently the Head of the Office of the High Commissioner for Human Rights in Bosnia and Herzegovina. Prior to her work in Bosnia and Herzegovina she practised as a lawyer in the

UK specialising in discrimination law. She has been involved in cases in both the European Court in Luxembourg and the Human Rights court in Strasbourg. She has also worked extensively in the UK and in Latin America on human rights issues, particularly in relation to women's rights and the rights of refugees.

Desiree E.M. Verweij is Associate Professor in philosophy and ethics at the Royal Military Academy of The Netherlands. Her research in moral philosophy is inspired by classical and present-day concepts of 'the art of living' and 'virtue ethics'. She is author of two books, one on Nietzsche and one on the subject of 'desire'. She published many articles on ethical perspectives on military issues and on gender. She is currently doing research on military virtues.

Suzanne Williams is Conflict and Gender Policy Adviser in Oxfam and co-ordinator of Oxfam's programme on violence against women. She has been Oxfam's Assistant Field Director in Brazil, and Country Representative in South Africa. She founded Oxfam's Gender and Development Unit, and was Oxfam's Basic Rights Policy Adviser. Her publications include *Child labour in Portugal*, published by Anti-Slavery International (1992); the *Oxfam gender training manual* (1994); the *Oxfam handbook for development and relief* (1995); and *Chronicle of a death foretold: the birth and death of Oxfam's gender unit*', in *Gender works* published by Oxfam (1999), and numerous journal articles and internal papers.

Dubravka Zarkov works as a senior lecturer at the Institute of Social Studies, the Hague. She studied sociology, anthropology and development studies in former Yugoslavia and the Netherlands, and worked at different Yugoslav and Dutch universities and research institutes. Her expertise is in the intersection of gender, sexuality and ethnicity in the contexts of nationalism and non violence and her special interest is in media representations of these intersections.

Index